SHAD
ANIMALS

"What we most dislike in others is often ourselves. We tend to project our shadow side—the aspects of ourselves we have repressed or denied—onto other people and situations. Recognizing and recalling such projections is a key to becoming whole and to healing all our relations. With her new book, Dawn Brunke makes a spirited and original contribution to shadow work, showing us how our buried histories and childhood fears take shape in our feelings and phobias around animals. She encourages us to ask: Is the spider or snake an aspect of my own power if I can move beyond fear in a conscious encounter? She reminds us that shadows are caused by the obstruction of light, and the clear light she turns on her subject includes personal dreams with the power of revelation and transformation. The book is worth its price for the chapter on bats alone. Studded with precious vignettes from mythology and folklore, honed with a naturalist's eyes for the social habits of the animal world, stocked with simple and effective meditations and exercises, *Shadow Animals* is a marvelous addition to the literature of shadow work and inter-species communication. Highly recommended."

ROBERT MOSS, AUTHOR OF *THE SECRET HISTORY OF DREAMING*

"*Shadow Animals* is a beautifully written, profound, and timely book. Brunke skillfully guides us to explore the shadow aspects of ourselves that we project onto animals. With helpful, practical exercises, she reveals how to reclaim those repressed or rejected aspects of ourselves and how to see the animals we once feared as teachers, guides, and healers. This book is particularly valuable given the increasing polarization in our world. By seeing and integrating our shadow aspects, we move toward wholeness, coming back into right relationship with ourselves, each other, and all sentient beings on our planet."

HEATHER ENSWORTH, PH.D., CLINICAL PSYCHOLOGIST, ASTROLOGER, AND AUTHOR OF *FINDING OUR CENTER* AND COAUTHOR OF *FROM TRAUMA TO FREEDOM*

"*Shadow Animals* focuses on your waking and dreaming animal connections, providing practices to uncover the profound treasures and transformative insights waiting there. Read this when you feel ready to go deeper into your psyche and return to the nature of nature. Highly recommended!"

ROBERT WAGGONER, AUTHOR OF
LUCID DREAMING: GATEWAY TO THE INNER SELF

"Brunke's *Shadow Animals* is a tour de force. Using the world's ancient mythologies and folktales to explore modern humanity's shadow, or hidden self, we learn from rats, bats, wolves, spiders, horses, and many other horned, hoofed, clawed, and winged creatures that can arouse fear in us. Sharing exercises, multicultural stories, and dream translations, Brunke's book holds a mirror to our psyche, gifting the reader access to the hidden, wounded, or shadow self that resides 'in the subterranean levels of the collective psyche.' A remarkable book, *Shadow Animals* shows how to respect and treasure these fascinating nonhuman beings, as they become our allies, teachers, protectors, and healers guiding us to wholeness on our shared journey home."

J. ZOHARA MEYERHOFF HIERONIMUS, D.H.L.,
AUTHOR OF *WHITE SPIRIT ANIMALS: PROPHETS OF CHANGE*

"*Shadow Animals* is a fascinating book that beautifully sheds light on the animals that help us to tap into fear-based emotions and the powerful role they play in our own inner transformational journeys. Dawn explains how each of these animals is in fact a bearer of light that has intentionally crossed our path to bring us their unique soul-healing medicine. She provides a rich and detailed history of the most common fear-triggering animals, their message and gift for you, and exercises to gently induce deep healing, safety, and peace. *Shadow Animals* is an important and much-needed book that I highly recommend!"

TAMMY BILLUPS, AUTHOR OF *ANIMAL WAYSHOWERS*,
ANIMAL SOUL CONTRACTS, AND *SOUL HEALING*
WITH OUR ANIMAL COMPANIONS

"A compelling read that makes you look at yourself and the relationships you have with your animals. *Shadow Animals* makes you delve a little deeper than normal, think, and then heal."

DIANE BUDD, AUTHOR OF *ENERGY MEDICINE FOR ANIMALS*

SHADOW ANIMALS

HOW ANIMALS WE FEAR CAN HELP US
HEAL, TRANSFORM, AND AWAKEN

DAWN BAUMANN BRUNKE

Bear & Company
Rochester, Vermont

Bear & Company
One Park Street
Rochester, Vermont 05767
www.BearandCompanyBooks.com

Text stock is SFI certified

Bear & Company is a division of Inner Traditions International

Cataloging-in-Publication Data for this title is available from the Library of Congress

ISBN 978-1-59143-457-3 (print)
ISBN 978-1-59143-458-0 (ebook)

Printed and bound in the United States by Lake Book Manufacturing, Inc.
The text stock is SFI certified. The Sustainable Forestry Initiative® program
promotes sustainable forest management.

10 9 8 7 6 5 4 3 2 1

Text design and layout by Virginia Scott Bowman
This book was typeset in Garamond Premier Pro, Legacy Sans, and Gill Sans with
Minion Pro and Kapra Neue used as display typefaces

To send correspondence to the author of this book, mail a first-class letter to the
author c/o Inner Traditions • Bear & Company, One Park Street, Rochester, VT
05767, and we will forward the communication, or contact the author directly at
www.animalvoices.net.

■ ■ ■

For my mother, Carol Edler Baumann,
a woman of adventure and accomplishment,
humor and wisdom,
deep love and generosity of spirit.

August 11, 1932–November 6, 2021

Cheers to a life well lived!

Contents

The Cat, the Snake, and the Shadow

As a child I loved dogs. I couldn't understand why people would choose to live with cats when they could be living with dogs! I didn't dislike cats, but they were definitely not my favorite animal.

When I was nine years old, my mother, sister, and I visited one of my mother's friends who had several cats. We stayed the night and in the early morning, while everyone was still in bed, I went downstairs to get some milk. In front of the refrigerator, blocking the door, sat the eldest cat. She was dark gray with bright green eyes, and she looked at me in a very deliberate way. As my skin begin to prickle, a cold fear rose from my belly. I sensed the cat knew something about me, perhaps something that I didn't know or couldn't know, and found me wanting.

The rest is a blur: a sudden movement, a scream. I recall my feet pounding up the stairs, the cat at my heels. I remember racing through the open door to my mother's room, jumping on her bed, still screaming all the while.

The cat never touched me, but an indelible impression of her remains. It is my first memory of meeting a shadow animal, face to green-eyed face.

While I didn't have the concept at nine years old to define this as an encounter with the Shadow, future events would reveal it was so. I did not develop a fear or hatred of cats because of the incident, nor did I think that cats were out to get me; in fact, my general opinion of cats did not seem to change.

1

My body, however, had a very different opinion. Soon after the event, I developed an allergy to cats. My eyes became red and itchy, my nose stuffy, my skin prickly whenever I came near a cat. If I wanted to pet one, I had to immediately wash my hands and face. Eventually I found it easier to stay away from cats.

It wasn't until several decades later that I met the cat again—this time in my dreams. The cat appeared many times over the years, always in different settings: sitting on a table, lounging in a chair, perched atop a refrigerator. The cat was silent, watching me.

Cat

By this time I was fascinated with dreams and the messages they share from our subconscious world. The dreams nudged me to revisit my earlier experience. What was it that made me run from the cat? Did the cat truly see something within me—and if so, what? Was my body defending me from a perceived threat by developing an allergy to keep me away from cats? Was there a reason cats were never my favorite animal, even before the incident? What is it that Cat represents for me?

I now know Cat as a skilled guide and mentor. The cat—both the physical cat and the dream cat—did indeed know something about me, something I had hidden away a very long time ago. Wise and patient, Cat was watching me carefully, waiting until I was ripe for its teaching.

So, what is the Shadow? In psychological terms it refers to the hidden aspects of our personality that we prefer not to identify with: shame or guilt, greed or arrogance, weakness or incompetence. Because we don't want to see ego-deflating aspects of self, we keep them in the dark, tucked away in the deep psyche. The Shadow holds all those parts of the self that we judge or disown—our secret fears, suppressed emotions, hidden prejudices, and dark beliefs. We each have our own Shadow and each family, society, and nation has its collective Shadow as well.

It's ironic—and yet fitting—that just as much as we ignore or refuse to know our Shadow, so the Shadow yearns to be known by us. It seeks to be seen, craving our acknowledgment of its existence—for it, too, is who we are.

The more we repress the Shadow, the more it works to make us aware of itself. It sometimes sneaks out in unsuspecting ways. Shadow images may appear in our dreams and daydreams or push their way into daily life via events and encounters that leave us feeling unbalanced and upset.

We may also glimpse our Shadow in the attributes that we project onto others. Instead of acknowledging qualities we do not like in ourselves, we subconsciously fling them outward—onto friends and family, politicians and the government, other races, and other countries. We also routinely do this to animals. Thus snakes are evil, spiders and bats creepy, rats dirty, and cockroaches downright disgusting.

The book you are about to read is not really about shadow animals. Rather, it is about humans and the many ways we suppress, ignore, and avoid our Shadow—and the ways that animals can help us to find it and begin to heal.

Several years ago I dreamt of an enormous snake. Larger than life, ancient and archetypal, it scrutinized me with its huge, gold-flecked eyes. On waking, I became fascinated with snakes. The more I read and learned about Snake—ancient creator deity, guardian to royalty, protector to gods and goddesses, mentor to those who sought wisdom,

Snake

healing, and enlightenment—the more curious I became as to how this once-trusted ally had become so despised by humankind. I knew then that Snake held a powerful secret for us all.

I wrote a book about Snake, focusing on how this premier example of a shadow animal had so very much to teach us—not only about snakes, but also about ourselves. While working on the book, I was challenged by Snake in personal ways. And I came to appreciate the life-changing insights that such shadow animals can bring to our lives, if only we are open and willing to work on ourselves. I learned the power of what these animals hold for us—the insights, clues, and pathways to deepening that can help us to know ourselves in clearer, more expansive ways.

Although I planned a writing break after sending my Snake manuscript to the publisher, the idea for this book rose to consciousness with a pressing need. I felt the book nudging me, insisting there was something here that wanted—*needed*—to be expressed.

What is the value of shadow animals? Why do we need to know about them? What can they teach us? And why are they so important right now?

As Carl Jung once wrote, "The world hangs by a thin thread, and that is the psyche of man."[1] Jung believed that *humans* are the great danger to our planet. And that is why he felt shadow work to be so vital. Without acknowledging and retrieving our shadow material, without becoming aware of our deep self, we remain disconnected from ourselves, from each other, and from our planet. Thus we begin to act out in some very destructive ways.

We live in alarmingly volatile and contentious times. Obsession with building walls and blaming others, knee-jerk reactions to project our faults and fears onto anyone but ourselves, and a stubborn refusal to acknowledge our own shadow material has led to a deep confusion about who we are. The collective Shadow is expressing itself in a multitude of metaphors: erratic weather conditions, megalomaniacal rulers, skyrocketing illness and puzzling medical conditions, a proliferation of extremist views and small-minded prejudices, and escalating acts of violence. Not only is the personal Shadow running amok, but the global Shadow is growing larger and darker.

Near the end of his life, Jung had a vision of worldwide catastrophe. His daughter took notes on the vision and, after his death, gave them to her father's friend and collaborator, Jungian analyst Marie-Louise von Franz. While von Franz was reticent to comment on the subject, she finally remarked, "I think that if not more people try to reflect and take back their projections and take the opposites within themselves, there will be a total destruction."[2]

Failure to acknowledge our Shadow can lead to all sorts of outbursts: rage, phobias, addictions, anxiety, depression, self-hatred, deceit, hypocrisy, and lies. That is why finding and integrating our Shadow is currently the most important work each of us can do. In fact, it is vital—our very survival as a species depends upon it. Remember this: the real danger does not come from meeting our Shadow, but rather from refusing to meet it.

This book looks at the powerful medicine shadow animals offer in helping us to identify, explore, and integrate our own shadow material. Why animals?

We have a long history of connecting with the animal world. Ancient peoples often identified animals as their ancestors, and many early gods and goddesses were represented in animal form. Some humans journeyed with spirit animals while others learned healing secrets and new perspectives from observing animals in the wild. Animals offered us protection, advice, inspiration, and wisdom.

Shadow animals are unique teachers that can help us find and better understand the lost and wounded pieces of ourselves of which we are not fully aware. Some hold clues to repressed memories of trauma or abuse. Some are guides, helping us to explore the puzzling or guarded aspects of our psyche.

Shadow animals may appear frightening at first, for they may reflect those aspects of self that we most fear knowing. But it is by exploring the Shadow that we can eventually face our fears and find—within those fears—our strengths, abilities, and wisdom. Shadow animals can help us discover and embrace what we have judged, forgotten, or marginalized.

It's important to remember that no animal is a shadow animal in itself. Rather, we make it that way. Events conspire to help create the perfect conditions for us to see our Shadow in an animal. Thus a perfectly nice, gray, green-eyed cat triggers a reaction that stays with us for decades.

Said another way, shadow animals are only shadow in relation to ourselves. They are the handy surface onto which we project our inner Shadow. Rats are not dirty. Snakes are not evil. It is only we who believe they are.

By showing us the outer shape of our Shadow, shadow animals offer clues to that which obstructs the inner radiance of our light. Their great gift is in helping us to see what we have hidden within.

The first part of this book offers an introduction to animals as teachers and guides. Whether domesticated or wild, in physical or spirit form, appearing only a moment or staying with us for a lifetime, such animals offer insightful messages tailored to our individual needs. We'll further explore the human Shadow and why we choose certain animals to hold our darkest projections and represent those aspects of our psyche that we deny, ignore, or suppress.

The second part of this book explores a variety of species that many may think of as shadowy—spiders, snakes, rats, and bats—as well as those that seem shadowy only to some, such as dogs, cats, horses. So too will we explore meeting the Shadow in ourselves and in our fellow humans—and why it is so timely and important to begin the work of integrating both the personal and collective Shadow.

Each of the thirteen "Shadow Animals" chapters features an exercise in working with shadow material. While these exercises are inspired by the animal representatives of each chapter, they are designed to be used with any animal or aspect of Shadow that you choose to explore. Thus the book provides thirteen different ways of working with your Shadow.

We'll ask a lot of questions along the way: *Why do we fear a particular animal? By exploring what irritates or frightens us about that animal, what will we learn? What gift does this particular creature offer that we have yet to see?* And, through stories and exercises, we'll consider different answers to these questions.

This is not a book with dictionary definitions of what various shadow animals mean, but rather a book about better understanding the animals that we dislike or fear and, in doing so, learning more about what we unconsciously fear and dislike in ourselves. Additionally, you may be surprised to find that reading about some animals you don't consider Shadow can be helpful in awakening knowledge of inner selves that have been disowned or disregarded for a very long time.

Ignoring the Shadow diminishes our energy. But by acknowledging its presence and opening to it, we begin to nourish ourselves. That is why shadow work is not only a process of self-education but also of healing and awakening.

Shadow work can help us to find the core of our phobias, anxieties, anger, frustration, arrogance, and small-minded beliefs. It can help us reclaim those parts of ourselves that we have forgotten or put away for what was once a very good reason: protection from childhood abuse, trauma, or debilitating fear. Shadow work allows for the healing of our core wounding—all that we don't want to see, yet that so desperately needs to be acknowledged.

By exploring and working with our Shadow, we begin to accept lost qualities of self rather than ignoring, avoiding, or repressing them. We begin to clear away what is untrue. In reclaiming our projections we become more realistic. We stop trying to toss away qualities we don't like onto others. We stop lying to ourselves about who we think we are or want to be, because we begin to like ourselves as we are.

By freeing our holds about the Shadow, we ignite creativity, increase clarity, and deepen our compassion for self and others. In uncovering more of our authentic self, we discover hidden talents and strengths, refine our abilities, expand our dreams, and begin to live in a way that celebrates our life's purpose.

To consciously work with one's Shadow is both powerful and life changing. It is to embark upon a spiritual process that not only heals but welcomes us home to who we are. Lucky for us, a great many animals offer their support along the way—protecting and advising, challenging and encouraging, inspiring and cheering us on, awaiting our heartfelt return.

Are you ready?

A SHORT GUIDE
TO THE SHADOW

Animal Teachers

In the beginning of all things, wisdom and knowledge were with the animals, for Tirawa, the One Above, did not speak directly to man. He sent certain animals to tell men that he showed himself through the beasts, and that from them, and from the stars and the sun and the moon should man learn.

Eagle Chief Letakots-Lesa,
"Introduction to the Pawnee Songs"

Humans have always been fascinated with animals. Since ancient times, we've been inspired by their speed, strength, and beauty, enthralled by their ability to fly or breathe underwater, intrigued by how they shed their skin or camouflage to become invisible in plain sight.

Through observation we recognized that each animal species offers a precious gift to planet Earth—a particular talent, unique perspective, or notable medicine that it both expresses and represents in our world.

Monkey reminds us to be inquisitive yet playful, to trust our curiosity in order to better innovate and problem solve. Fox reveals how to be cunning and alert, to step lightly and remain unseen. Beaver demonstrates the value of engineering, construction, hard work, and the importance of planning. By paying attention to animals, we learned—and continue to learn—many skills and secrets.

Early humans deepened in relationship with animals that offered guidance and knowledge. Shamans allied with animal spirits to journey through inner and other-dimensional worlds in order to bring back healing and insights. Hunters wore claws, fur, or feathers, attempting to become like an animal, to partake of its ability to stalk or pounce. Healers sought the counsel of animal mentors willing to share their expertise. As we crafted stories that celebrated their specialized gifts, animal teachers appeared in our art, folklore, and mythology, helping us to better understand both the natural world and ourselves.

Some myths note a mingling of human and animal form. Gods and goddesses were often depicted with animal heads or bodies. Bastet, ancient Egyptian goddess of protection, wore the head of a cat or lion, while the sky god Horus was depicted as a falcon or a man with a falcon head. In early forms Zeus, the king of Mount Olympus, was portrayed as Snake.

Some deities sought counsel from trusted animals. Athena, goddess of wisdom, drew counsel from Owl, and Diana, goddess of the wilderness, allied with Deer. Other divine beings depended on animal transport. Brahma, god of creation, travels on a swan; Durga, the

Lion goddess statuette from Egypt, circa 1069 to 644 BCE, displays the merging of human, animal, and divine features.

warrior goddess of India, rides a lion; and Ganesha, elephant-headed god and remover of obstacles, is carried by a rat.

A VARIETY OF EXPERIENCES

We may meet a wide variety of animal teachers throughout our life and relate to each in different ways. Guardians offer protection or emotional safeguarding through challenges and danger. Guides and advisors provide passage through underworlds or knowledge needed to complete a task. And companions share warmth and love.

Some animal teachers take form as physical beings living in our homes or in the wild. Some are spirit-based, and some carry a vast presence that conveys the teachings of their species or realm.

Birds, for example, may share elevated perspectives to assist us in accessing higher levels of consciousness. Water animals may help us sink into the fluidity of our unconscious and engage creativity. Reptiles may teach transformation or metamorphosis, encouraging us to get comfortable with change. And animals that live underground may remind us to burrow deep, showing us how to extract wisdom from buried or hidden spaces.

Spirit animal, power animal, totem, animal guide: all these terms refer to an animal's power and medicine—the unique teaching it embodies and expresses in our world. Animals may share based on personal experience or through a collective voice that taps into the specialized knowledge of their species. The larger energy of spirit animals may be expressed through a living animal. Or we may access the wisdom of past, future, and parallel worlds through ancestral animal spirits or dreamtime animals that provide an expansive history of their land or realm. Some humans celebrate a communal relationship with a totem animal that unites the clan, tribe, family, or group by conveying its protection, wisdom, and skills.

We intuitively sense both the playful and protective power of animals when we give our young children stuffed toys—plush elephants, tigers, and teddy bears. We still yearn to align with animals, and so we assign totemic animal images to vehicles, sports teams, and different brands or products in the marketplace: Jaguar, Mustang, the Miami Dolphins,

Spirit of Lion and Cat

the Milwaukee Bucks, Puma running shoes, Red Bull drinks, even the imprint of this book, Bear & Company. Our connection with the animal world is deep-seated, not only in our language but in our being.

It doesn't matter so much how we identify a particular animal—whether we call it guide, totem, or spirit animal—but rather that we appreciate and honor the animal that has come. For every animal offers a gift, a teaching, a perspective, another point of view. The more attentive we are in noting the animal teacher that appears, the more easily we sense the help, wisdom, and guidance that is offered.

You might meet your animal spirit or power animal through a planned ritual, meditation, or inner journey. But powerful experiences with animal helpers can come at any time or place, often unexpectedly.

One early morning many years ago, while standing outside in a mountainous area, I was struck with a compelling insight. While I had been confused the night before, the sudden clarity of the insight was so exceptional that I gasped aloud.

Despite the grandeur of the revelation, I felt the stirrings of doubt only a few moments later. Perhaps I had been opened too wide, too quickly, for my mind tumbled into skepticism and uncertainty, and I wondered if the experience had been real.

It was exactly then that a large gray dog who lived on the premises raced toward me, seemingly out of nowhere. Pausing in front of me, he pushed his soft muzzle into the curve of my hand. He then backed up and looked me straight in the eye. Holding my gaze, he wagged his tail and barked loudly—*one, two, three times!*—then raced away.

I shook my head in astonishment once again. *What just happened?* Had the dog sensed my excitement at the insight, or my doubt in believing it was true? What force caused him to run to me, to touch me, and to bark at me those magical three times, as if to say, "*Yes! yes! yes! What you just experienced is real!*"[1]

WHEN ANIMAL TEACHERS VISIT

Some animals show up in passing, their arrival unforeseen yet perfectly timed, their appearance igniting something inside of us. Some bring flashes of spiritual insight, others a summons to move, or a caution to stop. In crucial moments they may offer hint or warning, nudge or reminder, encouragement or call to awareness.

Afterward, we may remark on the strange synchronicity and auspicious revelation—that sudden vision of the soaring eagle overhead, suggesting we might consider a larger, wider, or more upraised point of view; the glimpse of a mouse peeping from the tiny entrance to its home, reminding us that sometimes it is wise to observe quietly from a safe position.

Such encounters can trigger something inside us—a deeper form of knowing or an opening to relationship, both with that animal teacher and also with ourselves.

Sometimes animals act as portals, allowing other energies to flow through them. A friend told me a story about a man she had been dating for several months. While she found him reserved and distant, on one particular day, while sitting face to face at a picnic table at the edge of a forest, she sensed a shift in his emotions. The man was sharing that his mother had died when he was nine years old and how the event had affected him deeply for many decades. He was only now noticing how he held his feelings tight inside as a result. As he spoke with teary eyes, my friend saw a movement behind the man.

She watched a red fox emerge from the woods and stand in an open clearing a short distance from their table. While it was strange for a fox to come out of the woods in the bright light of noon, my friend sensed its appearance was opportune.

She suggested to the man that he turn slowly to see their visitor, and he did as she requested. When he turned back several moments later, his expression was one of startled amazement.

A visit from Fox

"It's my mother," he whispered. "She always loved foxes. She had so many photos and paintings and little knickknacks of foxes in her house. I think she sent that fox, to let me know she is okay."

A sense of deep healing pervaded the moment, and the two sat quiet and still in the sunshine, both of them watching the fox until it trotted back into the woods. My friend reported that when the man turned back to face her, his eyes were shining with tears—no longer from grief, but with gratitude.

▪ ▪ ▪

While some animal teachers stay only a moment to deliver their message, others arrive for longer periods of time. Perhaps we are at a crossroads or facing a crucial life decision. An animal helper may arrive to offer guidance in addressing our challenge. Such animals may offer support as we deal with adversity or grief, or clues to healing, or insights to help us to better understand our situation and find the best path forward. As we move through the challenge, our teacher may move on as well—a sign of our completion.

Some power animals are with us for our whole lives. Sometimes we are only dimly aware of their presence working behind the scenes of our consciousness, and other times we know them from the start: an intuitive sense of kinship with Dog or Horse as a child, a deep fondness for Wolf or Whale. Like master teachers, these animals help us to grow spiritually. They may challenge us and nudge us to learn from our mistakes. They may encourage us to work at deepened levels of being as we address our life's purpose.

LEARNING, SHARING, AWAKENING

When we seek in the spirit of genuinely wanting to know, the world around us responds. Answers, clues, and messages come to us in the most amazing ways, tailored to our individual needs. So too may animals seek us out, sharing their worldview so that we may expand our perspectives and share with others.

I was once snorkeling in a secluded bay in Hawaii known for its turtle population. Happily watching the turtles gliding past me, I was surprised when one approached so closely it touched my face mask. I veered left to give it space, and it veered left; I dove, and it followed. Although we were told not to harass the turtles, it seemed this turtle wanted to engage.

After several minutes of swimming together, the turtle led me over a shallow reef. The water was only inches deep and the rocks below were sharp, the surge strong. I was reluctant to continue, but the turtle, now ahead, turned to look at me several times, as if encouraging.

A few yards further and the bay suddenly deepened ten feet or

Turtle scout

more. There were hollows in the volcanic rock and big circles of open sand below. And there were turtles—many turtles!—resting on the bottom. My heart beat faster with the realization that this was turtle sanctuary, created not by humans but by the turtles themselves. The secluded space was quiet and peaceful, a restful refuge from noisy tourists. As I floated on the surface and gazed down at the turtles, I could feel their ancient wisdom flowing through me. And so I lost track of time.

When I realized that I needed to return to shore, my turtle guide appeared and began leading me past the sanctuary—not to shore, as I expected, but further along the coastline. I felt the same reluctance I had on crossing the shallow reef. But only a moment later we passed another volcanic ridge and clearing of sand, and there an enormous turtle looked up at me from below. It seemed very old, very wise, an Elder Turtle of the Bay. I felt such a rush of emotions—astonishment, gratitude, joy—as it rose toward me and we glided together along the circumference of the sanctuary.

The old turtle shared its experience as protector of this bay. It pointed out coral formations and rock placements that had significance, a kind of sacred geomancy in this part of the ocean, serving as an anchor of energy. I sensed how turtle scouts swam beyond the area to engage swimmers and bring them here to deepen, rest, and commune in this peaceful space. And I understood that when we open like this—heart, mind, and soul joined—we know that we are all participants in the adventure of awakening.

As well as being personally moving, the experience reveals how animal teachers can test our engagement skills: Are we open to their invitation to learn more? Are we willing to move just a bit beyond our doubts and fears? Do we desire to share in experiences that may initially seem strange, different, or unfamiliar to us? In short, are we ready for the teaching?

Animal wisdom is all around us, all the time. It's up to us to be aware, to tune in, look, listen, sense, and feel.

If an animal teacher shows up in your life, there's a reason why: a lesson you may need to learn, advice that may help you with your next step, an offering of long-term assistance. Such teachers come to us because we are ready.

Sometimes we call on them, intuitively knowing we need the strength of Elephant or cunning of Coyote. There are no fixed rules. Creative possibilities are as open as we are. As we honor and celebrate the unique qualities we see in animals, we begin to awaken those qualities in ourselves.

SHADOW TEACHERS

While we may admire a variety of animal teachers, so too are there some that frighten or cause unease. Shadow animals are the ones that challenge us. They are often animals we would not ordinarily choose to interact with, and yet they come, offering very special lessons indeed.

Shadow animals encourage us to see our fears, to explore the dark corners of our psyche, to discover what is hidden, repressed, or buried deep within ourselves. We may initially judge these animals. We may be disgusted by them or have phobias against them. And we may come up with all kinds of reasons why this is so—*They look scary! They could harm us! They are aligned with the devil!*

We are fearful of shadow animals because they reflect the darkness of our inner world. That is why working with them and opening to their teachings is so valuable—for through them we can begin to see a clearer perspective of who we really are.

Shadow animals can help us to clear issues that trigger heavy emotions. They may appear at times of crisis or adversity, or when we are confused, angry, depressed, grief-stricken, or devastated. Perhaps we are stuck in a mode of thinking or behavior not helpful to our spiritual growth. Perhaps we keep repeating the same confused mistake or negative pattern. What to do?

Unique among animal teachers, shadow animals reveal the hard lessons we have not yet learned or would prefer to ignore. They seem dark because they come from our own darkness, but their goal is to help us see whatever is blocking us from our inner light.

Some may appear larger than life, intimidating, ferocious, or terrifying. Why? Because they are *shadow* animals, both reflecting and representing our inner fears. Patient and persistent, some may continue to appear until we begin to change or heal. Working with shadow animals may not always be easy, but if we go the course, they often become some of our most powerful guides.

What is required from us is to pay attention and be present, to open ourselves to deeper connections and different perceptions, to be willing to explore and expand our paradigms, and to be honest with ourselves and with others. Throughout the journey we may learn humility and find courage. So, too, will we discover why it is so important for each of us to shine our personal gifts in the world.

As we open in relationship to animals and their teachings, a part of us awakens. As we begin to embrace the shadowy parts of ourselves, we become more alive, more complete. We sense our deep kinship not only with animals, but with the natural world and ourselves. As teachers and guides, allies and friends, animals remind us what we have lost, what we have forgotten, what we yet need to discover, and who we truly are.

Shadow Animal Teachers

*No matter how far you travel, you can never get away from
yourself. It's like your shadow. It follows you everywhere.*
HARUKI MURAKAMI, *AFTER THE QUAKE*

In the mid-1500s the people of Warsaw, Poland, were convinced that
a basilisk was terrorizing their town. The mythological creature was
described as a large animal with snakelike skin, a long, curved tail, a
hooked beak, and sharp claws. It sometimes had bat wings or the head
of a rooster, but always a prominent crown-shaped crest, which is why it
was also called the King of Snakes.

The basilisk was said to be so venomous that it could kill with a
glance, wither vegetation with a single breath, and leave a trail of deadly
venom wherever it roamed. As Roman naturalist Pliny the Elder noted
in his first-century *Natural History,* "all who behold its eyes, fall dead
upon the spot."[1]

Although described differently in various cultures, countries, and
times, in sixteenth-century Warsaw the basilisk was believed to sleep
during the day in the basement of a crumbling castle. It only came out
at night to wander the town, eating livestock, stealing riches, destroying
crops, setting fires, and turning any humans who crossed its path into
stone. How to kill such a beast? Many individuals had tried, only to end
up as lifeless statues.

We can learn a lot about any group by considering the fearsome animals they conjure in myth and legend. A great many terrifying animals

Basilisk with snakes, from a Latin bestiary
(a treatise on real and mythical animals), circa 1200–1300

arise from the collective psyche, and it's not surprising—for life can be terrifying. Thus, world mythology includes the fire-breathing chimera of Greece, with its lion's head, goat's body, and serpent tail; the spiny, blood-sucking Chupacabra of Puerto Rico and South America; the deadly, cave-dwelling Grootslang of South Africa; and the monstrous, squid-like Kraken, whose immense tentacles could pull an entire ship down into cold Nordic waters.

We have always sensed the presence of shadow animals. From the earliest of times, dreamers and writers, poets and artists have projected our collective fears outward, creating an archetypal shadow beast that lives "out there," just beyond the village. They may dwell underground or in remote, wild places—the dark jungle, the windswept desert, the briny deep. They may hole up in tunnels, caves, chasms, even dilapidated castle basements. Most often they are creatures of the night, showing themselves only between the bewitching hours of dusk and dawn.

Sometimes the creatures are hybrids, blending human and animal traits. A human face merged with a hairy body and scaly tail hints that the monster is connected to our shadow self.

Mythic shadow animals are ferocious and intimidating, for they

Kraken attacking merchant ship, by Pierre Denys de Monfort, 1809

hold our deepest secrets and fears. They represent the underbelly of the group—that which is untamed and uncivilized, a conglomeration of all that is deemed deviant or depraved and needs to be locked away.

Shadow animals know us because their energy lives within us. Investigating them thus offers some excellent clues about what we do not want to know or see or feel. As with almost anything we choose to disown, however, repressing the Shadow forces it to express itself in some other way. And so, the basilisk roams the town.

How to deal with such a shadow animal? The Warsaw legend tells of a traveler who, upon hearing of the town's dilemma, creates a plan. He enters the basilisk's basement lair early in the morning while it is still asleep and holds a large mirror in front of its nose. Awakened by the noise, the basilisk opens its eyes. As it gazes into the mirror, it is greeted by its own reflection—and turns to stone. The traveler is so excited by his success that he drops the mirror, which shatters into many pieces. The shards catch the rays of the rising sun through a tiny window far above, the room brightens, and all the stone-turned humans come to life once again.

This folktale illustrates both how one group of people perceived their collective Shadow and how they banished it—at least for a time. Let's examine the tale for a few clues and connections to better understand its meaning.

The basilisk lives in the basement of a crumbling castle. Said another way, the Shadow resides in the subterranean levels of the collective psyche. Because this place is described as a royal structure in disrepair, we might assume that the sovereign structure of the group has been falling apart for some time. No wonder a shadow creature has emerged!

Woodblock print of a basilisk by Ulisse Aldrovandi,
from *Serpentum et draconum historia*, 1640

While benign during the daylight, the basilisk comes out at night to wreak havoc on the conveniences of civilized life: food, wealth, safety, and home. The potential loss of nourishment, security, shelter, and family are understandable fears for any town. But there's more. The basilisk stops all who oppose it by turning them into stone. While this hints at the fear of death, to be turned to stone is very specific. Does it reflect an unyielding or uncompromising attitude of the group? Statues are stationary, immobile, most often firmly set in their space. It's interesting that the stone castle is crumbling and yet the basilisk turns people to stone. Perhaps the group is fearful of imminent change and yearns for permanence?

The plan to stop the basilisk comes from someone outside the group—someone who is free to see beyond the constraints of the collective paradigm. The traveler's tool is simple yet powerful: a mirror, a device of reflection. The mirror's large size highlights it as a special object in this story.

Mirrors always hold a bit of magic. As symbols, they emphasize appearances—how we perceive ourselves or how we want others to perceive us. But magic mirrors mentioned in myths also reflect a desire to see the inner, deep, or true self. Accommodating our quest for insight, mirrors may reveal visions from the deep psyche, dream world, or shadow realm. In this story the mirror is the tool used to reflect the beast's image back to itself, thus turning it to stone.

The dropping of the mirror causes the reflected shadow image to shatter (the group thus no longer has the whole of Shadow to contend with, but only pieces), and so the town's fear begins to shatter as well. The mirror shards reflect sunlight from a window above. As symbols, windows offer light, new perspectives, and freedom. And when the room brightens with the reflected light from above, the basilisk's stone-casting spell is broken. While it's not a full resolution of shadow material, it is a clever start.

In the everyday world shadows are created when something solid—a body or object—comes between rays of light and a surface. The brighter the light, the darker the shadow. In the subconscious world Shadow is created when something is hidden away, repressed, or disowned. The darker the Shadow, the more fearful and disowned.

Shadows seem mysterious or frightening because they are formed from an obstruction of light. And this is exactly why exploring the Shadow can be so helpful—because it shows us that which obstructs our light!

As we face our Shadow clearly, we become aware that the qualities we hoped were "out there" are actually "in here," inside ourselves. We want to deny it, of course, but eventually we realize how that which we have shunned in ourselves has simply been projected outward onto others. This is true for individuals as well as groups or villages or nations.

The problem isn't that we project on animals (or life in general), for projections can be helpful in revealing what we cannot see in ourselves. The problem occurs when we believe our projection is a reality rather than a reflection of ourselves. The basilisk is always born from within.

To better understand why we cast our Shadow onto animals and others, let's explore how we acquire shadow material in the first place.

ACCUMULATING SHADOW

From an early age we are encouraged to develop the compliant side of our personality—the bright, smart, socially desirable side. Our parents tell us to sit still, behave nicely, and get good grades. In order to feel loved and accepted, we quickly learn to accentuate certain traits in our personality and reject others.

Poet and Shadow explorer Robert Bly refers to the Shadow as "the long bag we drag behind us."[2] As very small children we learn to stuff our bag with all that is not loved or valued by others. Each family, group, community, culture, and nationality has different ideas about what we should put in our bag.

Throughout our life we are encouraged to behave in certain ways, believe certain things, and accept certain rules and ways of being. Some of this is helpful and reasonable, of course, but it also causes us to suppress distinctive and creative energies that are unaligned with collective thinking.

Trauma in childhood may also cause us to repress certain experiences and fears. So too can intuitive abilities or natural gender yearnings not approved by society be stuffed in the long bag. Thus we put away whatever feels shameful or is judged untrue or abnormal. We usually aren't aware of forming our Shadow, nor do we realize how we carry it with us everywhere we go. It feels natural because it has become a part of who we are.

The origin of some shadow material may not make sense to us as adults. The events from childhood that once triggered us to stuff the bag may now seem insignificant—a cross word, an angry look, something our friends or parents disliked—yet at the time, to our small selves, these experiences were large and weighty. We are no longer our child self; now a chasm separates us from our Shadow and the reasons why we started a bag in the first place.

Although we may prefer to remain distanced from the bag, what's inside it is alive and kicking. In fact, elements from the bag often control us—sometimes overtly, sometimes in subtle yet powerful ways that we aren't aware of. Desires and urges from the Shadow can cause us to fear, judge, overreact, and act out, and we no longer know why. In addition, as Bly notes, the bigger or longer our bag, the less energy available to us.[3]

Shadow selves are not bad or wrong. Sometimes they shield us from harm. That is why some shadow animals stand guard over forgotten memories or valuable skills that may help us later in life.

The Shadow holds all that we reject and ignore, and there in the bag, all those judged qualities—all those lost pieces of ourselves—sit sulking, feeling unloved and unwanted. The longer these parts brood in the bag, the larger, more dissatisfied, and more desperate to be acknowledged they become.

As Bly notes, "We can only see the contents of our own bag by throwing them innocently, as we say, out into the world. Spiders then become evil, snakes cunning, goats oversexed . . ."[4] And this is how we eventually create our shadow animals.

IDENTIFYING SHADOW QUALITIES

Working with the Shadow is not always easy. And yet to be summoned by a shadow animal and offered its teaching or guidance shows that we are ready to evolve.

Our shadow animal may illuminate key pieces of our personal puzzle: past pains we continue to hold, deep yearnings we suppress, traumatic events not yet resolved. Or our shadow animal may offer clarification, help with re-visioning self and world, and ways to access and integrate lost energies.

Shadow animals are personal and distinct to each individual. A spider may be a wise teacher with helpful skills to one, a curious eight-legged creature to another, and a terrifying animal to a third. In other words, Shadow to one person is not necessarily Shadow to another.

All animal teachers work in different ways, each uniquely creative when addressing our individual challenges. Even if two people have the same species of shadow animal, it may appear very differently to each and work in differing ways.

Shadow animals help us to face ourselves, to view the roots of our anger or judgments, our self-righteous arrogance, or the shameful emotions that we project onto others. In this way, they offer potential release from that which holds us captive, providing guidance to freedom and a pathway to retrieving our power and wisdom.

How do you know if you've found your shadow animal? Ask yourself: how do I feel about this animal? If seeing, touching, or thinking about it gives rise to sensations of fear, anger, revulsion, or nausea, chances are that you have found a shadow animal!

To begin, here is a very simple yet powerful practice that serves as a great introduction to learning more about your shadow projections.

◆ ◆ **Consider This** ◆ ◆

Animal Projections

It is best to do this with a paper and pencil. It's also helpful to refrain from reading the full instructions in advance. Rather, read and complete each step before moving to the next.

1. Divide your paper into four quadrants, as shown in the figure below.

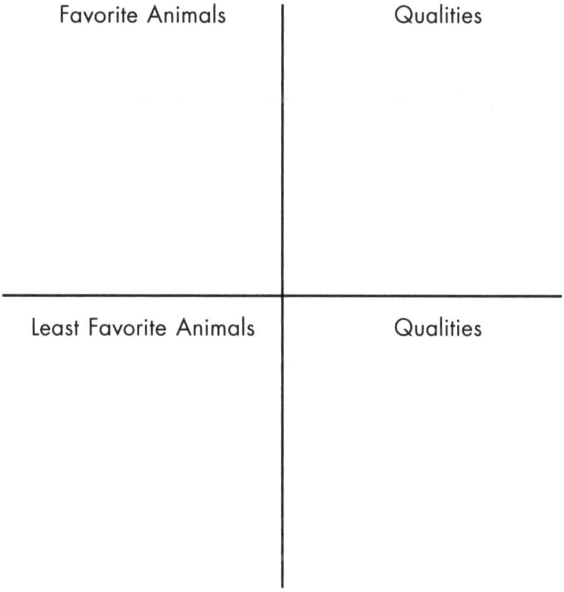

Favorite Animals	Qualities
Least Favorite Animals	Qualities

2. On the top left list two or three of your favorite animal species—the ones you admire or feel connected to in a positive way. For example, I might include: *Whale, Polar Bear, Dog.*

3. On the bottom left list several animal species that scare you—the ones you don't like or cause you to cringe. For example: *Alligator, Weasel.*

4. Going back to the top of the paper, contemplate your favorite animals and jot down on the right side what you like about these animals or why you find them interesting and amazing. For example, I might write about whales: *Large and graceful. Communicate in unique ways. Have expansive energy. Hold diverse connections and create pathways to inter-dimensional worlds.*

5. Now look at your least favorite animals and describe why you feel fear or unease around these animals. What bothers you the most? For example, Alligators: *Sneaky. Always watchful without being seen. Quick to bite, with sharp teeth and strong jaws that snap shut. Hold prey firmly, pulling into water and not letting go.*

6. Now fold your paper lengthwise, and consider all the animal qualities listed on the right side of paper. Forgetting the animals that these qualities describe, ask yourself: What do these qualities reflect about me? Be as honest as you can; this is just for you.

For example, when I consider expansive energy and diverse connections to inter-dimensional worlds, I can relate; I see a part of myself that I admire. Likewise, I perceive that I sometimes have a sneaky nature and can be sharp with my comments. I also tend to hold on to things that bother me for a very long time.

Projections can help us to see ourselves in larger ways. They offer us clues and clarity into a wider, deeper vision of ourselves—both the things we admire and the things we deny or don't care to acknowledge.

If you have no sense of what the qualities you've identified might say about you, that's okay. Allow them to simmer in the back of your mind. It may be helpful to save and refer to this list when working with some of the exercises in the next part of the book, or whenever you want to consider your projections, both positive and negative, in more depth.

SEEKING THE SHADOW

Shadow exploration can entail some confusion and frustration. Such adventures require us to engage our inner world. We need to be patient at times and quick acting at other times. We must be willing to acknowledge parts of ourselves that we may not like. We need to trust the process and ourselves. We also need to commit to the process in order to allow change to occur. We are confronting our dark side— at times not only personally, but communally and collectively. We will likely face obstacles, barriers, quicksand, and dark oceans. But so also will we find amazing vistas, buried treasure, golden secrets, and most precious of all, our true self.

Because of the work involved in facing repressed fears or triggers to heavy or dark emotions, shadow teachers may initially test us to determine if we are ready for the power of their lessons. Perhaps they come

Shadow animals may first observe or challenge us to make sure
we are ready for their teachings.

as nightmares: angry lions, wild horses, charging bears. By representing our fears they may appear as predators chasing us, snarling at us, intimidating us. They may snap or growl. The fangs are bared.

Do we run and hide? Do we fight back? Do we stand our ground? Do we have what it takes to face a shadow creature that threatens to turn us to stone? Our thoughts, feelings, and actions show us where we are in relation to ourselves, our shadow animals, and our readiness to work with Shadow.

If we are not ready for the teaching of a shadow animal, it can be dangerous for us. That is why some shadow animals come time and again—challenging us, testing us with their particular teaching. For example, it wasn't until decades after I met the cat mentioned in the introduction that I was able to recall its presence in a conscious way. When I finally did, I realized it had been carefully observing me in my dreams for over twenty years! At last, I had worked enough on my psyche for my shadow animal to determine I was ready for its teaching.

Forming a meaningful relationship with shadow animal teachers depends upon our ability to form a deep, honest relationship with ourselves. As representatives of our dark side, shadow animals want to be acknowledged. They come to us so that we can see our strengths and weaknesses more clearly. By working with them we engage more of ourselves, each lesson a stepping-stone to greater confidence, authenticity, and awareness.

Working with the Shadow

Everything that irritates us about others can lead us to an understanding of ourselves.
CARL JUNG, *MEMORIES, DREAMS AND REFLECTIONS*

Whenever a shadow animal shows up in our life, we are offered an invitation to explore a deeper side of ourselves. Accepting the invitation involves some courage, for we may be facing parts of ourselves that are scary, uncomfortable, or unflattering. And yet, this is precisely what leads us to our gold.

We may initially feel less than thrilled with the shadow animal that comes to us offering insight or advice. Let's say it's Rat. *Oh no! Rats are dirty, nasty hoarders with beady eyes and bald tails; what can this creepy animal possibly have to show me? What can I learn from Rat?*

Remember, we create shadow animals by pushing all the things we do not like about ourselves out there, onto others, like rats. We tend to marginalize that which we disown. Thus we dismiss the idea that rats have skills, or we belittle others by calling them dirty rats. That's our projection—and projection is always much more about ourselves than anything else.

Accepting an invitation from a shadow animal involves committing ourselves to deeper exploration. It requires engaging curiosity and an open mind as we earnestly consider what the animal presents to us. Once we allow ourselves to investigate, we might begin to see what's actually there.

Maybe we do a little research about Rat. Perhaps we are surprised to learn that rats are very clean and clever. In fact, rats are not only intelligent, but strong and strategic survivors. And so we ask ourselves again—this time with budding curiosity—*What can I learn from Rat?*

Rat's skills include resourcefulness, persistence, and adaptability.

If we are humble enough to ponder Rat, we may be surprised at the insights Rat and the rodent kingdom have to share! That's why it is wise to stay the course; to observe carefully, without judgment; to trust that the animal that shows up is the one we need. As we open to Rat's teaching, we may be pleased at how perfectly appropriate and helpful its presence can be.

Let's say we're stuck in a situation that never seems to resolve. We've tried to handle it various ways but nothing seems to work. Enter Rat. Maybe we dream about a rat or see a rat in the wild or on television. It gets us to thinking how rats are good with mazes, and how they can squeeze their way in and out of tight places. Perhaps we can learn something from Rat after all.

If we want to see what is, rather than what we want to see or fear, then it's wise to let go of expectations and rigid ideas of how we think things should be. Instead of holding firm to old beliefs or stereotypical prejudices about Rat, we open our mind to learn more about this animal. And thus we may discover that the situation we thought we were stuck in begins to open as well.

While on the surface of consciousness we may think we don't like rats or snakes or spiders, deep down there's something else going on. We fear shadow animals for the unattractive truths they show us about ourselves. Animals that have toxins or venom, for example, may help us see our own toxic nature—ways we manipulate or sting others to get what we want.

It is easier to project dislikes onto an animal than to accept what it reveals about us. And that's exactly why shadow teachers can be so valuable in helping us to find our true self.

Working with shadow animals involves paying attention to our thoughts and feelings. It takes time and requires self-honesty. After all, we're working to find what we don't know or cannot see clearly about ourselves. We'll be exploring what we deny, suppress, judge, repress, ignore, and disown. We may need to reconcile long-forgotten aspects of ourselves that are barely recognizable now. It can be a challenging, ongoing process.

Once we embrace our shadow animal, however, it often becomes a powerful guide, a trusted ally in our adventures through both everyday life and our private dreamscape. The very act of acknowledging our shadow animal propels us forward, onto a pathway that leads to clarity and enlightenment.

THE FIVE STAGES

In his very insightful *A Little Book on the Human Shadow*, Robert Bly observes five stages in working with the Shadow.[1] Bly notes that we don't live wholly in one stage all the time but rather "are in all five stages simultaneously, as we send out or receive back various rejected qualities, projected substances, abandoned powers, each absent in different degrees, or retrievable with different schedules."[2]

Although your practical experience of shadow work may be more fluid, Bly's neatly structured overview is quite helpful in understanding how we create, avoid, oppose, recover, and integrate shadow material.

Projection

Projection is the process of casting outward that which we don't want to see in ourselves. We fling unwanted character traits away from us, exiling their energy because we deem them too difficult to acknowledge or accept. *Bye, bye possessiveness, shame, and greed!* If we can successfully project our shadow material outward, onto others, we can disown it. In fact, we may disconnect in such a thorough and adamant way that we believe the energy is not our creation, but part of a problem "out there."

The Waver

This phase begins when we notice that something doesn't quite fit with our projection. Say we have projected a shameful aspect of self onto snakes. Snakes are really repulsive we have decided. But then one day we see a woman holding a brilliant green snake. Its bright scales glimmer in the sunshine and we notice how peaceful both woman and snake seem and how beautiful the scene. But wait, that's not right; snakes are disgusting!

It's a confusing time because our unwavering belief that snakes are loathsome is beginning to waver. That means our projection isn't as consistent or reliable as we thought it was. We sense the stirrings of disillusionment. Maybe snakes aren't as awful as we imagined?

We might feel anger, for what we thought was successfully projected out there is now threatening to return. We might feel sad or depressed, for now we sense our connection to what we thought was safely away from us. We may be nervous and anxious. What does it mean if some snakes are calm and somewhat appealing? We probably feel confused and unsettled too. We might not acknowledge any of this mentally or consciously, but we will *feel* it.

Attempting to Repair the Waver

At this point we know deep down we need to change our beliefs, but we don't really want to, and so we fight to keep things as they are. *Hello, rationalization and justification!* We can't stand the uncomfortable idea that some snakes may be gentle and peaceful, so we try our best to convince ourselves otherwise. We may secretly relish reading stories of snake horrors on the internet or talking trash about snakes. But, alas, this desperate attempt is short-lived.

The psychological term is *cognitive dissonance*—the discomfort or uneasiness we feel when trying to hold two or more contradictory beliefs or values. What we are actually angry, sad, nervous, and confused about is the disconnect that caused us to be inauthentic with our feelings in the first place. Our old, habitual script contends that all snakes are repulsive, but here's a woman interacting with a snake in a beautiful and loving way. Reality exposes our bias and judgment. It's not fun to feel dissonant, so we try to avoid seeing or feeling it. Thus we run away, time and again, from the approach of our shadow self.

Diminishment

At this point we're tired of trying to reconcile old beliefs with what is. It's a losing battle and we know it. As we give up the struggle, we begin to note what we have been missing—enjoying the beauty of snakes for example. We may feel tired at this point, exhausted even. It's been a long struggle and we realize that when we deny our Shadow, we are being inauthentic with ourselves and the world. While this is an ending stage, it can feel a bit sad because some of our beloved beliefs, cherished ideas, and idealized projections have begun to wither and die.

Retrieving the Shadow

At this stage we recover our projected shadow parts and begin to integrate them. While we may still feel some sorrow from the last stage, we feel passion too. A spontaneity of life returns, and humor as well—a deep, wise, joyful humor about life. Perhaps we tell good-natured jokes about snakes or educate ourselves and share amazing snake facts with others. We embrace our feelings, respect our limitations, and acknowledge who we really are. We might never want to live with snakes or even touch them, but we respect their right to live and appreciate their contributions to the world. A deeper form of wisdom awakens within.

Bly calls this stage eating the Shadow. It's a slow process that doesn't happen all at once, but many, many times. As we retrieve and ingest our shadow parts, we reclaim lost energy and nourish ourselves. By doing so, we become more authentic. As Bly puts it, "So the person who has eaten his shadow spreads calmness, and shows more grief than anger. If the ancients were right that darkness contains intelligence and nourishment

Hello, Snake!

and even information, then the person who has eaten some of his or her shadow is more energetic as well as more intelligent."[3]

EATING THE SHADOW

The problem with projection is that when we give away a part of ourselves (even a part we judge unwelcome or unlovable), we give away part of our energy. And that is why finding our Shadow can be so helpful. By identifying our shadow material in a projection, we may recognize what we disown in ourselves and begin to appreciate it.

So, how do we retrieve our projections and eat the Shadow so as to nourish ourselves? One of the first steps is to shake up our habitual way of seeing the world. We might begin by engaging our shadow animal in an artful, attentive, lighthearted way. We could watch or follow it in nature or mimic its movements or sounds. We might draw, paint, or sculpt it, coaxing it into consciousness by celebrating its unique gift. No matter what we do, Bly emphasizes that it must be playful.[4] For example, if Snake is your shadow animal, you might add a sensual slither to your movements or a sibilant *hissss* to your whispers.

By activating our imagination and sparking creativity, we open new neural pathways, inviting ourselves to fresh ways of perceiving, thinking, and being. Utilizing an inquisitive, intuitive approach can deepen our curiosity and assure our shadow animal that we are open to learning new things.

Remember, shadow animals are helping us to look at what we've disconnected from or ignored in our life. By learning more about the animal, we begin to see ourselves from different perspectives, which can lead to life blossoming in surprising, exciting ways.

Because we may have cast out and disowned parts of our Shadow for quite some time, we may not sense immediate or direct correlations in our shadow animal. Understanding its teachings may require us to use metaphor and allusion, to be open to twisting paths of one thing leading to another. It helps to relax and leave judgments aside.

It is also helpful to ease into discussions with the Shadow, to spend time considering our thoughts and feelings. Our shadow animal may be testing us. Are we serious with our desire to learn?

Remember, this is no small journey we are embarking upon! Shadow animal teachers offer us a bridge to our deeper self, a pathway to awakening.

WORKING WITH SHADOW ANIMALS

There are many creative ways to engage and work with our shadow animals. These include meditation and vision quests, inner voyages and dream work. As noted, we may engage our animal artistically by drawing or painting, or by dancing and singing. We can emulate our shadow animal, watching its behavior and trying on its habits. We can honor our animal by creating an altar or preparing a meal in its honor. We can converse with our shadow animal and learn from its skills or perspectives. And we can play! Some of these ways are explored in more depth in the next part.

Some techniques may work better for you than others. And some may be more effective at certain stages along the journey. That's why this book offers a buffet of tips and techniques. It's always wise (and fun!) to try different things to see what works best for you. This book also asks many questions—all of them threads of inquiry that you can tailor to your unique situation when encountering your shadow animal.

What we are doing in most of the exercises is building bridges between realms and learning to travel through different worlds. We are attempting to link inner and outer, dream states with waking consciousness, meditative images with practicality. We are explorers, forging paths to develop deeper, richer, more fulfilling relationships with animals and ourselves.

Working with shadow animals may seem difficult at times. It may require effort and patience. We may become frustrated or anxious, or arrive at what seem to be dead ends. But remember, you are not alone. Most animal teachers are sensitive to our efforts and appreciate our endeavors, especially when we convey our genuine feelings, along with desire and gratitude for their help.

◆ ◆ **Consider This** ◆ ◆

Ways to Better Know Your Shadow Animal

To research is to re-search: to see again. Once you have identified your shadow animal, it is helpful to investigate who and what this creature is through a variety of perspectives so that you can begin to know it in a more holistic way.

As a naturalist, you can gather information by watching it in the wild or on nature documentaries. Are you intrigued by certain mannerisms, or by the way it moves or sleeps or eats?

With scientific eyes you may learn about its biology, habits, and habitats. What about its unique form makes it special? Does it have any surprising abilities?

With the eyes of an artist, you might focus on the visual beauty of your animal's design. Use a magnifying glass to behold details. Sketch features—wings, ears, tails, paws—that appeal to or interest you.

As an archaeologist you can dig up facts about the history of your animal species, including how it has evolved and diversified throughout time. What are the strengths and weaknesses of this group of animals?

As a psychologist or symbolic anthropologist, you can explore your animal's role in myth, legends, stories, art, films, and popular culture. How has it been honored or vilified? Has the animal appeared in your dreams? If so, how did it present itself and how did you relate to it in the dreamworld?

Our shadow animal may appear in different ways at different times and in different realms. For example, we might encounter Lizard as a living animal (such as this Boyd's forest dragon, *Lophosaurus boydii*) or as a mythic dragon expressed through a work of art.

All of this offers us helpful information. But to deepen in relationship with an animal teacher, we need to relax and allow ourselves to deepen as well. That is why when collecting and collating insights, it's helpful to pay attention to the thoughts, emotions, and intuitive nudges that arise. Notice what bothers you or makes you queasy. Make note of how (and where in your body) you are triggered when considering certain aspects of your animal. This will help you in later exercises to perceive why you have projected your Shadow and how it might be retrieved.

WHAT THE SHADOW KNOWS

The exercises included in the next part of this book are designed to help you identify, investigate, and integrate shadow material. By exploring a variety of exercises, you can assemble your own inner toolbox of tested techniques. As you experiment and fine-tune these, you'll know how to work with any shadow animal teacher that presents itself.

The shadow world journey is an adventure of self-discovery starring you! While it can be helpful to consider the opinions of others regarding your animal teacher, it's often best to initially spend time pondering and playfully simmering ideas yourself. Invite that Snake Spirit for a cup of tea and conversation! We can hone our abilities by contemplating, dreaming, and utilizing our inner wealth of knowledge to come up with personal insights and clues. What we find may delight, deepen curiosity, and inspire more questions. Afterward, consulting books or online resources about animal symbology can supplement your findings or offer ideas you haven't yet considered.

Remember, there is no one way to work with Shadow or deepen your acquaintance with an animal teacher. At times certain techniques will work better than others, but you'll only discover this by experimenting. So be brave and receptive and creative! Try on different ideas and modify methods to fit your own needs. This is how we begin to see not only our shadow animal but also ourselves from fresh perspectives. Let us begin!

SHADOW ANIMALS

1

Arachnophobia

Come on, let's go find that spider. And let's find your mom to take care of that spider. Honey, we're in the living room. We need you to kill a spider!

ARACHNOPHOBIA, 1990 (FILM)

Shortly after deciding to write this book, I witnessed the disturbing intensity of arachnophobia.

Spider and her web

I was descending a stairwell in a medical building when I heard a shout from below. "*Stop, stop! Please help!*" screamed a woman, clearly in distress. Racing down the stairs—was this an assault? an abduction?—I turned 180 degrees to descend the second flight of stairs into the lobby.

Frozen in a hunched position, right hand extended with an accusing finger pointing downward, was a middle-aged woman shrieking loudly, "*Someone kill it, please!*" Just then, a young man bolted from the lobby coffee shop. Halting in front of the woman, he raised his foot high above the dark, dime-sized object of her terror: a spider.

"No!" I cried, rushing toward them, attempting to intervene. I could easily scoop up the spider and relocate it to a non-offending area of the lobby.

But it was too late. Down came the young man's boot, making an audible *stomp* on the hard tile floor. As if to make sure the spider was extra-dead, the man twisted his foot—one, two, three times—grinding the tiny spider's body into the cold beige tile.

Disaster averted (for the woman, but not the spider), the young man turned to leave.

"I have a terrible spider phobia," said the woman, still frozen to the spot.

The situation seemed overly dramatic: the shrieking woman, the exaggerated stomping, grinding, and killing of the beastly spider. My adrenaline was tweaked and my frustration level high as I made my way to the front door. "*Idiots,*" I muttered under my breath.

Hours later I realized that I had lost a perfect opportunity to learn more about arachnophobia. I could have engaged the woman, attempted to understand how she felt and why. On further contemplation I recognized the scenario had also exposed some of my own Shadow. I knew then that I would be facing some deeply personal judgments and prejudices on this journey to better understanding the fear and power and importance of shadow animals in our lives.

SPIDER FEAR

Arachnophobia: the term comes from the Greek *arakhne* (spider) and *phobos* (fear) and was first used a century ago to diagnose the irrational

Spider engenders beauty and mystery for some, terror and revulsion for others.

and debilitating fear of spiders. As one of the oldest recorded and most common of phobias, arachnophobia affects 3.5 to 6 percent of the global population.[1] In addition to clinical diagnosis, a general fear of spiders is reported by a whopping one-third of the world's human population—even in countries where no venomous spiders exist.

For arachnophobes, seeing a spider or its web (or even the image or thought of one) can trigger great unease: trembling, sweating, crying, screaming, heart palpitations, hot flashes, rapid breathing, nausea, dizziness, and fainting. A panic attack may ensue and the person may not be able to enter or cross the area where the spider or web was seen. The individual may also judge the spider to be larger, closer, and more "ferocious" than it actually is, thus amplifying anxiety. Indeed, the fear of spiders may be so strong and persistent that basic functioning is impaired.

It will crawl up my leg, jump on my face, creep up my nose! It will drop into my mouth while I am sleeping and lay its eggs inside of me! It will bite and maim or kill me! Most people know these are irrational fears, yet many feel there is nothing they can do about it. On encountering a spider they may run and scream or freeze, for generally arachnophobes are unable to remove or kill the spider by themselves.

Humans have identified over 49,000 species of spiders.[2] While almost all spiders are venomous, only about twenty-five species (or 1/20 of 1 percent) have venom that may cause illness in humans. Clearly, the actual threat of spiders to our survival is incredibly small, especially when compared to other animals that pose a much greater threat. In fact, you are three times more likely to be killed by a horse, five times more likely to be killed by a dog, and over 2,500 times more likely to be killed by a fellow human than by a spider.

Arachnophobia is a learned phobia, mostly influenced by cultural beliefs and experience. Having been bitten by a spider or unnerved by walking into a spider's web gives rise to personal fears. That spiders are commonly depicted as scary and threatening in our society reinforces the fear. Add to that a disgust response to multiple eyes and hairy legs, fast movements, sticky webs, and a heaping dose of media predilection to display dramatic spider bites or cast spiders as villains in films, and it is easy to see why spiders have such a bad rap in Western culture.

As with treating most phobias, the trick is to shift fear to curiosity. Because arachnophobes usually don't know much about spiders, they tend to believe the worst. But a learned set of beliefs can be unlearned and replaced with new, factual understanding. Treatments that combine education and experience thus generally work best, for the more we know about spiders, the more interesting they become. And when agitation yields to amazement, the more likely we are to release irrational fears. An impressive 90 percent of those seeking treatment for arachnophobia show clinical improvement in anxiety.

> Once you begin watching spiders, you haven't time for much else—the world is really loaded with them. I do not find them repulsive or revolting, any more than I find anything in nature repulsive or revolting, and I think it is too bad that children are often corrupted by their elders in this hate campaign. Spiders are skillful, amusing and useful, and only in rare instances has anybody ever come to grief because of a spider.
>
> E. B. WHITE, IN A LETTER TO HIS EDITOR ON WHY HE CHOSE
> A SPIDER TO BE THE HEROINE OF HIS
> 1952 CHILDREN'S STORY *CHARLOTTE'S WEB*

THE SHADOW SIDE OF SPIDER

If spiders present so little of an actual threat to our survival, why do we fear them so much? Shadow animals represent that which we repress, disown, or judge in ourselves. Is it possible that tiny Spider possesses some very big medicine—something so powerful that nearly a third of all humans don't want to see or even think about it?

The first spiders scurried over the earth 400 million years ago. But it took another 100 million years for them to become successful as the clever arachnids they are today. Aeronauts, architects, designers, divers, weavers, and engineers—spiders not only astonish and mystify, but are incredibly diverse and accomplished.

Some stalk, some hunt with bolas, some throw nets, some wait in burrows, and some use pheromones to catch their prey. No matter how they do it, all spiders are predators—skillful, calculating hunters that know exactly how to use their talents to fulfill their needs.

While almost all spiders are venomous, very few are dangerous to

A brown orb weaver spider wraps lunch. Orb weavers are known for their circular wheel-shaped webs. While not all orb weavers build webs, those that do often build a new web every day.

humans. Spider venom is not designed to harm large creatures such as ourselves, though it can sometimes trigger an allergy, cause pain, illness, or in very rare cases death. With the development of antivenins, however, death by spider bite rarely occurs anywhere in the world, especially in North America.

Most spiders are delicate and nonaggressive. While they generally avoid human activity, they are nonetheless incredibly beneficial to us. By eating a vast amount of insects—aphids, fleas, roaches, mosquitoes, and more—spiders help the world to maintain ecological balance.

These are facts. But in the throes of terror, facts are forgotten. In exploring shadow animals throughout this book, detective work is key. There is no one-size-fits-all answer as to what wisdom or special teaching Spider holds for you. Rather, we each need to deepen our focus, consult our feelings, question ourselves, and follow the clues.

There is an art to feeling what resonates within. *Breathe deep; sink down; listen, sense, intuit.* We need to be patient and allow our curiosity to open us. By paying attention to feelings, we can sense when something is not quite right or gives us a queasy little tug. That is our subconscious whispering, *Yes, look here—what's this uncomfortable feeling?* By trusting ourselves to follow such clues, we begin to discover more about who we are.

SPIDER'S SECRET SKILLS

So, what is it about Spider that really bothers you?

All those eyes! All those legs—so hairy and fast! And those fat, squishy bodies too!

Long ago, before we were squeamish about spiders, we were enthralled. The ancients recognized Spider as a master of creation, communication, and cosmic design. Producing magical threads from its body, patiently joining one silken strand to another, weaving a unified pattern of wholeness, Spider both forms and reveals the universal tapestry of life. Positioned in the center of their webs, eight long legs splayed forth, multiple pairs of eyes gazing in all directions, spiders were once viewed as mystical creatures that guarded the secrets of sacred knowledge.

All spiders have eight legs (an easy way to distinguish them from

Female jumping spider, *Hyllus brevitarsus*. There are over 6,000 species of jumping spiders, all of which are noted for their excellent eyesight.

six-legged insects), most have eight eyes (though some have six, four, two, or none at all), and many have a body divided into two segments that resemble a figure eight. This is why ancient peoples also associated Spider with the lemniscate, the symbol for infinity and the endless flow of energy.

Venerated in countless myths and legends, Spider creates the universe, initiates the flow of cosmic order, and oversees the divine plans of creation. So too does Spider inspire poets and artists and offer wise counsel to kings and rulers throughout the ages.

In ancient Sumeria, Uttu—the celebrated goddess of weaving—was envisioned as a spider creating a web. Both Mayan goddess of procreation (Ixchel) and Egyptian goddess of hunting (Neith) were associated with spiders. And in India Spider is linked to the great goddess Maya, the weaver of illusion and reality, reminding us that things are not always what they seem, nor all as it appears to be.

In some myths Spider is the guardian and keeper of words. By spinning designs upon her web, she creates the primordial alphabet—the roots of written communication—teaching humans how to record their thoughts

Tarantula (*Pamphobeteus cf. nigricolor*) and lemniscate. While the size and coloring of their 1,000-plus species varies, tarantulas are among the world's largest spiders.

and share knowledge with others, both at a distance and through time.

In the Native American world, Grandmother Spider spins the great Web of Life, linking past and future, connecting all beings in her creation. Weaving loose threads into a living work of art, Spider not only designs the plan of existence, but awakens our creativity and intuitive ability to discern connections.

Weaving is just one of Spider's many skills.

Ts'its'tsi'nako, Thought-Woman,
is sitting in her room
and whatever she thinks about
appears.

She thought of her sisters,
Nau'ts'ity'i and I'tcts'ity'i,
and together they created the Universe
this world
and the four worlds below.

Thought-Woman, the spider,
named things and
as she named them
they appeared.

She is sitting in her room
thinking of a story now . . .

LESLIE MARMON SILKO,
OPENING TO CEREMONY

Spider reminds us that as we are all part of the eternal web of creation, we can access ancient wisdom. At the same time, Spider reveals the limitless ongoing possibilities of creation and teaches us how to spin our thought-webs (our plans, ideas, dreams) to bring us what we need.

Spiders are patient and persistent. A Scottish legend notes that when Robert the Bruce was badly defeated in battle against the English in the early 1300s, he retreated to a cave where he noticed a spider building its web. Day after day the spider failed to secure its threads on the damp walls or, having secured several threads, had them carelessly brushed away. When the spider finally succeeded in constructing its web, the king of Scots recognized the power of tenacity and perseverance. Revitalized by Spider's lesson of persisting even after failure, he rallied his troops and won independence for Scotland.

THE TWO SIDES OF SPIDER

Intimately connected with intuitive knowledge of the earth, Spider is often depicted as an archetype of divine feminine energy. She is associated with magic because of her creative powers and ability to spin a web, and is linked to tapestry, basketry, and net and knot making.

But there is also a male side to Spider—sometimes portrayed as a shapeshifting trickster who blends wisdom and folly.

In West Africa, Anansi is the sly spider god who uses wit and trickery to turn the tables—though sometimes the tables are turned on him. In one story Anansi steals the world's wisdom and tries to keep it for himself. But the pot he places it in breaks. The wisdom spills, is washed down a stream, into the ocean, and back to the world.

Several Native American tribes note similar trickster qualities in Spider. The Lakota, for example, tell tales of Iktomi, a shapeshifting spider spirit with a propensity for mischief who occasionally offers aid.

Some tribes call upon Spider's protective power by adding a decorative web to warrior clothing. As a symbol of invisibility, the design safeguards the wearer by guiding arrows and bullets through the spaces of the web. Somewhat similarly, both Muslim and Jewish tales involve spiders weaving webs across openings in caves to make the entrance invisible so that fleeing prophets and heroes are hidden from harm.

From cloaks of invisibility to dew-laden webs shimmering in the early morning light, Spider's web can both obscure and illuminate. Spider's delicate silk—deceptively fragile yet incredibly strong—can be woven into a web of beauty as well as entrapment. Like many shadow animals, Spider is at home in the paradox of in-between. Uniting strength and sensitivity, elegance and simplicity, creation and extermination, Spider balances the seen and unseen.

For some, the appearance of a spider heralds breakthrough and completion. On the day I finished writing my first book about animals, a spider descended from a thread upon the ceiling and hovered before my eyes. While I didn't know what this meant, I felt it as a reassuring sign. With every following book, Spider has appeared to me soon after I finished. At first I felt Spider was cheering me on, but as I later

Spider's elegant web

learned of Spider's association with words and writing, I deepened in appreciation for the larger significance of Spider's appearance.

> I remember Spider Woman from the first page of Leslie's [Marmon Silko] novel *Ceremony*. She is the Thought Woman who names things and so brings them into being. Until then, I had imagined myself alone in believing that spiders should be the totem of writers. Both go into a space alone and spin out of their own bodies a reality that has never existed before.
>
> GLORIA STEINEM, *MY LIFE ON THE ROAD*

WHAT CAN WE LEARN FROM SPIDER?

In ancient Greece a noblewoman named Arachne was celebrated as a weaver. So spectacular were her creations that Athena, goddess of wisdom and the arts, challenged her to a competition. When Arachne created the perfect tapestry, Athena cursed her and poor Arachne hung herself. With later regret and humility, Athena brought Arachne back to life as a spider—the original arachnid—to be acknowledged forevermore as the most accomplished weaver in the world.

As a master weaver, Spider summons design and integration. Spider reminds us that all we envision and do in the world is part of what we create and that all aspects of our life—and all life—are linked and

Spiders have been creating webs for at least 100 million years. Webs can be positioned horizontally, vertically, or at any angle in-between. Their diverse designs include tangle webs (or cobwebs), funnel webs, mesh webs, sheet webs, and orb webs.

interrelated. Spider can thus help us to align our thoughts, discern connections between ideas, and more consciously design our life as we spin our path and weave our reality.

By working with Spider, we can learn to unravel patterns that frustrate or hold us in knots. Spider can help us to bring together disparate threads—to recover lost selves, for example, or recall forgotten aspects of the past. By contemplating the various threads of our web, we can discover viewpoints we had not considered or connections we did not see. Webs do not have to ensnare or tangle us; they may offer a means to see the larger whole and connect with others in unexpected ways.

Spider reminds us to hone our receptivity, pay attention to subtle details, and *feel* the web of life supporting us. With patience we can better weave our reality web into one that helps us achieve our goals and appreciate our life's design.

ASKING QUESTIONS, FOLLOWING THREADS

When people say they hate spiders what they often mean is that they fear spiders. For many of us it's easier to hate than admit fear. And yet that's what this book is all about: facing our fears, whatever they may be. What does Spider evoke in you? What is it that you fear so deeply in yourself that you project hatred onto spider?

To uncover any shadow animal's teaching, you might begin by considering and describing your fears. Sketch them or paint them; dream them or dance them out of your body. Like a spider creating a web, throw out your foundational thread of fear and watch where it lands and what form it takes.

To discern Spider's teaching can be simple and elegant: follow a strand and see where it takes you. Look for connections; sense the deeper links. By trying different things, we find what doesn't work and what does.

Like all shadow animals, Spider can help us to discover that which is hidden, forgotten, judged, or disowned. If the thought of Spider brings uncomfortable or uneasy feelings, we have only to look at the web of self. Which of our threads quiver with tension because they are stretched too tight? Which are too loose or need repair? To create a strong web, release what does not work and reinforce what does.

Spider reminds us to consider multiple angles and viewpoints in order to be more conscious of the interconnections in our web. In the following exercise we'll be exploring what is hiding beneath fear.

◆ ◆ **Exercise** ◆ ◆
Spider's Web of Intrigue

Part One

For this exercise choose an animal that you fear or dislike. Copy the facing figure on paper or in a notebook. You will be answering two sets of related questions. Take time to be thoughtful with each question and write your answers with as much description as you like. Then, summarize each answer and write a few key words in the corresponding numbered area of the web. The more specific and clear you are with your answers, the more easily patterns and connections may be recognized.

QUESTIONS, PART ONE

1. What do I most dislike/fear about this animal?
2. How do I feel when I think about or encounter this animal?
3. Where in my body do I feel this emotion?

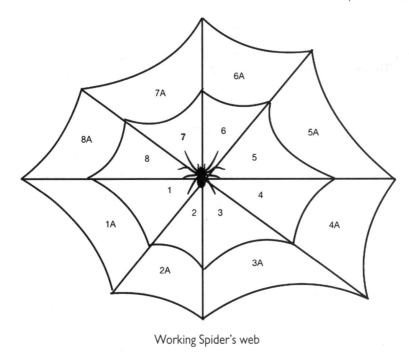

Working Spider's web

4. What are my physical feelings in that part of my body?
5. What are the top three adjectives I would use to describe this animal?
6. How do these words make me feel?
7. What would I most like to do when I encounter this animal?
8. Why do I think this animal repulses, frightens, or causes me unease?

Part Two

As Carl Jung often noted, it is precisely that which irritates us about others that can help us to better understand ourselves. Creating the second level of this web is a way to uncover clues about *why* this particular animal holds some of your Shadow. Take your time answering the questions, for surprising yet meaningful connections may occur as you ponder, wonder, and contemplate.

Just as a spider creates its web by linking threads, you'll be linking answers in this exercise. Consult your corresponding answer from part one as you answer each of the following questions. For example, look at your answer to 1 before answering question 1A, and so on. As in part one, answer each of the following questions with as much detail as you like, then summarize your answers in the second tier of web spaces.

QUESTIONS, PART TWO

1A. What does my fear or dislike about this animal remind me about myself?

2A. Have I always felt this way about this animal? Is there an event from my past that relates to my feelings about this animal?

3A. What is the main action or function of the part of the body in which I feel fear or repulsion to this animal? (For example, legs help us move, belly digests, chest muscles help us breathe.)

4A. How do my physical feelings relate to my thoughts and emotional feelings about this animal?

5A. What aspects of myself might these three adjectives describe?

6A. If this animal could offer me a gift or teaching, what would it be?

7A. How would I prefer to feel when I encounter this animal?

8A. What does this animal represent in me?

For further exploration you can expand your web with additional levels by asking your own questions or re-asking those from part two a second time. Consider waiting several hours or days between rounds. Allowing questions to simmer in the subconscious often yields helpful insights.

Part Three

The last stage of the exercise is about making connections, discerning patterns, and following clues. Because our shadow animals reflect deeper fears, we may need to dig beneath the superficially apparent to find helpful hints and keys.

For this part of the exercise, view the overall web and consider how your answers connect and interrelate. Are there any repeated words or ideas in the web spaces? Do you sense a common theme or pattern? What are the main threads linking your answers?

The following answers come from my friend Barb Techel who agreed to test-run this exercise shortly after I created it. We were both amazed by how a collection of simple questions can dramatically open and illuminate experiences from the past that continue to hold us captive.

After finishing parts one and two, Barb worked with her answers by following loose threads, noting patterns, and contemplating the connections in her life. While not all of her answers are included below, the gist of how she followed her clues may be helpful to you.

Barb began by noting that what she most dislikes about spiders is that they are "fast and sneaky—all of a sudden, there they are!" The three adjectives she used to describe spiders were "Creepy. Sneaky. Fast." A bit surprised by these words, Barb further noted, "Creepy makes me feel dirty. Sneaky makes me feel like you're hiding something from me. And fast is a control thing—I can't control you coming at me so fast."

On the second round Barb explored how her fear of spiders reminded her of herself: "I second-guess myself a lot—so that fast and sneaky part—I don't always trust what I first get but when I go back it's usually right. It reminds me of how we might describe the typical salesman—trying to pull a fast one. Trust is big for me; it takes a lot to earn my trust and even when you do, I still might question it. That's when I go back and say, *See, I knew!*"

Barb then pondered what the three adjectives might describe in relation to herself. "Creepy—hmmm, how would I define creepy? Dirty. Why is creepy dirty? Oh! I'm just recalling now a childhood wound of abuse! That situation was creepy—dirty. And it was fast and sneaky. Not the person doing it, but the situation. Fast because it was a control issue—I felt I had no control. There's also something about Spider getting its prey and holding it in its web. That's how I felt. Whew!"

Adrift in a rush of emotions, Barb's answer to what this animal might offer as a gift or teaching was both surprising and profound: "I'm reminded of the book and film *Charlotte's Web*. I'm picturing Charlotte the spider when she's resting and talking to Wilbur, looking at him with her big, kind eyes, and reassuring him that everything is going to be okay. That is one of my favorite scenes with Charlotte—and I read this so many times as a child. Everything is going to be okay—and, oh my God, everything *is* okay!"

To the last question—what does Spider represent in me?—Barb answered, "I feel Spider represents a trauma to me—something crawling on my body that wasn't meant to be there. There's no doubt in my mind about that."

As we finished I asked Barb if she felt any changes. "I had some tension in my body just thinking about Spider, but I'm so much more relaxed now. I feel that physically, but there was another shift as well. Once you face something traumatic and move through it, there's a lightening. I feel lighter. I also feel like I'm going to have more respect for Spider. Now that I feel this shift, I'm curious to see if Spider is going to show up in other ways in my life."

Over the course of several weeks, Barb deepened in understanding of her past trauma with the help of Spider. With research she noted that eight—often connected with Spider—was the numerological number of her birthdate and that Spider's connection to the Wheel of Life was of great significance to her.

In meditation she engaged Charlotte, taking refuge in Spider's protective nature. She later saw herself as Charlotte, a spider that "listened and really heard and believed" the traumatized little girl inside.

This led Barb to contemplate why some spiders seem scary to her and others loving—and how spiders trapping prey in webs are one thing and spiders weaving a beautiful web, "like a work of art," are another. Barb observed that while "dark, dirty, creepy" spiders may hold us captive, a Spider encountered as a kind and gentle teacher, like Charlotte, can set us free.

"Who would have thought all of this would have come?" Barb exclaimed. "Sometimes you just have to trust. You feel a thread and follow it and trust where it leads. In this way Spider helps us connect the dots."

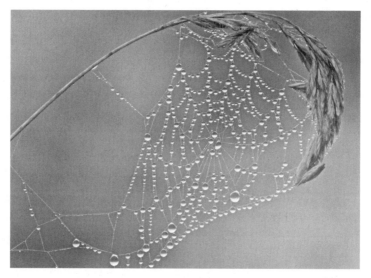

Contemplating Spider's web can help us follow threads of inquiry, link thoughts and ideas, and connect the dots.

2

Hidden Treasures

But there was more to it than that. As the Amazing Maurice said, it was just a story about people and rats. And the difficult part of it was deciding who the people were, and who were the rats.

TERRY PRATCHETT, *THE AMAZING MAURICE AND HIS EDUCATED RODENTS*

Most humans have very strong feelings about rats. They are often seen as filthy, sneaky carriers of disease that inspire hate, loathing, and disgust. And that is why we refer to them in our language the way we do.

To call someone a rat is to describe a despicable person—a liar, a cheat, a dirty double-crosser, an individual thoroughly deserving our contempt. To rat on someone is to spill their secrets, snitch, or betray. Such ratty disloyalty commonly happens in the rat race, that fierce and exhausting competition in which participants struggle for wealth and power. To pack rat is to hoard, to rathole is to hide stolen goods, and to smell a rat is to sense that something is very wrong indeed.

Considered unclean creatures; bad omens; harbingers of the plague; symbols of pestilence, decay, and death, rats have been feared throughout the ages. Living in garbage dumps and subterranean spaces in crowded cities all over the world, rats will gnaw through almost anything—wood, brick, cement, insulation, electric cables, lead pipes—stealing food, causing panic, and proliferating like there's no tomorrow. Sly and secretive and wholly misunderstood, no wonder Rat is one of humanity's prime candidates for a shadow animal!

Wherever humans are found, so too are rats. Swimming through sewers, scavenging in trash bins and basements, they are privy to the human underworld. Thus they are familiar with our shadow, especially that which we reject, discard, or deem as dirty. And that is just one reason why, more than any creature, Rat both reveals and represents the shadow side of human civilization.

It's true that rats cause damage. They infest buildings, destroy crops, and like other animals, can carry disease. But public opinion of rats is par-

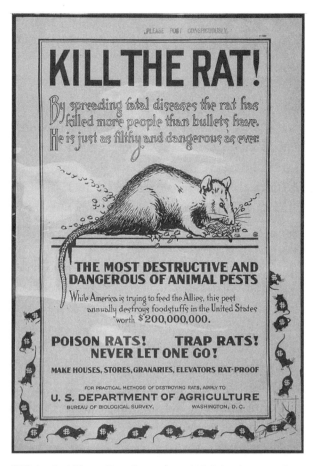

"Kill the Rat! Please Post Conspicuously." Advertisement from the U.S. Department of Agriculture, 1918–1919.

ticularly harsh. For over 700 years we blamed rats for the spread of medieval plagues that killed tens of millions of humans in Europe, Asia, and North Africa. Recent findings indicate, however, that a combination of poor human hygiene, body lice, and fleas was much more likely the culprit.[1]

Ratting

So hated were rats in the nineteenth century that Ratting—pitting a dog against hundreds of rats in an enclosure—was a popular blood sport. In 1862 a bull terrier named Jacko was championed for killing one hundred rats in under six minutes.

RATTING—" THE GRAHAM ARMS," GRAHAM STREET. '

Illustration of *Ratting,* from Henry Mayhew's London Labour and the London Poor, 1861

Rats have lived among us for over 3.5 million years. Most species originated in Asia, and all learned quite quickly that it was beneficial to follow humans. Thus rats traveled with explorers and merchants and invading tribes, hitching rides on boats and barges, carts and caravans, exuberantly multiplying and colonizing along trade routes and in distant lands. With the exception of Antarctica, there is no continent where rats are not currently found.

Alert to opportunity, clever at problem solving, and able to squeeze or gnaw through almost anything, rats go where they want, when they want. It's one of the things that most frustrates us about them. And yet so much of what infuriates us about rats might also be admired.

Smart and savvy, rats are persistent and adaptable. Though they live near filth, they are remarkably clean. Hard to trap and wily at escaping, they have an uncanny knack for survival. We want to control them, but we can't—at least not for long. Their rowdy antics and shrewd, secretive nature, their association with dirt, disease, and unrestrained sexual reproduction are an affront to our desire for order, morality, cleanliness, and purity. Thus we despise and insult the rat.

What better animal to be the repository of the collective human Shadow? The rat is always out there, hiding inside our structures, skittering through our rubbish, sneaking into our language and stories. So many of the qualities we project onto rats mirror our own unpleasant problems: overpopulation, pollution, epidemics, indecency, and scandal. Rat offends us, activating awareness of all that we don't want to see in ourselves . . . which is why we hate them so.

What is it about rats that we don't want to see in ourselves?

RAT FACTS

Humans have identified sixty-five rat species in the genus *Rattus,* or true rats, including the ones we are most familiar with: brown rats (*Rattus norvegicus,* also known as Norway rats) and black rats (*Rattus rattus,* also known as ship rats or roof rats).[2] Some species not of the *Rattus* genus look and behave in similar ways, and so we also call them rats. Small rat species may be only 5 inches long, but some grow quite large. The Gambian pouched rat of Africa, for example, can measure 3 feet long from nose to tail.

Though we sometimes think of rats as loners, they aren't. Most live in small family communities that sleep, play, and groom together. Rat groups—called *mischiefs*—can be territorial and protective of their own. Most rats are omnivores and like to scavenge; some kill small insects or animals, and some are vegetarians.

Well known for their fecundity, a female rat can mate up to 500 times in the six hours of receptivity she experiences about fifteen times a year. Gestation is only three weeks long, and most litters are of six to ten pups (though there may be up to twenty-two). At three months old most rats are sexually mature. This means that a single pair of rats may produce up to 2,000 offspring and descendants in just one year.[3]

Amazing Rat Abilities

- Can swim—some species over a mile
- Can tread water for three days without drowning
- Can hold their breath for three minutes
- Can squeeze through an opening the size of a quarter
- Can fall 50 feet without injury
- Can jump to 3 feet vertically from a standing position
- Can survive being flushed down the toilet, and return via the same route[4]

The amazing rat!

In addition to their notable survival abilities, rats also have an endearing quality—they laugh! In the late 1990s neuroscientist Jaak Panksepp unexpectedly discovered that during playtime lab rats—especially juveniles—made high-frequency chirps that resembled human laughter.[5] To test his theory the scientist conducted rat-tickling experiments. Though he initially considered tickling rats with a machine, Panksepp realized this would not be tickling at all, for "tickling has to be done in a joyful way. It has to have the characteristics of play. . . . Give an animal a really good time, you know?"[6]

Panksepp discovered that rats are ticklish (especially on the back of the neck) and the ones that emitted the most laugh-chirps seemed to be the most playful. He also observed that tickling created a bond between rat and human.[7]

What does this tell us? Perhaps that rats have more in common with humans than we realize. Or that by making an attempt to understand rats we may better understand ourselves. As Panksepp noted, the more we know about our animal emotions, "the more ideas we will have about how to be better people. As we follow the old philosophical advice to 'know thyself,' the more options we will have for being good to others and the world."[8]

Rats have a sense of humor. Rats, in fact, think the world is very funny. And they are right, reader. They are right.

KATE DiCAMILLO,
THE TALE OF DESPEREAUX

FOR THE LOVE OF RAT

"Dear Tatti: I love you, and I miss you. Of all the animals who've lived with me, you were physically the closest. You were on my body so much of the time: on my shoulder, my arm, my lap, in my hand. It was an intimacy of

touch, of warmth, of the senses. I loved your ratty smell, your delicate pads, always clean, scrupulously groomed. I loved your long tail that freaked out so many people. I loved your profuse whiskers, your round translucent ears, your little black, shiny eyes, your warm white underbelly . . ."[9]

So begins a love letter from the late performance artist, author, and animal activist Rachel Rosenthal to her cherished rat, Tatti Wattles. Rosenthal was fond of rats, particularly Wattles, who appeared in her performances and accompanied her to parties and workshops. Tatti Wattles not only helped Rosenthal teach humans about the virtues of rats, but was honored as "a very famous art rat."[10]

Some may find it hard to believe that a human could so love a rat, yet those who live with rats as friends and companions wholly understand. *They are so smart, so affectionate, so cute and clean and clever!* rat aficionados affirm. These humans acknowledge and appreciate the positive qualities of rats—their intelligence and empathy, their eagerness to play, their loyalty and sensitivity to stress in others. In short, they respect, admire, and love rats.

Contrary to common public opinion, rats are very clean. They keep tidy nests and are attentive and affectionate to their offspring. In fact, rats are kind, friendly, sociable animals that have been observed

Some humans find rats to be lively friends and loving companions.

sharing food with one another, caring for the sick and injured, and even attempting to free other rats from traps.

The truth about rats is far from our stereotype. And some humans find that to be an interesting aspect to stimulate change. In the early 1980s a French graffiti artist who called himself Blek Le Rat stenciled large images of black rats running along brick walls throughout Paris. Inspired to spread street art as a means of raising awareness of social issues—homelessness, war, urban decay, poverty—Blek championed the rat's ability to outsmart and survive.

Twenty years later the British graffiti artist known as Banksy similarly used rat images on bridges and buildings all over the world. "They exist without permission," Banksy wrote about rats in his autobiographical *Wall and Piece*. "They are hated, hunted and persecuted. They live in quiet desperation amongst the filth. And yet they are capable of bringing entire civilizations to their knees. If you are dirty, insignificant and unloved then rats are the ultimate role model."[11]

Not only is Rat an anagram of *Art*, there's also a telling link between Rat and street artist. Creative, clever, and not easily controlled, both Rat and graffiti artist understand self-preservation by skillfully using stealth, anonymity, and the cover of darkness to avoid detection. Inventive and resourceful, they dare to challenge the confines of conventional reality and escape being caged by small-minded ways of thinking.

Street rat photographer, by Banksy. What does Rat
see about us that we do not acknowledge?

IN THE SHADOW OF THE HUMAN PSYCHE

Despite the animosity humans hold for them, rats survive. Indeed, one of Rat's many gifts is the ability to continue regardless of the opinions of others. That is why in Eastern cultures Rat is often associated with good fortune, success in business, and the capacity to withstand negative public opinion.

As rats are frequently found with food, they were early on associated with prosperity and wealth. In some Asian countries Rat is also a symbol of fertility, children, and good luck. Daikoku, the Japanese god of wealth and happiness, has a companion white rat, also regarded as a symbol of the deity.

In Chinese mythology Rat brings the gift of rice—a symbol of wealth and wisdom—to humans. Rat is also the first animal of the Chinese zodiac. Those born in the Year of the Rat are perceptive and creative, with good imagination and curiosity. Like Rat, such people are quick thinkers, sensitive yet savvy, and alert to opportunity. As luck would have it, this chapter was written in the Year of the Rat.

God of good fortune and happiness, Daikoku, sits against a full rice bag with his pet rat. Japanese calendar print by Katsukawa Shunzen, 1792.

In India the elephant-headed god Ganesh rides a rat. Ganesh, Lord of Abundance, is most known for his ability to remove obstacles, and his *vahana* (Sanskrit for "vehicle," usually denoting the animal or mythical being used by a deity for transportation) shares this ability. Rat is relentless in finding ways in and out, squeezing through narrow pathways, gnawing through barriers and obstructions. There is something humorous yet appropriate in the pairing of pot-bellied Ganesh and long-tailed Rat, moving together, triumphing over obstacles, and making clear the way.

Ganesh on his bejeweled vahana, Rat. Color print, bazaar art, 1910.

While Eastern perspectives of Rat may celebrate good luck and prosperity, it's a different story in the West. One of our oldest and most famous rat tales is *Der Rattenfänger von Hameln*. This legend from the late thirteenth century tells the story of a colorfully dressed traveler who is hired to exterminate rats in the German town of Hamlin. The rat catcher uses a magical pipe to lure the rats to a river, where they drowned. But when the mayor refuses to pay for his services, the piper retaliates by enchanting the children of the town and leading them to a distant place—a mountain, a cave, a river—where they are never seen again.

Gruss aus Hameln, lithograph, 1902

From street to street he piped advancing,
And step for step they followed dancing,
ROBERT BROWNING, *THE PIED PIPER OF HAMELIN*

The story speaks to something deep in the human psyche, for it has been told and retold many times throughout the ages—as an opera, a folktale by the Brothers Grimm, in poems by Goethe and Robert Browning, and as children's stories and films.

The town's collective fears—disease, crowding, infestation—are conveniently projected onto rats. How wonderful that a mysterious piper agrees to get rid of them! After the rats are gone, however, the town reneges on the deal, either refusing payment or offering much less. This twist to the story is the crux of what happens when we try to cheat or shortcut our work with Shadow.

While the townspeople may think they have cleverly disposed of the dark forces that lurk within their psyche, their collective Shadow emerges in other forms: greed, arrogance, fraud, betrayal. The town continues to project its Shadow because it is not yet ready to be responsible. As author Terry Pratchett notes in his smart and humorous take on the tale in *The Amazing Maurice and His Educated Rodents,* here is a story about people and rats in which it's difficult to discern who are the people and who are the rats.

Could the same be true of how we use lab rats in scientific experiments? Along with mice, rats make up 95 percent of all laboratory animals currently used in medical research.[12] Rats are well suited for psychological experiments because they are small, smart, trainable, and quick to solve puzzles and problems.

First used scientifically in the 1850s because of their close resemblance to human physiology and genetic makeup, rats became our biomedical stand-ins. We have since controlled their movements with implanted electronics, electrically shocked them as negative stimulus, induced heart failure to test new drugs, and re-created human diseases in them through genetic engineering.

Whether we should use rats—or any animal at all—in medical experiments is a complicated and controversial subject. But this should not divert us from recognizing the immense gift that rats have contributed to our health and well-being. Experiments with rats have helped humans learn about Alzheimer's, cardiovascular disease, cancer, diabetes, HIV, and many other infectious diseases. As noted by the Foundation for Biomedical Research, "Human medicine would not be where it is today without the incredible contributions of these small yet mighty animals."[13]

Because rats are quick to move through mazes and solve puzzles, they are sometimes used in scientific experiments to better understand the human brain.

And yet, instead of thanking rats for the many treatments, cures, and therapies their sacrifice has given us, we toss them aside. At the end of experimentation, the majority of lab rats and mice (an estimated 100 million a year) are killed by lethal injection, decapitation, or suffocation with carbon dioxide.[14] Clearly this tells us much more about the human psyche than it does about rats.

What would happen if we respected rats for the helpful skills they offer to humans and treat them as the heroes they may be? APOPO, a nonprofit organization based in Tanzania, has done exactly that. Their mission—to "protect people and the planet with innovative solutions using trained rats and other scent detection animals"—has included training over 800 African giant pouched rats over the last twenty years to detect tuberculosis as well as hidden landmines that still plague humans in over fifty countries.*

Drawing upon their intelligence and acute sense of smell, the trained "HeroRATs" have helped humans to save time, money, and lives. A single HeroRAT can search a potential landmine area the size of a tennis court in thirty minutes, while a human deminer could take up to four days to cover the same area with a metal detector. Similarly, a human technician using a microscope can take up to four days to check a hundred sputum samples for tuberculosis (TB), while a HeroRAT can successfully accomplish the same task in only twenty minutes.

As APOPO notes, the rats are "sociable, clean and intelligent animals and it is very satisfying to see how they respond to our training methods and how hard they work. Many people still think of rats as dirty and stupid animals but they are actually very smart and likable. The rats all have unique personalities. Some are very energetic, constantly moving and running about, while others are more relaxed. A few of the rats are very vocal, happily squeaking when they are about to be fed, while they are being handled, and sometimes while they are working."[15]

With their own care-taking staff that makes sure they are well fed, happy, and healthy, HeroRATs work only a few hours a day. And, unlike lab rats, a HeroRAT retires in comfort. Notes APOPO, "We

*In 1975 pet rat owner Bart Weetjens envisioned scent-detecting rats as a solution to the global landmine problem. The APOPO project was launched in 1997. See their website at Apopo.org for more details.

HeroRAT at work, sniffing for landmines
Photo courtesy of Aaron Gekoski/APOPO

allow them to work as long as they are performing well, still feel like working, and pass weekly health checks. We notice that the rats are generally enthusiastic to work but when they are growing old, some simply don't feel like getting out of their cage to work anymore. If that happens or when a rat's performance has declined or it is not healthy enough to continue working, the rat is retired to its home cage. When they are retired to their cages, they receive a healthy diet, are regularly taken out

Bart and Chavez, working partners
Photo courtesy of APOPO

to play and exercise, and continue to receive weekly health checks. If a rat is clearly suffering in its old age or from an untreatable disease, it is humanely euthanized."[16]

Because they are too light to set off the explosives, the rats are completely safe on the minefield; no rat has ever been harmed during training or operations. Yet their sensitive nose and willingness to work with humans have prevented countless deaths and tragedies (half of all landmine explosions involve children).

Let us remember that humans planted these explosives in the first place! What other forgotten landmines lurk within the human shadow that Rat may help us to retrieve?

RAT'S GIFTS

Author James Hillman tells the story of a kind man who was failing in his new career in real estate. Then the man dreamed of a figure he called Rat. Hillman recounts as follows:

> Rat began accompanying him on sales calls. They talked in the car before he walked into a house. Our man began to find quick answers, which sprang to his lips to his great surprise, instead of vague sales talk that he had learned on tape. He began to avoid traps laid for him and showed some teeth when cornered. And, he spent the late nights studying, under Rat's tutelage, wising up about zonings and regulations, about the maze of laws and small print in bank loans. (Remember, rats are used by high-tech science for their learning capacity.)
>
> He also began to look out for number one, himself, thereby gaining confidence and being less paranoid that he was always being taken, being deceived by everyone. Until he knew Rat, he only knew the rat's unconscious effects, those shadowy suspicions of others and gnawing doubts about himself.[17]

Discernment, innovative thinking, and excellence at problem solving—these are only some of the qualities Rat can offer when we ask for help. On the lookout for opportunity yet wary of traps, Rat knows that it is better to assess before acting, and that what may seem longer or harder may actually be our best choice. What makes rats extra clever is that they don't always choose the obvious.

So when Rat shows up in our life, we might begin to ask ourselves some questions.

Are we involved in exasperating circumstances? Do we need to discover a way out or do we need the fortitude to keep on keeping on? Rat knows how to do both, and has the wisdom to know which is best. Rats sense when situations are hopeless (always look to a rat when wondering whether to abandon ship), but so too are they focused and persistent, rarely giving up. Rat can help those who feel trapped or need to escape sticky situations.

Is there a part of us that we have typecast as a rat? Do we scurry to survive, do dirty work, wear shabby clothes, or settle for ratty relationships? Is there a part of ourselves that we have repeatedly disregarded or undervalued? Rat can help us find what we have abandoned or degraded so that we may begin to embrace the hurt, resentful, neglected, or rejected parts of self that cause us to act in the ways we do.

Rat's Special Talents

- Resourcefulness
- Determination
- Resiliency
- Adaptability
- Creativity
- Dexterity of mind and body
- Nonconformance

Rats are skillful scavengers and find value in what others have discarded. An expert in repurposing, Rat offers creative, unconventional solutions.

Rats are commonly known to hoard. We use the term *pack rat* to describe both a ratlike rodent that collects sticks and debris in its nest as well as a person who saves and stockpiles. Although hoarding can easily spiral out of control, there is wisdom in Rat's advice to be mindful of the many resources that are all around us. For Rat knows that it is at home, in ourselves, that we often find our most useful hidden treasures.

◆ ◆ **Exercise** ◆ ◆

Rat's Treasures, Three Ways

The following exercises feature journaling, placement, and collage as ways to learn more about your relationship with Shadow. Based on Rat's advice to make good use of resources, each activity focuses on gathering thoughts, images, and objects that hold shadow material for you. You may enjoy doing all three exercises, for each offers a different facet of collecting and curating.

Shadow Journal

Think of it as a safe place to release pent-up feelings or troubling emotions. A journal is a space of expression, not judgment. Be brave and record the dreams or events in daily life that trigger revulsion, disgust, sorrow, shame, embarrassment. Did you have an encounter with a frightening animal or see one that made you shudder? Collecting such observations can help you to notice patterns and themes. By recording encounters with Shadow and noting perceptions about our experiences, we can better understand and love ourselves.

Shadow Shrine

A shrine contains sacred objects, meaningful relics, or memorabilia. Create a shrine to display representations of your shadow animal (such as images, statues, fur, or feathers). You might focus on what frightens you or other emotions your animal evokes—anger, anxiety, negligence, regret. Following Rat's guidance, survey your stash of resources by seeking out objects you may have put away or stored for safekeeping. Why did you box them up? Do they represent something lost or abandoned?

Place your altar in a prominent position to be more aware of Shadow on a daily basis. Play with moving, adding, or subtracting objects as your views of Shadow change. Add a candle to observe the ongoing interplay of light and dark.

Shadow Card

It can be very revealing to collage our perceptions while working with a shadow animal. Use printed material, sketch your own, or pull from the internet the designs, words, and images that speak to you. I created the card below to feature the aspects of Rat most significant to me while writing this chapter—companion, small animal that needs to eat, pirate scavenger who knows of buried treasure, and commemorated figure in story and legend. I was amused to find that Rat lives in the middle of narrator. In many ways this is what I most admire about Rat—that it is the narrator of its own life, regardless of our opinion.

Rat Card created by collecting, arranging, and layering images and words.

3

Suspense
and Suspension

Between me and the moonlight flitted a great bat,
coming and going in great, whirling circles.

BRAM STOKER, *DRACULA*

Like rats, bats are routinely feared and very much misunderstood. In older times they were called flittermice, derived from the German word *fledermause,* or flying mouse. While bats may look like fluttery-winged rodents, they are actually more closely related to humans. In fact, the similarity between the bones in our hands and the elongated bones in bat wings is very close—which is why we gave their taxonomic order the name Chiroptera, Greek for "hand-wing."

As the only mammal that can fly, bats have mystified humans since ancient times. Sleeping upside down in dark, secluded spaces— in caves, under bridges, inside hollow trees—leathery wings wrapped around their bodies like a cloak, a shroud, there is a Gothic quality about bats. Some have gargoyle-like faces and some drink blood, and so we sometimes associate them with the nefarious and sinister.

It's understandable how bats speak to our fears, for so much about them is suspect. Like many shadow animals, they are creatures of the night, active between dusk and dawn. Spreading their dark wings against the moonlit sky, bats embody nocturnal mysteries.

Flying bat with outstretched wings. Humans and bats have the same number and types of bones in the forearm. Note the wrist bones ending in four elongated "finger" bones (covered by the wing membrane) and one "thumb," extending at the top of each wing as a small claw.

As a teacher Bat often appears when things are breaking down, when the old is ready to release, when loss is imminent. At home in the uncertain space between endings and beginnings, Bat can help us view life from a different perspective. We may not like it, but sometimes we need our world turned upside down in order to truly see.

With its head inverted Bat offers unexpected frames of reference. Hang with Bat and new vantage points may be explored, new visions stirred, new truths perceived. Bat promises change—if we are willing to venture outside our comfort zone and stay the course.

A small animal with strong medicine, Bat can be a powerful initiator and ally, especially in times of uncertainty. More than anything, however, Bat challenges us to face our fears. If we are not ready for it, Bat's guidance can be disturbing. As the Guardian of Night, Bat signals dark mysteries of the Unknown.

Die Fledermaus, by Vincent van Gogh, 1885

THE BAT GODS

In ancient Babylonia bats represented the souls of the dead. To the Maya they were a symbol of transformation and rebirth. And in medieval Europe, they were likened to miniature dragons.

Many early peoples were fascinated by the unusual appearance and habits of bats, but intrigue was strongest in South America. As more bats and bat species live in the South American tropics than anywhere else, it makes sense that bats figure prominently there in folklore and legend. One myth features a Bat-Man who teaches humans all they need to know. The Inca sometimes added bat fur to the silky wool of the vicuna for royal vestments, and Atahualpa, last of the Incan rulers, was said to wear a cape made entirely from the skins of bats—the "birds that fly at night."

A variety of pre-Columbian artifacts depict human figures with bat-like features: large, pointy ears; open mouths with sharp teeth; arms merging into wings; and ornate, facial "nose leafs," unique to several families of bats.

For the Maya the greatest bat deity was Camazotz, the Death Bat, a cave-dwelling creature with a human body, large bat wings, and knife-like nose. Known for decapitation, Camazotz was often shown carrying a sword or sacrificial knife in one hand and a human head in the other.

Stories in the sacred Popol Vuh (a collection of oral legends, later recorded in 1550) describe the trials of twin brothers in the

Chiroptera from Ernst Haeckel's *Kunstformen der Natur*, 1904, includes drawings of the big-eared woolly bat, the flower-faced bat, the greater spear-nosed bat, the thumbless bat, and the spectral bat.

underworld. One challenge involves spending an entire night in the House of Bats, a labyrinthine cave overseen by Camazotz. The men crouch and hide to escape swarms of screeching killer bats. When the bat creatures are finally silent, one brother raises his head to see if the sun has risen. It has not and, in his haste, the man is promptly decapitated by Camazotz, who carries his head to the ball court to be used by the gods in a game.

Mesoamerica tribes associated bats not only with death and rebirth, but also with sacrifice—especially in the form of decapitation. It's an interesting connection that might have originated like this: Bats sleep in caves, portals to the underworld and deep transformation. When they emerge from these dark chambers of deathlike slumber, they feast upon the blood of animals. Perhaps they do this to appease Camazotz? Perhaps we should follow suit and offer human blood to the Death Bat, so that we may live longer, stronger lives?

Blood sacrifice to the gods (often obtained by human decapitation) occurred in many ancient New World cultures. And bats—creatures of both skyward and subterranean realms, connectors of heaven and earth—were a powerful symbol for that sacrifice. In one legend Bat gives humans a special knife for sacred decapitation. Thus Bat figures and bat deities are present on many pre-Columbian ceremonial artifacts, including swords, knives, sacrificial bowls, and funerary urns (see photo on page 82).

Some tribes had folktales about bats biting humans and draining their blood. This may have derived from observations of a small bat that drinks blood from the neck and shoulder of cattle and other large mammals. More likely, however, the association was linked to imagined fears about the great false vampire bat (*Vampyrum spectrum*). As the largest carnivorous bat, with an impressive wingspan of over 3 feet, the false vampire (depicted on page 82) eats rodents, birds, and other bats by grabbing a prey's neck in its powerful jaw, often killing with a single bite.

OF VAMPIRES AND VAMPIRE BATS

For thousands of years before European explorers witnessed tiny bats in South America drinking blood, vampires were firmly entrenched in

Zapotec ceramic funerary urn with the head of a Bat God. Found in the tombs at Monte Alban, a pre-Columbian archaeological site in Oaxaca, Mexico.

The great false vampire bat (*Vampyrum spectrum*), also known as the spectral bat, is a large carnivorous bat found in Central and South America. Drawing by German zoologist Eduard Oscar Schmidt, mid-1800s.

myth and folklore. Ancient tales from Babylonia, India, Greece, and China describe troubled souls wandering the night, killing humans for blood. These were the undead, the bloodthirsty, the early vampires.

The most descriptive stories came from Eastern Europe, and it is from the Hungarian word *vampir* (meaning "blood drunkenness") that we get the word *vampire*. Early legends noted that vampires could travel as flame or smoke, or shapeshift into other animals such as horses, dogs, cats, snakes, and fleas—but never bats.

As the tales migrated to western Europe, exaggerated claims about vampires skulking the night to drain humans of their blood incited waves of mass hysteria. The black plague, smallpox, and other epidemics that wiped out entire villages were often blamed as the work of vampires.

When Spanish explorers first observed little bats consuming blood from cattle in the mid-1500s, they called them "vampires" to distinguish them from other species of bats. Perhaps the name was a witty jest for the explorers, who were astonished to find bats with such extreme food specialization.

There are only three species of vampire bats, and all live in Central and South America. These include the hairy-legged vampire bat, the white-winged vampire bat, and most well known, the common vampire bat, *Desmodus rotundus* (see page 84). Weighing only 2 ounces, this petite, 4-inch bat has pointy ears, small round eyes, and a snouty nose leaf that houses heat-sensing pits.

Among the most agile of bats, the common vampire lands near the neck of its sleeping prey. Gently licking the area, it makes a small incision with its sharp teeth and daintily laps the blood, rather like a kitten lapping milk. The tiny bat can only drink 2 tablespoons of blood a day—certainly not enough to kill a cow, horse, chicken, or pig.

It wasn't until Bram Stoker published *Dracula* in 1897 that a vampire takes the form of a bat. It was an inspired connection that linked the strange truths of nature with our fears of the supernatural. Stoker's Dracula is bat-like in appearance: pointed ears, sharp teeth, and a flowing black cape. Like bats, he is active at night and sleeps during the day in a dark, enclosed space. Like earlier forms of vampires, he is able to shapeshift, taking the form of a wolf, a dog, a fog, and—most

Vampire bat (*Desmodus rotundus*). Researchers have discovered this bat's saliva contains a powerful anticoagulant (nicknamed draculin after Stoker's Count Dracula) that may prove helpful in treating blood clots and strokes.
Photo by Uwe Schmidt, CC BY-SA 4.0

notably—a bat. The association became archetypal, and Stoker's link between vampires and bats would forever change the way many of us think about both.

A COMPLETELY DIFFERENT VIEW

In parts of Asia, China especially, there is nothing nefarious about bats. Rather, Bat is all about health, wealth, and longevity. The word *bat* in traditional Chinese sounds similar to the word for "good fortune," another reason why bats are considered lucky animals.

From the early 1600s to the end of imperial China in the early 1900s, bats were routinely painted on palace walls and vases, carved into furniture and thrones, embroidered on expensive clothing and royal robes, all to influence prosperity and well-being. As symbols of good luck, bat images were also used in classical feng shui to attract happiness and auspicious dreams.

Woman's ceremonial bat medallion robe, featuring metallic thread embroidered on silk satin, circa first half of the eighteenth century, China

With their acute sensing abilities, bats can navigate quickly and efficiently to find what they need. For this reason, the Chinese believed they were masters at locating good *chi*. Bat designs were commonly used to augment positive energy, security, and joy in the home. Bat charms attached to gold coins and red tassels were hung by doors or outside windows, both to welcome prosperity and prevent disease from entering. Doubly talented, Bat draws in the good and repels the bad.

Zhong Kui, the Demon Queller, was a popular deity in Chinese mythology from the early 600s onward. As a guardian spirit he was called upon to vanquish ghosts and evil spirits. Bats were his special helpers in locating hidden demons since they could see in the dark. As the myths evolved Zhong Kui became a vehicle of good luck and fortune, and a grouping of five bats pictured near the deity represented *WuFu,* the five blessings: long life, health, wealth, happiness, and a natural death in old age.

Zhong Kui, the Demon Queller, waves his sword to invoke good fortune and ward off harm. The five bats on his left represent WuFu, the five blessings. Wood engraving on paper from late nineteenth to early twentieth century, China.

Over 1,000 years later and a continent away, Americans were introduced to a modern-day demon queller who called himself Batman. The origin story in a 1939 *Detective Comics* shows millionaire Bruce Wayne in his study contemplating ideas for his new persona. "Criminals are a superstitious and cowardly lot, so my disguise must be able to strike terror into their hearts," he says to himself. "I must be a creature of the night, black, terrible . . ."

In the next frame, as if in answer to his contemplation, a huge bat flies through the open window. "A bat!" exclaims Wayne. "That's it! It's an omen. I shall become a bat!" Thus is born this "weird figure of the dark," reads the top bar. "This avenger of evil—'The Batman.'"[1]

BAT FACTS

From blood-drunk vampire to Demon Queller, from symbol of wealth and happy dreams to feared shadow creature, the ideas and representations we hold of Bat span a great spectrum. But these are human projections upon Bat not facts.

Over 1,300 species strong, bats are widely diverse in size and behavior. The world's smallest mammal is a bat: the Kitti's hog-nosed bat, also known as the bumblebee bat, less than 2 inches long with a wingspan of less than 6 inches. At the other extreme the giant golden-crowned flying fox can weigh over 4 pounds, with a wingspan up to 6 feet wide.

Humans classify bats by dividing them into two suborders: Megachiroptera and Microchiroptera. Megabats, sometimes called flying foxes or fruit bats, are medium- to large-sized bats that mostly eat fruit, pollen, and nectar. Their ears are small, their snouts long, and their eyes large to help them see well in twilight.

Left: The Sulawesi flying fox (*Acerodon celebensis*) is an endangered fruit-eating bat endemic to Sulawesi and several other Indonesian islands.
Right: The grey-headed flying fox (*Pteropus poliocephalus*), with a wingspan of up to 40 inches, is the largest bat in Australia. Its long fur is streaked gray and, unique to the *Pteropus* genus, extends all the way to its ankle.

Microchiroptera are little bats with pushed-in snouts and elaborate nostrils. Their eyes are small and their ears are large since they rely on echolocation to navigate and find food. Unlike their fruit-loving cousins, microbats are carnivores. Some eat fish, frogs, and other bats, but most eat insects: flies, grasshoppers, mosquitoes, beetles, cockroaches, and more.

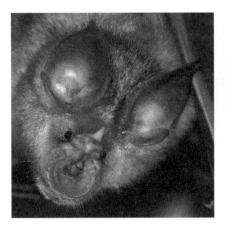 

Left: The greater horseshoe bat (*Rhinolophus ferrumequinum*) is the largest of the horseshoe bats, all of which have a distinctive horseshoe shape in the lower portion of their nose leaf that helps to focus ultrasound.
Right: The brown long-eared bat (*Plecotus auritus*), also called the common long-eared bat, is a small Eurasian bat with long ears that feature a distinctive fold. Their excellent hearing allows them to sense the subtle flutter of a moth in flight.

Chiroptera have survived more than 50 million years, and it's a good thing for humans that they have. While Bat provides us with an array of powerful teachings, the wide variety of bat species contribute to a healthy environment by providing us free pollination, fertilization, and pest control.

The Benefits of Bats

If you like tequila, thank a bat! Macrobats are the major pollinators of many flowers, cacti, and fruit trees, including avocado, banana, date, fig, mango, cashew, and blue agave—used to make tequila. Bats help to pollinate over 1,000 plant species worldwide, and in the tropics over 500 species of flowering plants rely on bats as a major or exclusive pollinator.[2]

Microbats provide an equally awesome service to the world in the form of nontoxic pest control. As the best bug killers on the planet, bats can eat half their weight in insects a night. They not only take a huge bite out of bugs that damage crops or spread disease—such as malaria and West Nile virus—but also reduce the need for

Nectar-eating bats are nocturnal pollinators.
They are most attracted to large, fragrant, pale-colored blooms.

pesticides. The little brown bat can eat 1,200 mosquitos an hour. And an immense (1.5 million) colony of Mexican free-tail bats living under a bridge in Austin, Texas, eats over 15 tons of insects nightly. A recent study of the economic importance of bats to North American agriculture estimates their value in pest-control to be between 3.7 and 53 billion dollars a year![3]

Bats also serve an important ecological role in the form of guano. Many cave animals, fungi, and bacteria—entire cave ecosystems, in fact—are dependent upon bats for the nutrients their guano provides. Rich in carbon, nitrogen, potassium, and phosphorous, bat droppings are not only a powerful fertilizer, but were once used to make gunpowder and explosives. Scientists are now exploring guano bacteria and enzymes for other potential benefits.

BAT'S TEACHINGS

One of the easiest ways to discern the teaching of any animal is simple observation. What are this animal's habits? How is it unique? What might we learn from this animal's expertise? Let us consider Bat . . .

Inversion

While an inverted sleeping posture may seem strange or strenuous to us, for bats it makes perfect sense. Hanging in high spaces allows bats to hide safely from the reach of predators. Because bats can't launch from the ground, the hanging position is also ideal for a quick takeoff. Further, the upside-down weight of their body causes a bat's talons to lock in place. For bats, it's a relaxing position.

Are you struggling to hang on or see things in a different way? Bat can help us grasp what we need in an easy manner, even when it seems that everything is pulling us down. Shifting away from routine and viewing the world from a reversed, transposed, or inverted perspective opens us to different viewpoints. And a safe, quiet space away from others affords us peaceful contemplation. Bat reminds us to retreat and repose, allowing alternate points of view to unfold as we await change.

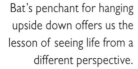

Bat's penchant for hanging upside down offers us the lesson of seeing life from a different perspective.

Right Timing

Bats undergo torpor to slow down their metabolism and conserve energy when inactive. They can do this for just a few hours on chilly days or for extended periods when hibernating. Female bats can also keep their embryos in stasis until conditions are more favorable for birth.

Bat reminds us to pay attention to the pulse of life when discerning the most appropriate time for rest, change, and birth. Bat's teaching requires us to stay the course so that we may fully release the old and successfully birth the new. It's seldom a quick change. If we hurry ahead or quit prematurely, we may end up like the brother in the Popol Vuh story and lose our head.

Heightened Sensing

Humans once believed bats were blind since they fluttered in erratic patterns. Bats are not blind, and many have excellent eyesight, sometimes better than humans.

Extremely sensitive to its surroundings and attuned to a wide spectrum of frequencies, Bat can help us fine-tune our abilities to perceive. Indeed, studying with Bat may involve lessons in seeing what is not seen, or hearing what is not said. Bat reminds us to stay alert, pay attention, and consider a range of perspectives.

Some bats are particularly gifted in the dark, using echolocation to "see" in the absence of light. Night vision allows bats to perceive what is obscured. As a shadow ally, Bat can teach us to see through illusion and deception, or to discern hidden messages and meanings. Bat can also help us to locate our blind spots and uncover the secrets we hide from ourselves.

Because they often live in caves, bats are sometimes connected with the dreamworld. Bat can help us heighten awareness in dreamtime, develop intuitive abilities, and hone perceptions in non-ordinary realities. To do that, however, we need to see past our fears—most of which, Bat reminds us, are self-generated.

Maneuverability

Unlike insects and birds, bats have very flexible wings. Similar to human hands, the many bones and joints in bat forelimbs allow them to spread and twist their wings in a great many ways. Thus they can weave and dive and soar, slicing through the air on folded wings or swooping through the night sky to snatch insects on the fly. A master of maneuverability, Bat can help us increase flexibility and move with greater ease.

But so too can those wings wrap around Bat like a warm blanket, a personal blackout curtain. Bat reminds us that sometimes we need to take a break and shut off outer world distractions so that we can focus inward. Enfolding ourselves when needed, we can settle into the dark and allow insight to occur.

Death

The sudden appearance of Bat often signifies the imminence of powerful change. What is broken and can no longer be repaired? Bat does not simply nudge us to take a chance on change. Rather, Bat announces that a shift is needed—now!

We often fear transitions—and Bat's arrival may coincide with great loss, calamity, disorder, or disease. Sometimes we need the enormity of crisis to slow us down, to prod us into the quiet, dark cave of self so that we can release what no longer serves.

Bat offers a shamanic death. Indeed, one of Bat's greatest gifts is instigating death of the old so that we can birth the new.

Dark Soul Journey

As I wrote this chapter, a friend reminded me that his "dark soul journey" was announced by a bat that had lost its way. "There are no coincidences," he noted.

"It was several days after my dog died. I had just left my home, family, friends, and job. I had decided to change my point of view from outside to inside and, with this, to step away from the old, falling-apart life. I was renting a farmer's house in the middle of nowhere. All at once I heard a noise at the window and there I saw her, the little bat. She looked so fragile. She had somehow got in through the open window but could not get out. I gently held her with the curtain and—whoosh!—she was gone."

Thus began a very dark time for my friend. "It was a deep fall into the dark, yes," he told me, "but more importantly it was a fall into the trust. My old life could not be cemented anymore; too much had fallen apart. In retrospect, I understand that daring to step out of this tragedy was important. Only then did the bat show herself. She did not announce joy and sunshine, but many, many different emotions and a lot of darkness until the point of death. To me, it felt like the most natural question in the world: do you want to stay on this earth or go back into the light? This experience was not joyful, but it was necessary to gain clarity and silence. In the end, it felt like dismemberment and repair of the soul."

Rebirth

Sleeping in the dark, womb-like belly of the earth during the day, bats awaken and emerge from caves at twilight. Early humans thus associated bats with rebirth and resurrection.

Let us remember, however, that Bat is reborn not into the light, but into the night. Best not to expect fairy-tale endings. Bat leads us to something much more powerful, much more mysterious. Bat initiates birth into the Great Unknown.

Bat's Expertise

- Fine-tunes perception
- Enhances intuitive abilities
- Reveals alternate perspectives
- Deepens stillness
- Improves mental and physical agility
- Connects endings and beginnings
- Initiates the Great Mystery

Bats gliding through the twilight skies of Sydney, Australia

FACING OUR FEARS

What are you avoiding? What causes you angst, dread, or trepidation?

Bat is an expert in helping us to face our fears. While this may seem a daunting task, we are usually much worse off imagining those fears than confronting them. Just as the untreated bite of a rabid bat can lead to madness, so too can unchecked fears lead to anxiety, apprehension, phobia, and terror if we allow them to rule.

Bat is an exacting teacher and will not tolerate half-hearted work. Perhaps Bat is so demanding because its teaching can be difficult or dangerous to those who are not yet ready. We may be required to deepen in shadow exploration, open to radical transformation, or embrace a major life change.

Bat reminds us that great work is done in the dark. It's where seeds sprout and healing occurs. By exploring our own darkness we may awaken inner vision and discover a greater lightness of being. Being with Bat is about gaining wisdom and accepting and implementing the necessary changes for our ever-evolving self.

◆ ◆   **Exercise**   ◆ ◆

Be-ing with Bat

While visiting Carlsbad Cavern many years ago, I stood in a large chamber deep in the caves with a group of others. "You don't know dark until you've been in a cavern," announced our guide. As he abruptly killed the lights, we were plunged into a black expanse. My heart quickened as I lost all sense of perspective. I could not see my body, my hands, or anything at all. I was amazed, frightened, exhilarated—and surprised by how quickly I felt at home there, in the dark. A part of me longed for more.

The following exercise may be helpful when you feel stuck in relation to shadow material. All you'll need is a large, soft, lightweight blanket (fleece or puffy down is a good choice) and a very dark space—a closet, a basement, a windowless room.

Make sure you have plenty of time (at least twenty minutes) and will not be disturbed. Find a relaxed position and drape the blanket over your head and back. Holding two corner edges, extend your arms, and wrap your soft "bat wings" around to enclose your body.

Spend a few minutes getting comfortable, breathing calmly, familiarizing yourself with this dark, quiet, peaceful space. You are protected and at ease, at home in your Self.

Folding its wings, bat gently wraps itself for sleep.

If you like, invite Bat to be present with you in the stillness, or to offer guidance.

Allow your body to relax, your mind to loosen. If your thoughts wander, gently shift awareness back to your breath, to the quiet, to the present.

Let go, deeper and deeper, until you feel suspended in the vast expanse of dark. Sometimes we need a dark space to help open the darkness within—sadness or grief or unhappiness that has been stuffed away. Sometimes we need a dark space to help us awaken inner vision. Sometimes we need to stop do-do-doing so that we can be.

This is an exercise of trust. Even if it seems as if nothing much is happening, you may be surprised to discover that you emerge feeling more at ease and capable. You may receive an insight, a vision, or sudden knowing. The exercise helps to awaken internal processes deep in the caverns of our psyche.

You may want to do this exercise several times, spending longer periods in the space of Self, accepting Bat's invitation to deepen your presence and being.

4

The Knower of Secrets

I am the cat of cats. I am
The everlasting cat!
Cunning, and old, and sleek as jam,
The everlasting cat!
  WILLIAM BRIGHTY RANDS, *THE CAT OF CATS*

As noted in the introduction, the first shadow animal I recall from childhood was a cat. Her coat was dark gray, her eyes bright green, and when she gazed at me in an eerily deliberate way, I felt a cold fear rising in my belly that caused me to run. I later sensed that the cat perceived something hidden within me—some secret about myself of which I was unaware.

In my twenties I dreamed of an orange cat sitting on a table. The cat wore a small, ornate fez made from copper, with a black tassel at the side that ended in a feather. Still and silent, she stared at me with a sense of knowing.

For many years the cat appeared in my dreams in various settings: resting atop a refrigerator, lounging on a shelf, perched upon a window ledge. Within the dreams I often realized that I had seen the cat before, and sometimes I became lucid—knowing, within the dream, that I was dreaming. While lucid, I often recalled the previous dreams in which this cat appeared. I also knew that on waking I would forget the dream. How frustrating! It took many years until I was finally able to consciously recall this series of dreams.

Once I was able to remember the dream cat in waking life, she

Cat: Shadow animal, dream guide, knower of secrets

appeared more frequently. She did not speak but rather looked *into* me, and a sense of connection linked us so completely that I understood her thoughts and feelings. I recognized the cat as a teacher, and was eventually able to communicate with her both while waking and dreaming.

The cat told me that she appeared in my dreams at different times as a way to measure my readiness for her teachings. It was not only my ability to recall the dreams in waking life that revealed readiness, said the cat, but also the way in which I related to her presence. The cat explained that one's approach to a mentor is an indication of how one attunes to guidance—as well as a reflection of the type of teaching that might be offered in return.

Most often we teach respect by being respectful, said my cat in the hat as she reviewed with me the many times she had appeared in my dreams: always quietly watching, waiting for me to notice her. I understood that her presence in the dreams was a teaching in itself, her quiet approach allowing me the respect of unfolding at my own rate.[1]

So, what was the secret the cat knew about me? What did she see that I did not? This may be one of the most potent gifts from our shadow animals: guidance to the revelation of that which is forgotten, disowned, or buried deep within ourselves. And it is at this ability that Cat excels.

CAT'S SECRETS

Sly, stealthy, and sometimes scheming, cats are no strangers to secrets. Capable of seeing in the dark, they can perceive what we do not. While domestic cats are mostly crepuscular (active at dusk and dawn), feral cats as well as big cats in the wild tend to be nocturnal. At home in the shadows, cats are often linked with magic, mystery, dreams, and the unknown.

In some myths Cat is guardian to the underworld—as well as other worlds. Privy to signs from spirit, voices and images from other dimensions, Cat offers a bridge between seen and unseen. Thus the Druids called upon Cat's guidance and knowledge to access magical realms.

An old English proverb notes that a cat has nine lives: for three she plays, for three she strays, and for three she stays. Several cultures note that cats have multiple lives—sometimes seven, other times six, but almost always more than one.

Why should we imagine that a cat has so many lives? Perhaps it is because cats are incredibly agile, capable of falling great distances (up to thirty-two stories!) at great speeds (up to 60 mph!) and surviving.[2] Perhaps we imagine these impressive abilities to sidestep death must mean that cats have extra lives to draw upon.

In Celtic legend the Sith—a large black cat with a white spot upon its chest, said to haunt the Scottish highlands—was believed to be a witch who could transform into a cat nine times, freely the first eight times, but on the ninth time remaining a cat for the rest of her life.

No culture was more enthusiastic about cats than the ancient Egyptians. Valued for their hunting abilities, small cats were domesticated in Egypt about 5,000 years ago. Not only did they kill grain-stealing rodents, venomous snakes, and scorpions, but they guarded temple gates and pharaohs, and warded away evil. So valued were cats that they were often mummified when they died and buried in special tombs, along with mice to eat and bowls of milk to drink. Some

A group of mummied cats in painted linen,
Twentieth Dynasty, ancient Egypt, circa 1100 BCE

Egyptian cat cemeteries were enormous—one dating to 2000 BCE housed over 100,000 mummified cats and kittens.

Regal, intuitive, and graceful, cats were often linked to the divine in Egypt—especially the Goddess.

Mut, a Mother goddess originally portrayed as giving birth to the world, was later represented by several animals, including lioness and cat. Mafdet, one of the earliest and most fiercely protective cat-headed (sometimes leopard-headed) goddesses in Egypt, was said to rip out the heart of anyone who wished the pharaoh harm, placing the bloody organ at his feet just as a cat might offer a bird or mouse.

Bastet and Sekhmet were both popular in ancient Egypt and sometimes recognized as two aspects of the same deity. With the head of a lioness, Sekhmet was best known as a powerful warrior goddess who

Left: Granite statue of Sekhmet from the Temple of Mut, Luxor, Egypt,
circa 1403–1365 BCE
Right: Associated with the goddess Bastet, this seated cat has golden earrings,
a golden scarab inlaid on the forehead, and wears a pendant displaying
a goddess nursing a young Harpokrates, the god of
silence and secrets, Egypt, circa 664–350 BCE.

created the desert with her breath. She not only protected the pharaoh
but led his army into battle and fallen warriors to the afterlife.

Originally lioness-headed, Bastet was later depicted with the head
of a cat. As she evolved to reveal a gentler form of the goddess, Bastet
was increasingly associated with home, fertility, birth, and feminine
mysteries. Because living cats were viewed as physical representatives of
Bastet, killing a cat was a serious crime.

The Egyptians' extreme devotion to cats may also have led to their
demise. A legend notes that in 525 BCE Cambyses led the First Persian
Empire in a battle against Egypt. Observing their worship of cats and
strong aversion to harming them, Cambyses ordered his soldiers to carry
cats onto the battlefield. As the Egyptians refused to shoot, Cambyses
won the battle and seized the throne.

When Egypt became a Roman province in 30 BCE, rulers dis-

King Cambyses slinging cats at the Siege of Peluse,
painting by Paul-Marie Lenoir, 1872

couraged the "pagan" practice of worshipping cats. Cat temples were
destroyed, cat-headed goddesses disdained, and the mummification and
burial of cats prohibited.

Almost all cultures have cat myths. Villain or demon, protector
or deity, Cat is both venerated and feared. What is it about Cat that
speaks so deeply to our psyche? What feline mystery stirs our imagination causing Cat to appear in so many different ways in fables, myths,
and legends?

In ancient Rome, Cat was guardian of homes and domesticity, and
sacred to the moon goddess Diana. Considered a blessing on fertility
and birth, Cat was often linked with children and family. Freya, Norse
goddess of love and divination, said to bring the art of magic to the
gods, is pulled on her chariot by two male cats (illustrated on page 102).
And Cerridwen, Celtic goddess of wisdom and magic, only trusted cats
to deliver her messages to humans—though if the human was unable to
understand, it was no fault of the feline.

Domesticated throughout Europe, Cat made itself at home wherever it roamed: on caravans and ships, in barns and castles. Free-spirited

Freya in her cat-drawn chariot, drawing
from Alexander Murray's 1874 *Manual of Mythology*

and inquisitive travelers, cats spread their numbers along trade routes through the Middle East, India, China, and arrived in the New World with traders, explorers, and colonists.

While cats were relied upon in medieval Europe to hunt mice and rats, so too were they feared to be the companions of witches. Some believed witches could shapeshift into cat form or be reborn as cats, especially black cats. The belief was deep-rooted and when settlers came to America they brought cats as hunters and companions, as well as their superstitions about cats. As fear of the supernatural increased, many cats were drowned, tortured, dismembered, or hung beside their "witch" companion.

What so deeply frightens a group of people that they would do such a thing? What terror resides within a collective consciousness that it must be projected outward onto a small, furry animal?

Because cats can see in the dark and often hunt at night, they were associated with darkness, secrets, and magic. Because they can be independent and aloof, they were judged unpredictable and untrustworthy. And because they can move in slinky, sensual ways, cats were considered in alliance with seductive and suspicious females.

When things are not understood, our fears can ignite. Just as seventeenth-century midwives and herbalists were persecuted as witches and condemned to die, so too were cats deemed in league with the devil, and thus they had to be destroyed.

THE VARIETY AND ENIGMA OF CAT

There are approximately thirty-eight species of the family *Felidae* on the planet today. We generally recognize two groups: *Panthera*—the big cats that roar, and *Felis*—the small- to medium-sized cats that purr. Interestingly, purring and roaring are mutually exclusive, so while all big cats (lion, tiger, jaguar, and leopard) can roar, they cannot purr, while cats that purr are unable to roar.

The Roar and Purr

Roars are possible due to a flexible hyoid bone, a stretchable ligament in the voice box, and flat, square-shaped vocal cords. As air passes across the vocal cords, a loud, deep-pitched sound is produced. Purrs occur from a fixed, hardened hyoid, and divided, triangle-shaped vocal cords. By breathing in and out, an audible vibration is thus created. Whether a cat can roar or purr has nothing to do with its size, but rather with its anatomy. Used mostly to frighten predators, roars are impressive—but purrs also have a purpose. Scientists have found that besides being calming, rhythmical cat purring can both improve bone density and promote healing.[3]

Roar!

No matter its size or ability to purr or roar, all cats are built to hunt: to stalk, leap, chase, and pounce upon prey. These abilities serve them well, for all cats are carnivores; in fact, they are obligate carnivores, which means they require meat in order to survive.

Humans describe, categorize, and define cats in a variety of ways. We sometimes think that by naming animals we can know them. But not so with Cat.

Consider the puma, said to have more names than any other animal. Because these cats once ranged extensively throughout the Western Hemisphere, they were called different names in different areas. Thus *Puma concolor* is Lord of the Forest to the Cherokee, Cat of God to the Chickasaw, panther or painter in Appalachia, catamount in New England, and mountain lion, American lion, cougar, el leon, or fire cat elsewhere, depending on where it is found.[4]

What's in a Name?

As T. S. Eliot notes in his book of poems *Old Possum's Book of Practical Cats,* a cat must have three different names: one familial (an everyday, sensible name used by the cat's family); one particular (a fancier, more dignified, strong, and unique name); and one secretive—known only to the cat.

When you notice a cat in profound meditation,
The reason, I tell you, is always the same:
His mind is engaged in a rapt contemplation
Of the thought, of the thought, of the thought of his name:
　　　　His ineffable effable
　　　　Effanineffable
　　　　　　Deep and inscrutable singular Name.

ELIOT, "THE NAMING OF CATS"

As the only tamed cat species, *Felis catus* is often called domestic cat to distinguish it from its wilder cousins—cheetah, jungle cat, bobcat, ocelot, serval, lynx, and more. The International Cat Association recognizes seventy-one breeds of domestic cats. From the tailless manx to the luxurious Turkish angora, from the popular American shorthair to the exotic Japanese bobtail, domestic cats enjoy a wide range of coat length, tail shape, body size, and fur pattern.

Some of the Many Faces of *Felis catus*

Top left: A naturally occurring genetic mutation causes hairlessness in cats, but it was selective breeding in the 1960s that created the sphynx, known for its lack of fur.

Top right: Descended from an ancient Italian breed of cats, the modern Persian, with its fine, silky hair, was created as longhair cats from Persia and Turkey were added to the bloodline in the sixteenth and seventeenth centuries.

Bottom left: Legendary temple cat to the king of Siam, the elegant Siamese has been refined by breeding to accentuate its sleek body, almond-shaped eyes, and triangular-shaped head.

Bottom right: A blend of wild and tame, the Bengal is a hybrid of the domestic cat (often the Egyptian mau) and the Asian leopard cat, *Prionailurus bengalensis*, from which it gets its name.

Just as each domesticated cat breed has its unique appearance, outlook, and teaching, each big cat species has its distinctive gifts as well. But appearances can be deceiving and, once again, Cat surprises. Lion and tiger, for example, are almost identical anatomically. And yet, as author James Hillman notes, "the manner in which they walk through our dreams and into our societal imagination—as different as day and night."[5]

Lion and Tiger

Up to 13 feet long and 660 pounds, tiger (*Panthera tigris*) is the largest of the big cats, followed by lion (*Panthera leo*), up to 10 feet long and 500 pounds. While tigers may be the biggest big cat, lions are the loudest. As resonant as a boom of thunder, the roar of a lion can be heard up to 5 miles away.

Lions roam the open plains of Africa and live in groups appropriately called prides. Tigers slink on solitary treks through thickets and dense Asian forests. Lion's tawny yellow coat links it to the golden warmth of the sun, while Tiger sports bold contraries—stripes of orange or white and black.

With its impressive size, strength, and regal bearing, Lion is considered a king. Symbol of monarchs and nobility, Lion represents courage, dignity, and devotion, and thus appears on the emblem of heroes and royal coats of arms. Originally associated with the goddess and the energy of an open, awakened heart, the tribe of Lion is proud and powerful, bright, sunny, and shining.

Tiger is also a king, but for different reasons. Independent, cunning, brave, and confident, Tiger rules the forest. Symbolic of passion, power, battle, and inspiration, Tiger fuels enthusiasm, provides protection, repels evil spirits, and, in the tantric perspective, transforms anger into insight. The fiery, fearless sign of the Chinese zodiac, Tiger is the national animal of several Asian countries and carries Durga, protective goddess and mother of the Hindu universe, upon its back.

While Lion represents rule and order, Tiger breaks rules. Lion teaches how to use personal power and command respect, while Tiger is the ancient initiator, challenging us to activate our raw power as we enter dark realms of the unknown. Like day and night, yin and yang,

Durga, Hindu goddess of war and protection,
Slayer of Demons, on her Tiger
Wellcome Collection

both Lion and Tiger are necessary aspects to Cat—a keen reminder that no one interpretation or singular view of Cat is ever the full story.

As always when working with Shadow, we must consider the animals that come to us with an open, inquisitive mind. Best to let go of stereotypes and superficial ideas or beliefs. If Cat appears in your dream, how does it present: resting, purring, roaring, pouncing? What form of Cat visits you: powerful puma, streetwise alleycat, exotic serval? How do you feel on meeting it—what secret fear or desire is stirred in your heart? Cat can help us discover unseen truths about ourselves if we are willing to venture into shadowy realms with curiosity and sincerity.

STALKING THE SHADOW:
ADVICE FROM CAT

When I created an animal-inspired tarot deck, I linked Cat with the second card in the major arcana, the High Priestess. In tarot symbology the High Priestess sits at the gateway to the Unconscious, guarding the veil between everyday awareness and mysteries beyond.

Cat, Knower of Secrets, from *Spirit Animal Tarot* by Dawn Baumann Brunke, illustration by Ola Liola
Courtesy of CICO Books

As the Knower of Secrets, Cat may invite us to move past the veil so that we can search for what is hidden within. Nudging us to trust our instincts and notice meaningful connections, Cat can help us to see in the dark—to perceive beyond the surface of appearances. Cat tends not to explain, but rather encourages us to experience with our own deep, feline wisdom. To learn more about Shadow stalking, consider the teachings from the following different Cats.

Cheetah—Focus

As the fastest land animal in the world, the cheetah (*Acinonyx jubatas*) is long and lean and built for speed. Cheetahs can reach 60 mph in only a few seconds. But even with this impressive ability, cheetahs rely first and foremost on focus. Alert to prey, cheetahs hold a motionless stare before stealthily and silently stalking. Only when very close will they expend the energy to run and pounce.

All cats have fully retractible claws—except the cheetah. Retracting claws protects and prevents them from wearing down. Cheetahs, however, depend upon their claws for extra traction while running. Their genus—*Acinonyx*—means "unmoving claw."

Cheetah reminds us that without clear focus it doesn't matter how fast we run—in fact, running without focus can work against us. Avoid self-sabotage by racing to assumptions and conjecture. Don't lose your way with diversions and distractions. Cheetah encourages self-scrutiny and keen perception to maintain focus on what you really want.

Jaguar—Consult the Inner World

The ancient Maya knew Jaguar (*Panthera onca*)—"he who kills with one leap"—as both a formidable warrior and accomplished guide to the spirit world. Jaguars have unique rosette patterns with central spots, as if to emphasize that their teaching is about going within. Companion to shamans, healers, and explorers of consciousness, Jaguar journeys inward, helping us to release fears, awaken inner vision, and investigate interior worlds where secrets of self can be found.

Confer with Jaguar while investigating dreams or considering voices and visions. With fearless intent and strong self-confidence, Jaguar offers courage to see clearly, hone intuition, trust experiences, and follow hints of the heart.

Jaguar is the largest New World native cat and third largest of the big cats.
Worshipped as a god in many ancient cultures, Jaguar was known
by the Maya as a skilled spirit world guide.

Snow Leopard—Step out of the Ordinary

Known by a variety of names, the snow leopard (*Panthera uncia* or *Uncia uncia*) is sometimes considered a big cat—and sometimes not. Although it cannot roar, neither can it purr—just one of the several ways this cat defies the boxes of human categorization. Snow Leopard reminds us to break through the small-minded views of others or self-limiting paradigms we have accepted about ourselves.

Living in cold, remote, mountainous areas, snow leopards are rarely seen by humans—and thus considered one of the most mysterious of cats. Follow Snow Leopard when you're ready to move away from pack mentality and explore what is unorthodox or unconventional. Snow Leopard encourages independent thinking, helping us to step out of the ordinary in order to access the extraordinary and expand our ideas of what is possible in ourselves and the world.

Snow leopards are difficult to classify. Some taxonomists group them with the *Panthera* (lions, tigers, jaguars, and leopards) while others feel their unique characteristics warrant a distinct genus—*Uncia*.

Black Panther—Follow the Mystery

The black panther is not really a panther at all. Rather it is a black-coated jaguar or leopard with fur so dark it appears not to have spots. Linked to the mysteries (and misconceptions) of perception, Black Panther can be an excellent guide to discernment and fine-tuning awareness.

Walk with Black Panther to get used to the dark, to familiarize yourself with what is solid and steadfast in yourself, and what is distorted or deceptive. With incisive clarity this big cat can help us to acknowledge our abilities by exposing the dark, destructive projections that eclipse the power of who we really are. Call upon Black Panther when you're ready to release fear.

Black panther is not a species, but a general term to describe a big cat (usually a jaguar or leopard, though may also apply to tigers and pumas) with black fur. The melanism—or black coloring—comes from a gene variant that produces dark pigment.

PLAYING WITH PROJECTIONS

Astute, resourceful, intelligent, and independent. Aloof, selfish, finicky, and occasionally obnoxious. Playful and fierce, mysterious and practical, Cat is a freethinker who sometimes sees what we cannot. But is the cat we see a true version of Cat or simply our projection?

Robert Bly compares projections to a thin roll of film we carry inside of us. All of the many intriguing, annoying, hideous, and striking figures of our psyche rolled up as images, conveniently ready to be cast upon those around us. "Our psyches then are natural projection machines: images that we stored in a can we can bring out while still rolled up, and run them for others, or on others."[6]

While working with Shadow, it is wise to be suspicious of our favorite scripts, to notice the images we habitually jump on to judge and project: idiot driver, incompetent salesperson, money-grubbing lawyer, arrogant world leader. Not only do such projections reflect aspects of our own psyche, but they are quite often believed—very adamantly—to be about *those* people and have nothing whatsoever to do with ourselves.

The Shadow is that which is hidden and repressed in self but happily projected onto others. The problem isn't so much the projection, for projections can help us to see *out there* what we don't see inside ourselves. The problem is when we believe the projection is real—that the trouble is all out there, and not at all about the insecurity, anger, pain, or confusion that triggered us to bring out our roll of film in the first place.

What we need to ask ourselves is: What movie are we running? What story are we telling ourselves? What theme or plot or script are we playing, projecting onto people and animals and situations again and again, in an endless variety of ways?

Projections hold secrets about ourselves. The projection is the mirror. The secret is that the reflection is us.

The following exercise is a playful approach to becoming more aware of how and what we project.

◆ ◆ **Exercise** ◆ ◆

That Cat—It's Just a Story We Are Telling Ourselves

Projections are neither good nor bad. They are simply the stories that we are telling ourselves. Our projections mirror our judgments, beliefs, secret fears, and desires. They are unique to each of us and may change over time.

In the photo below we see a cat. But what kind of cat? Consider these three stories:

That Cat

1. That cat is magnificent! Still and silent, she sits like a Queen—dignified, regal, self-assured. Her gaze is steady, her bearing proud. She looks confident, purposeful, and in control. Clearly, she needs no one to validate her existence!

2. That cat is planning something! Superior, sneaky, self-involved—what an attitude! What a poser! Clearly he's up to no good—probably waiting for the perfect moment to pounce, unleash his deadly claws,

and unfurl his plan of destruction. This is exactly why you can never trust a cat!

3. That cat is constipated! Look at its crabby face, uptight and ornery— what a sourpuss! It looks like it's impatient with others' stupidity! Its whole body seems constricted, as if it's holding everything inside. Clearly, it's awaiting a good release—no wonder it's cranky!

Noble being? Scheming assassin? Digestively impaired feline? While the cat in the photo hasn't changed, our ideas about the cat shift with the stories we tell. How we perceive the cat and what we choose to believe reveals much about ourselves—which is exactly why projections can be so valuable in helping us to identify Shadow material.

We can't explore our projections, however, until we are aware of them. And it can be tricky to perceive past all the emotionally heavy, belief-laden ideas we have constructed about ourselves and the world. The reason we project outward is that it's easier and much more ego-enhancing to believe the problem is "out there."

For this exercise observe the inept drivers, pushy store clerks, arrogant waiters, or pompous politicians that irk you in everyday life. Pay attention to what offends and annoys, what incites anger, resentment, or jealousy. Our irritation with others provides exceptionally good clues to shadow material that lurks within. The more emotive your story script, the more telling the projection.

Make notes in your Shadow Journal so that you can track the frequency, intensity, and variety of your internal scripts. Committing to this over a period of weeks or months allows for a clearer, broader perspective of your favorite projections. This in itself can be fascinating— and very revealing.

The focus of this exercise is to *identify* projections. So allow full range to your feelings—blast away with abundant, descriptive adjectives at what you find so galling, infuriating, inexcusable, and exasperating. The act of getting it all out on paper is not only emotionally satisfying, but can provide some excellent clues for future exploration.

In upcoming exercises we'll work to identify the core of our projections and begin to retrieve them. But for now be a cool cat and simply observe and record the various movie scripts that play in your everyday life.

5

Trust That Turns

The monster never dies.

STEPHEN KING, *Cujo*

In the horror novel *Cujo* by Stephen King, a big, friendly St. Bernard chases a wild rabbit through a grassy field, sticks his head into a small cave while sniffing it out, and is bitten on the nose by a rabid bat. Thus he transforms, slowly changing into a raging beast—foaming at the mouth, wild look in the eyes—attacking, biting, terrorizing, and killing humans.

Rabies is a viral disease that causes madness, and as King reminds us, it's not really the dog Cujo who is a monster, but the illness acting through him, causing him to lose control.

In the story humans lose control too—an affair, a business failure, domestic abuse, confusion, instability, and desperation. King notes that he was under drug and alcohol addiction while writing the novel, and barely remembers writing it at all.[1] Fittingly, what emerged from his muddled state of consciousness was a story that illustrates what happens when dark energies inside of us can no longer remain locked within. An accomplished author loses his grip; humans cast their pain on one another; a lovable dog becomes something other than itself. This is what happens when Shadow that is repressed too long makes an escape.

ALL ABOUT DOGS

Family *Canidae* consists of thirty-four species, including the domestic dog, various wolves, jackals, and foxes, as well as the coyote, dingo, dhole, and more. The smallest is the dainty, 2-pound fennec fox and the largest is the gray wolf—common ancestor to all domesticated dogs, weighing up to 180 pounds.

Left: Two fennec fox, also called desert fox as they are native to the Sahara and Arabian deserts
(Photo by Sumeet Moghe, CC BY-SA 4.0)
Right: Two gray wolves, native to Eurasia and North America

Dogs have lived with us since the tail end of the Paleolithic—for about 30,000 years. From very early times our lives were entwined with theirs. They hunted with us, protected us from intruders, played with our children, slept with us, and kept us warm at night. Reading our facial expressions and gestures, sensing our moods and emotions, dogs became members of our family and loved us, just as we loved them.

There are countless tales of loyal dogs saving lives, shielding humans from harm, and helping when we are sad, sick, lost, or disabled. Guiding and guarding, watching and warning, dogs can open our hearts, connecting us with the divine and what is good within ourselves—which is why some humans are keen to remind that *dog* spelled backward is God.

In ancient times we honored dogs as gods. We revered their fierce ability to defend, their steadfast nature to protect, and their savvy talent to guide—sometimes into other realms. In several cultures Dog is associated with death, and dogs were sometimes buried with the dead so as to lead them safely to the Underworld.

Ancient Dog Deities

Anubis: The Egyptian god of mummification, burial, and transformation. Sometimes portrayed as a black jackal, though more often a man with the pointy-eared head of a jackal, Anubis was both feared and honored in his role as a psychopomp—a conductor of souls into the afterlife. The association may have occurred from jackals lurking in graveyards, digging up and eating corpses. One of Anubis's many names was thus "The Dog who Swallows Millions."[2]

Statue of Anubis, 332 to 30 BCE, Egypt

Bau: Sumerian goddess of dogs, later known as Gula and Nininsina, often represented with a dog's head or with a dog beside her. Because a dog's licking of human wounds seemed to have a curative effect, Bau later became known as a goddess of healing.

Cerberus: The huge, three-headed dog who guards the entrance to Hades. As a vigilant watchdog Cerberus prevents the living from entering the Underworld, and the dead from escaping. As described in Ovid's *Metamorphoses,* "His three throats filled the air with triple barking, barks of frenzied rage, and spattered the green meadows with white spume."[3]

Illustration of Cerberus in pen, ink, and watercolor over
pencil and charcoal, by William Blake, 1824–1827

Xolotl: Aztec dog-headed god of lightning and death. Legend notes that Xolotl's twin, Quetzalcoatl, took the form of a dog while searching the Underworld for ancestral bones to create humans. Xolotl often took a monstrous form of Dog, and dogs were sometimes sacrificed to Xolotl to help humans journey beyond death.

Aztec sculpture representing the head
of Xolotl, circa 1250–1500

Dog presides as the eleventh sign in the Chinese zodiac, and shines as Orion's hunters in the constellations Canis Major and Canis Minor, as well as Sirius—the Dog Star, one of the brightest objects in the night sky. In some myths Dog brings fire to man, appears unexpectedly to help lost travelers find their way, and keeps young children safe from harm.

In the British Isles there are numerous tales of a malevolent Black Dog—a hellhound with glowing eyes that appears as a portent of death. In other cultures a large hairy dog called the Pesanta sneaks into bedrooms and sits upon the chests of sleeping humans to cause nightmares. Other legends tell of evil sorcerers and witches who transform into black dogs that prey on livestock.

Helpful watchdog, harmful demon—our ancestors sensed something two-sided about Dog. The notion lingers in our language. A dog can be an unattractive female, a rascal of a man, something worthless or undesirable, or a buddy or friend. When things go to the dogs they deteriorate, though to put on the dog is to bring forth an ostentatious display. If you don't have a dog's chance, there is no chance at all, but then again every dog has its day and at some point you will attain luck and success. What is it about Dog that gives us ambivalence?

A legend from thirteenth-century Wales tells of Prince Llywelyn and his faithful wolfhound Gelert.* One day on returning home, Llywelyn is stunned to find the room in shambles, his infant son missing, and cradle overturned, and Gelert with a blood-stained mouth. Believing the dog has killed his son, Gelert plunges his sword into his beloved hound. As it yelps in death, a baby cries, and Gelert discovers his son lying beside the body of an intruding wolf that Gelert had slain while defending the child. Filled with remorse, the prince buries his heroic hound and is said never to have smiled again.

Similar legends are told in different countries with minor variations, but always the theme is the same: a loyal canine saves the day, only to be falsely accused and killed.

As the story suggests, there is something about our relationship with dogs that causes doubt. But why? Dog proves its loyalty to Man by killing its own ancestor, Wolf. Man misinterprets the situation and, in

---

*The story is engraved on a memorial dedicated to Gelert in the village of Beddgelert, Wales.

Painting of the legendary Gelert protecting Prince Llywelyn's
infant son from a wolf, by Charles Burton Barber, 1894

confusion and haste, kills his faithful companion—revealing his uncertainty and latent suspicions about Dog.

Molecular testing reveals that all dogs (*Canis familiaris*) are descendants of wolves—specifically, the gray wolf (*Canis lupus*). Not only has the behavior of dogs changed with evolution, so too has their physiology—dogs are generally shorter in stature than wolves, with smaller teeth and muzzles. While all dogs share a common ancestor in the gray wolf, it was human intervention and selective breeding that created the many different breeds we know today. And yet, from Chihuahua to Great Dane, all dogs are basically domesticated wolves.

Descended from Wolves

While our domestication of dogs has spanned tens of thousands of years, most of the breeds we recognize today are only about 150 years old. Before that time dogs were grouped according to function: hunting dogs, herding dogs, lap dogs. In Victorian Britain the practice of selectively breeding dogs for desirable traits and aesthetics was enthusiastically embraced. Bloodlines were recorded, and the color of fur and shape of body, snout, ears, and tail all became standardized in breed classification. Some breeds were refined and others created through cross breeding. For example, in 1840 only two types of terrier were recognized. By 1900 there were ten, and today there are twenty-seven different terrier breeds.[4] The World Canine Organization (better known as the FCI, Fédération Cynologique Internationale) now recognizes over 340 breeds of dogs.

The many faces of Dog:

Top left: Golden retriever. Originally bred as gun dogs in Scotland during the 1840s, golden retrievers are known for their intelligence, friendly disposition, and bright golden fur. They excel as guide dogs, therapy dogs, and search-and-rescue dogs.

Top right: Pug. Believed to have originated in ancient China as a lapdog for royalty, the petite pug has a long history of charming its humans.

Bottom left: Alaskan malamute. Bred for its strength, energy, and thick coat, the Alaskan malamute was originally used by the Inuit to pull sleds across the snowy Arctic.

Bottom right: American pit bull terrier. Descended from now extinct terrier and bulldog breeds, the American pit bull terrier (APBT) was developed in the British Isles and brought to the United States in the mid-nineteenth century. Though sometimes given a bad rap, the APBT is noted by the United Kennel Club for its enthusiastic zest for life and willingness to please.

While many in the West adore dogs, this is not the case in all countries or cultures. Dogs are traditionally considered unclean in Judaism and Islam, and so too is cynophobia—the fear of dogs—fairly common worldwide. It is often listed as one of the top ten phobias, and an estimated 5 to 15 percent of humans report extreme anxiety around dogs. Some fear is not unfounded.

Approximately 90 million dogs live with humans in the United States. Every year about 4.5 million Americans are bitten by dogs. Most bites are minor, but hospitalization is required for between 6,000 to 13,000 people.[5] Moreover, an average of thirty to fifty people die each year in the United States due to dog attacks.[6] The accounts are shocking: a seventy-six-year-old disabled man pulled from his wheelchair and killed by four dogs in his front yard; a twenty-eight-year-old woman mauled to death by a dog she kept with her fiancé, a K-9 officer; a four-month-old girl attacked and killed by the family dog.[7] These are not attacks by wild dogs or rabid dogs; rather, they are dogs who live with friends and neighbors and family.

What some humans do to dogs is just as horrifying, and the accounts are equally difficult to read: dogs thrown, hung, starved, suffocated, electrocuted, mutilated, or beaten to death. Dog abuse ranges from failure to provide basic food, water, shelter, and care to torture, sexual abuse, and organized dog fighting. Mistreatment may also include hoarding, puppy mill abuse, and laboratory experimentation. In addition, 3.1 million dogs are taken in by shelters annually, with an average of 390,000 euthanized each year.[8]

What is happening here? Living in our homes, attuned to our daily lives, dogs often mirror the behaviors and emotions of their people, thus providing a good teaching about where we excel and where we are lacking. While the majority of humans and dogs form close, caring, and mutually loving bonds, the shadow side of our relationship exists nonetheless.

The core of our connection with Dog is rooted in the distant past—in that first, uneasy alliance forged between Wolf and our human ancestors. Early humans tamed wolves by feeding, sheltering, and caring for them. In exchange these wolves offered protection, companionship, and help with hunting. Wolves forfeited their wildness to align with humans, and humans accepted the role of caretaker. Both sides benefited, and so some wolves became dogs. And yet—as both dogs and humans intuit: some trace of Wolf remains.

THE BIG BAD WOLF

Like dogs, wolves are social animals. Keenly observant and intelligent, they excel at communication, cooperation, and community. They generally mate for life, are dedicated parents, and are loyal not only to their pups but to their pack.

Much of what we love about dogs is their social connection to us. They mostly do what we ask, come when we call, and obey our rules, while wolves do not. Wolves are wild—and that can be terrifying.

But this was not always the case. Helpful wolves in mythology include the she-wolf who suckled legendary twin founders of Rome, Romulus and Remus, and supernatural wolves Freki and Geri who traveled ahead of the Norse god Odin to report what they saw. In Asia, Wolf is often considered lucky and in some legends guards the doors not to Hades, but to the heavenly realms. Ancient Mongols believed they were descended from wolves, as was Genghis Khan, and so Wolf was championed as a noble, powerful warrior with strong instincts and a spiritual disposition.

In Europe and North America, however, Wolf was primarily viewed as a predator and associated with danger—often something dark, devious, and demonic. Wolves were linked to witchcraft in Northern Europe, and some Native American tribes believed witches took the form of wolves. Throughout Europe for hundreds of years, the fear of wolves was an ever-present theme. The Big Bad Wolf thus appeared in countless fables and folktales.

Because wolves have learned to live far from humans and avoid them, there are few human deaths by wolves in the modern world. However, there are many historical records of fatal wolf attacks, especially in France, which once had one of the largest wild wolf populations. Throughout the sixteenth and seventeenth centuries, most Europeans considered wolves a dire enemy. Fear was fueled by accounts of carnage and tragedy, and a remarkable number of attacks were cited.

Illustration of Little Red Riding Hood and the Big Bad Wolf, by Jessie Wilcox Smith, 1911, from *A Children's Book of Stories*. Variations of this folktale have been told for centuries in numerous countries. In many early versions, Little Red Riding Hood escapes on her own. When the Brothers Grimm published the story in the 1800s, however, they added a male huntsman to save the girl.

Many were attacks from rabid wolves, but so too were predatory attacks noted—and remembered. This gave rise to stories such as "the Beast," a monstrous wolflike canine with pointy ears, formidable teeth, and an exceptionally long tail, that terrorized the French province of Gévaudan by tearing out the throats of its victims (depicted on page 126).

Before Europeans arrived in North America, an abundance of wolves roamed freely. Early settlers and wolves avoided confrontation based on mutual unease. But as colonists penned pigs, cattle, sheep, and horses, hungry wolves sometimes helped themselves to an easy meal. This ignited an intense anger at wolves, inciting flames of violence, fear, and hatred that continued with each generation.

In the early 1900s the U.S. Forest Service sponsored wolf extermination. Wolves were trapped, mutilated, deliberately infected with mange, and killed. The effort was so successful that by the mid-1900s gray wolves were almost completely exterminated in the Lower

French print of the Beast of Gévaudan attacking a woman, circa 1765

48 states. In 1973 Congress enacted the Endangered Species Act and wolves were among the first species to receive federal protection. There are now approximately 6,000 gray wolves in the contiguous United States (another 12,000 live in Alaska) due to reintroduction programs. But some say this is far from recovery.[9]

There is still heated debate over the wolf—from farmers and ranchers who fear livestock predation, to environmentalists who seek to restore wolf populations; from hunters who feel wolves compete for deer and elk, to nature lovers who are thrilled to glimpse a wild wolf in its natural habitat.

WHICH WOLF TO FEED?

In a well-known parable, a grandfather tells his grandson about two wolves fighting inside himself. One wolf is full of anger, arrogance, and resentment. The other is peaceful, compassionate, and kind. The fight is constant, the old man comments, and it goes on within everyone. "Which wolf will win?" asks the young grandson. "The one you feed," responds grandfather. "The one you feed."

Gray wolf, Canada. There are more than thirty subspecies of *Canis lupus*.
In North America these include the Arctic, Northwestern, Great Plains,
Mexican, Eastern timber, and Alaskan tundra wolf.

For many years I shared this story with others. I liked the idea that by feeding the "good" wolf we can be more loving in the world. As I worked more consciously with shadow material, however, I realized the story was flawed. Would starving the "bad" wolf really cause it to wither and die? Or would it simply become enraged and ever more determined to escape?

Our emotions, thoughts, and behaviors have both dark and light sides. By feeding the good wolf, we may be praised by others and feel good about ourselves. But do we really believe that starving the dark wolf will banish its existence? This sounds suspiciously like something that creates shadow material in the first place!

As Robert Bly observes, Shadow that is ignored for too long eventually takes on a personality of its own.[10] Bly reminds us of Robert Louis Stevenson's tale about a man who consumes a potion that separates good from evil. At his best the man is the caring, virtuous Dr. Jekyll, while the worst becomes Mr. Hyde, a degenerate, violent man who shows up in other parts of the city to kill. "Every part of our personality that we do not love will become hostile to us," comments Bly. "We could add that it may move to a distant place and begin a revolt against us as well."[11]

While researching the origins of the wolf story, I discovered that it was sometimes claimed as a Native American legend, other times told by evangelistic preachers as a fundamentalist commentary on the ongoing war between good and evil.[12] There are several versions of the story, most involving two wolves, but sometimes two dogs—one white, one black. In almost all cases, however, the ending is the same: a moralistic prompt to feed only the "good" canine within.

In my favorite version of the story (which some claim is the original), a different perspective is offered. Grandfather explains that by failing to feed the dark wolf, disaster will ensue. The wolf will hide in the shadows and wait for us to become ill or distracted, then it will jump out to get what it needs. But if we feed the wolves right, Grandfather observes, both will win.

If we feed the wolves right, both will win. How exactly would we do that?

When unacknowledged, the dark wolf hides in the shadows, waiting, watching . . .

Perhaps to feed our wolves right is to acknowledge all aspects of who we are: light as well as dark, yin as well as yang. By doing so, we may discover that the dark wolf has something to teach us—something not initially apparent because of our own heavy judgments against it.

Our dark wolf has skills—such as cunning, strategy, the power of outrage. Sometimes anger, indignation, and grim tenacity is needed to face a bully or abuser, to fight corruption or injustice in the world. By acknowledging our dark wolf, we may find value in what we previously snubbed or suppressed.

We lose touch with the dark wolf by denying our negative energies and projecting them outward, pretending they have nothing to do with us. We point the finger, judging others as aggressive or deceitful so that we do not have to see those qualities within ourselves. In the short-term this may feel good, for obviously *they* are the problem, not us. And yet this is exactly how we lose our personal power—by failing to see the dark parts of ourself that clamor for our attention, that have wisdom to share, skills and strengths to offer.

To feed both wolves right is to acknowledge the teachings of both. Not only do both wolves win, but so do we. To be at peace with our inner light as well as our inner dark allows us to think clearly and act confidently, no longer at war inside ourselves.

Lucky for us, there are two members of family *Canidae* who are masters at balancing such energies. They teach in unconventional ways, through pretense and exaggeration and wild antics. Outrageous and unpredictable, they poke fun, inviting us to laugh at our fears and flaws so that we may better accept and embrace the diverse spectrum of our many selves within.

FOX AND COYOTE

One of the oldest known trickster animals is Huehuecoyotl (whose name means "Very Old Coyote"), an ancient Aztec god of storytelling, music, dance, mischief, merriment, and unrestrained sexuality. He is often imaged cavorting, with an ornate coyote head and fancifully decorated human hands and feet.

Huehuecoyotl, as depicted in the Codex Borgia, a Mesoamerican manuscript painted on folded animal skins, likely created between the thirteenth and fifteenth centuries.

For the Aztec, Coyote symbolized exuberant curiosity, unconventional wisdom, and a healthy dose of hilarity. As with later versions of the North American Coyote trickster, Huehuecoyotl plays tricks on both gods and humans, though sometimes the schemes backfire and cause problems for himself.

Like real coyotes, Coyote is cunning and resourceful, a clever survivor. Playful with a sly sense of humor, Coyote can transform into other animals or humans, shifting both shape and gender. An accomplished prankster fond of festivity, he is in many ways the original party animal.

In some myths Coyote brings the seeds of life—as well as man and woman—into the physical realm. He steals fire for humans, places the stars in the sky, and brings new ideas into being. By balancing dark and light, Coyote initiates shifts in the world, ending one way of life so that a new way can begin.

Creative shapeshifter and trickster, Coyote employs the art of deception to confuse and cajole to get what he wants. But so also is Coyote willing to play the fool. By mirroring our ability to deceive others as well as ourselves, Coyote reminds us to embrace the humor of life. Indeed, one of Coyote's most powerful tools is laughter—that potent, magical force that can open us to deep revelation and healing.

Like Coyote, Fox is also a trickster who knows how to use whatever life presents to its advantage. Both foxes and coyotes are fast and wily, with sharp senses and a keen ability to observe without being seen.

Left: Inquisitive red fox, Alaska. *Right:* Resting coyote, Death Valley, California.

Because most foxes are active at dusk and dawn, and live at the edges of forests and fields, Fox is linked to transitional times and places, often portrayed as a guardian of the in-between. In some myths Fox leads humans to special gateways that allow entrance to other realms.

In Asia, Fox is often liked to sexuality and seduction. Kitsune—the Japanese word for fox—is a magical fox spirit with supernatural powers. Like Coyote, Kitsune can shapeshift into human form, sometimes to trick others, sometimes to form love relationships. In some legends female kitsune live as foxes during the day and as beautiful women at night—often married to adoring husbands who are oblivious of their true identity.

In ancient Japan, fox and humans lived together as companions, which may be how the legends of kitsune evolved. Sometimes helpful, sometimes mischievous or even malicious, kitsune grow additional tails (up to nine total) and develop supernatural abilities as they gain wisdom and experience. Kitsune can fly, become invisible, and create lifelike illusions. Some kitsune manifest in human dreams, some bend time and space, and some transform into beguiling shapes, such as an incredibly tall tree or a second moon in the sky.

Prince Hansoku, bewitched by Lady Kayo, shown on the floor in her mortal human form and floating in the air in her true form: a nine-tailed fox kitsune. Illustration by Utagawa Kuniyoshi, circa 1855.

In Europe, during the late Middle Ages, a profusion of fables featured a red fox called Reynard (*Reinaert* in Dutch, *Reineke* in German, *Renartus* in Latin). Sly and bawdy, this rogue trickster's adventures involve deceiving others and turning the tables to gain advantage. The stories—often satires of politics, religion, and social morals—were so

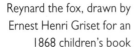

Reynard the fox, drawn by Ernest Henri Griset for an 1868 children's book

popular that *renard* became the standard French word for fox. Reynard appeared in children's stories as well as Chaucer's *The Canterbury Tales* (1392) and Goethe's epic poem *Reinecke Fuchs* (1793–1794).

Tricksters such as Coyote and Fox play with Shadow. Dashing between dark and light, reality and illusion, they blur opposites, opening us to wonder, reminding us to lighten up and laugh and love. They urge us to take a risk and trust the flow of life. Their stories offer portals to both collective and personal shadow material. As improbable guides, they challenge us to acknowledge and explore and accept all of our many selves within.

◆ ◆ **Exercise** ◆ ◆

Sitting with Dog

I love sitting beside my dog. Whether relaxing on the couch or on a grassy hill under sunny skies, this simple act inevitably brings a sense of calm. Without need of word or gesture, Dog offers us the gift of an open heart and unconditional acceptance of who we are.

For this exercise choose a shadow emotion you'd like to explore. Pick something that is recent or ongoing—sorrow, grief, anger, heartache, frustration, fear, whatever causes you discomfort.

Find a quiet, comfortable space. If you live with a dog, you might invite it to sit with you. Or ask Dog to be present in spirit as a guide or companion.

Sitting beside Dog, allow your breath to flow freely throughout your body. Take time to center and deepen.

When you are ready, invite the emotion you wish to explore to be present. *Hello, heartache. Greetings, fear.* Notice where it settles in your body: in your neck or head, your shoulders, hips, or heart? Notice how it manifests—does that area feel tight or heavy, hollow or achy, warm or cold? Focusing on the physical feeling of the emotion in our body can help us to better acknowledge and attune to its presence.

As you feel the emotion, avoid thoughts of *why* you feel it. It can be seductive to indulge the ego's rant of why we are entitled to feel a particular emotion. If you notice yourself thinking rather than feeling, simply redirect your attention back to physically sensing the emotion in your body.

Emotion is energy in motion—a constant flow of feelings that clamor to express themselves. Remember, you do not need to fix anything. You do not need to explain or justify. Simply feel.

Dog is patient; its presence may help you to persevere. As you deepen into feeling, staying fully present with your emotion, you may be surprised to notice that it suddenly shifts or dissipates.

"Tapping into that shaky and tender place has a transformative effect," writes Pema Chödrön in *The Places That Scare You.* "Being in this place may feel uncertain and edgy but it's also a big relief. Just to stay there, even for a moment, feels like a genuine act of kindness to ourselves. Being compassionate enough to accommodate our own fears takes courage, of course, and it definitely feels counterintuitive. But it's what we need to do."[13]

As your emotion fades or transforms, you may find your body softening, your breath flowing more freely, your heart resonating with a wave of love and compassion. Maybe it is for the person who caused you harm, maybe it is for the world in general. In any case—no *maybe* about it, it is also for you.

The trick is to *be* in your body with your feelings—not to oppose or direct or manipulate, not to offer rationalizations or visualizations or affirmations, but simply to be. To sit and watch and feel with an open heart. Like Dog.

My dog Deshka

6

Scapegoat

In other traditions demons are expelled externally.
But in my tradition demons are accepted with compassion.
MACHIK LABDRON, ELEVENTH-CENTURY
TIBETAN BUDDHIST TEACHER

A scapegoat is someone who takes the blame for the mistakes or wrong-doings of others. We now use the term figuratively, but in older times the *scapegoat* was an actual, living goat.

As far back as ancient Babylon, a ritual scapegoat was used to carry away communal sin. After confessing the community's transgressions, the high priest would symbolically place them upon the head of the goat. Sometimes a silver hoop was put around the goat's neck; other times its horns were wrapped with red fabric. The goat was the sin-bearer, sent to carry the heavy load of wickedness into the wild.

In ancient Greece similar rites were used to prevent plague, drought, and famine. The scapegoat—generally a human slave, criminal, or pauper—was first treated royally, with feast and fine clothes, before the sacrificial ceremony in which he would be beaten and chased into the wilderness as a means of warding off catastrophe. In seventeenth- to eighteenth-century Great Britain and Ireland, a local sin-eater would be paid to eat bread and salt placed upon the chest of the deceased. In this way the sin-eater would take on the sins of the departed so that he or she could enter heaven.

The Scapegoat, by Holman Hunt (1854–1856). Hunt created two versions of this painting. The larger version (shown here) features a light-haired goat with its horns wrapped in red cloth to represent the sins of the community. Hunt felt the Judaic view of the scapegoat was similar to and perhaps a prototype of the Christian's suffering Messiah.

Most often, however, a living goat was chosen to hold human sins. Sometimes individuals or families would attempt to transfer their bad luck or illness onto their own goat, which was then slaughtered and buried or eaten. One European folk remedy suggests allowing a goat to graze near a sick room; when the goat leaves, it carries the sickness with it.

The book of Leviticus describes how on the Hebrew Day of Atonement two goats are chosen: one as a blood sacrifice and one as the sin-bearer.[1] All the iniquities of the people shall be confessed and placed upon the head of the live goat, which is then sent with a designated person to a barren region. Thus Goat served in two ways: as sacrifice to honor the Lord and as atonement to free the people from their guilt.

The Merriam-Webster dictionary notes that the word *scapegoat* is modeled on a misreading of the Hebrew word *azāzēl,* which occurs in Leviticus 16:8.[2] Of the two goats noted in this passage, one is designated for the Lord and one for Azazel. Dispute remains as to exactly who or what Azazel is. Some suggest it was the name of the distant place where the goat was led. Some believe it refers to a fallen angel or a Hebrew demon. Others note it as a deity linked to goat sacrifice or a pagan god worshipped in the form of a goat.

In 1530 the medieval scholar William Tyndale translated *Azazel* as escape-goat, later shortened to scapegoat. Different Bible versions translated the word in similar ways: the emissary goat, the goat that departs, the goat sacrifice that is sent away. This general meaning stuck for some time, though some modern translations now use Azazel. So, depending on one's perspective, Azazel is a devil, a deity, or a sacrificial goat.

Demon, god, goat—is not the connection of these three elements intriguing? As a sacrifice the goat is neither good nor evil, but simply the vessel that carries the sins of the people into the wilderness. As such, Goat is a stand-in, a sly way for humans to avoid self-responsibility.

Loaded with the people's transgressions, the scapegoat ensures that the group's collective Shadow is sent away, somewhere barren, where it will not be faced or found—an interesting notion of how we encourage denial.

What happens to the goat in the wilderness? Does it live? What then? Other questions come to mind as well.

WHY GOAT?

Of all the animals why is Goat chosen to bear the sins of humanity when goats offer humans so very much?

Soon after dogs were domesticated, goats were too. In the early Neolithic, about 9,000 years ago, farmers began herding goats for milk, meat, and more. Goat milk could be used to make yogurt, cheese, and butter, and goat dung was used as fuel. Goat fur was made into rugs or warm wraps, the soft hairs woven to create clothes. Goat bones were used as tools, and sinew as thread for sewing. Goatskins were used as bags for wine or water as well as parchment for writing. Nothing was wasted!

Baby Zeus was suckled by the goat Amalthea, whose horns later became the cornucopia, symbol of abundance. In both myths and

Illustration of the goat Heidrun eating leaves from the tree Læraðr in Valhalla, from an Icelandic manuscript, circa 1765

reality, goats pulled carts and carriages. Bacchus, the Roman god of wine, had a goat-driven cart, and Thor, Norse god of thunder and lightning, employed two goats to draw his war chariot. The mythic goat Heidrun nibbled tender leaf buds from a special tree located at the top of Valhalla to produce mead for the gods and warriors.

We now recognize over 300 breeds of goat, from floppy-eared Nubian dairy goats to wild, mountain-dwelling ibex. There are alpine goats and pygmy goats, angora goats and fainting goats. Goats live in a variety of habitats, from low-altitude valleys to incredible mountain heights.

Like many shadow animals, goats represent a wide range of extremes. Female goats are often symbols of mothering and abundance, gentle nurturers that feed body and soul. But so too is there the lofty side of goat, ever climbing, defying gravity with daring leaps. Goat is the symbol of Capricorn, linked to ambition, persistence, and determination. Goats can also represent virility, lust, and uncontrolled passions, which is why we sometimes speak of lecherous old goats.

Teachings from Goat

Curiosity

Highly inquisitive, with lips that can grasp objects, goats scrutinize their environment. Like detectives, they investigate latches and locks, intrigued by how things work. Prompting curiosity and inquiry, Goat encourages us to awaken wonder and expand our intelligence by exploring everything.

From exploration and introspection to adaptability
and thrill-seeking, Goat's teachings span a wide range.

Contemplation

Goats are ruminants. To ruminate means to chew one's cud or think deeply about something. Goats do both, reminding us to ponder well when considering our options.

Agility and Stability

Sure-footed and steady with a keen ability to know how and where to step, goats are masters at navigating rocky, slippery, or difficult terrain. In addition to physical agility, goats engage mental agility to find creative ways of moving past obstacles. Combining a firm foundation with a flexible attitude, Goat reveals how to adapt and succeed when confronting a challenge.

Goat standing on rooftop

Independence
Though typically herd animals, goats are also freethinking and independent. Watch Goat to learn how to express individuality while remaining connected to the herd. Goat encourages us to follow our fascination to discover unique perspectives of self.

Joy
With sturdy legs, strong self-confidence, and a strategic outlook, goats climb steep mountains to access areas that other animals avoid. What a thrill! Goat nudges us to trust our abilities and embrace the flow of life to better follow our joy.

Those who live with goats generally find them to be clever, quick-witted, and fun-loving. But there are some who fear goats. The condition is called *capraphobia* (from the Latin *capra* for "goat"). As phobias go it is fairly uncommon. Those who get the goat-willies, however, sometimes link it to the uneasiness they experience in the presence of goats. With their strange slit-shaped pupils, earthy smells and hairy body, cloven hoofs and protruding horns, goats touch something deep and ancient in the human psyche that we have learned to fear.

GODS WITH
HOOFS AND HORNS

Representing fertility as well as virility, Goat was connected to several Old World gods and goddesses. In no deity was Goat's influence more apparent, however, than in the untamed nature god, Pan.

With the upper body of a man, and the horns, legs, and tail of a goat, Pan personifies and celebrates the Wild: animals and nature; rustic mountains, fields, and groves; music and merriment; intoxication and promiscuity. Pan is lustful, forever chasing nymphs and goats and shepherds. In one myth he seduces the moon goddess Selene to come down from the sky for a tryst in the woods.

Hairy, horned, and goat-footed, Pan revels in the natural world. In Roman myths he is Faunus, the horned god of field and forest. In the Celtic world he is linked to Cernunnos, god of animals and the wilderness, and in Egypt he is Banebdjedet, an ancient fertility god later known as the Goat of Mendes.

There are numerous versions of Pan—so many that the woodland god is sometimes referred to in the collective as the "Pans." As an ancient nature spirit, Pan precedes the Olympian pantheon. He is an old god, worshipped in the wilderness, in secluded glades and caves and grottos rather than temples or churches. There is a bit of the unpredictable trickster in Pan, especially in his displays of wild abandon.

Noisy and exuberant, lustful and laughing, Pan awakens sexuality, urging us to enjoy our body through sensual movement, dance, and song. Pan reminds us that we are connected to animals and nature in the web of life. But so too can Pan lead us to our wild side, to panic and pandemonium.

Satyrs and fauns romp through Greek and Roman myths as rowdy gods who cavort and carouse. In the early Greek tradition, satyrs are half-man, half-horse, but are later depicted similar to Roman fauns—men with goat ears, horns, legs, and tail. As followers of Pan and Dionysus (originally a nature god of fertility; later a god of wine who inspires song and dance through intoxication), satyrs frequent mountains, fields, and forests, where they frolic and seduce.

The Goat-God

Shackled by the Iron Age
Lost the Woodland heritage,
Heavy goes the heart of man
Parted from the light-foot Pan;
Wearily he wears the chain
Till the Goat-god comes again.

Dion Fortune, "The Rite of Pan,"
invocation to her novel *The Goat-Foot God*

Statue of Pan

Associated with primeval energies, Pan is an all-encompassing god. The Greek word *pan* means "whole, all, every." When combined to create other words—*pantheon, panacea, panorama, Pangaea*—Pan speaks to collectivity and inclusion. From Pan springs pantheism, a celebration of all gods, as well as the notion that all nature is God. As Dion Fortune noted, "Pan is greatest, Pan is least, Pan is all, and all is Pan; Look for him in every-man."[3]

A satyr, oil painting by Flemish artist Jacob Jordaens, 1630–1645

With their bawdy approach to life, the horned gods sparked roguish mischief and merriment. Living in the wilderness, drinking, dancing, and copulating, Pan was a favored god among rural people. But his overt sexuality and animal nature was an affront to religious morality, an example of what happens when libidinous desires run wild.

No wonder Pan invoked disgust in the medieval church. The unrestrained potency of the wild man must be dampened! And this is how demonization of the Goat-god Pan began.

FROM GOAT TO DEVIL:
AN EVOLUTION OF SHADOW IMAGERY

In the Middle Ages it was believed that goats could lead saints into temptation by whispering salacious thoughts in their ears. The connection between goats and seduction stemmed from earlier times. The ribald shenanigans of satyrs, the Pans, and ancient horned gods of the wilderness caused early Christians concern.

Separation of Sheep and Goats, reproduction of an early sixth-century Byzantine glass mosaic from the Basilica of Sant'Apollinare Nuovo, Ravenna, Italy

In the parable of the sheep and goats, Jesus separates the righteous from the neglectful as a shepherd separates sheep from goats.[4] The blessed (sheep) are put on the right to be given eternal life, while the cursed (goats) are put on the left to be condemned. The left side, classically considered the sinister side (from the Latin *sinistra*), refers to the corrupt, unlucky, or unchosen. A sixth-century depiction of this scene shows a red angel on the right with the sheep and a blue angel (sometimes identified as the fallen angel, Lucifer) with goats on the left.

Furry hindquarters and cloven hoofs; a penchant to live in remote areas; earthy, animal instincts with an exuberance of drink, song, dance, and lust—all this led early Christians to associate the horny goat-gods with promiscuity, depravity, and evil.

The iconographic evolution of goat to devil occurred bit by bit over the centuries. An amalgam of stories, symbols, and ideas from older religions led artists to portray the Devil with a hairy, beast-like face and large, curved, pointy horns. While horns traditionally signified wisdom, nature, and the abundance of life (as represented in the cornucopia), on the devil-

Satyr, from the Aberdeen Bestiary, a twelfth-century illustrated manuscript of real and mythical animals. Commentary notes the satyr holding his thyrsus (an ornamentally tipped staff carried by Dionysus and his followers) to be "used in his lustful and disorderly revels."[5]

goat they represented virility and aroused, unrestrained sexuality.

Medieval imagery commonly portrayed the Devil as a goat or goatlike, frequently with a small, pointy beard (later called a goatee). Sometimes the images included additional faces in unusual places: on the belly, knees, back, or arms. In the medieval world demons were considered fallen angels so their bodies were often depicted with distorted angelic features. Because angels were envisioned with feathery white wings, for example, demons were assigned the opposite: leathery, black bat wings.

The purposeful twisting of myth and imagery led to the gradual transformation of a pleasure-seeking, pagan nature god that was

An illustration of Pope Sylvester II and the Devil, 1460

revered and celebrated by local people, to Satan, the evil adversary feared by all. And this is how a God of Nature became a scapegoat called the Devil.

We can further observe how humans connect goats with devils and utilize the role of scapegoating via the evolution of tarot card imagery, as the fifteenth card of the major arcana (which features universal archetypes) represents the Devil—most often depicted with goatlike features.

In the early 1700s the Tarot of Marseilles presented the Devil with goat ears and twig-like horns, bat wings, a face on its belly, and eyes on its knees. Smaller male and female figures have matching goat ears and horns, slim tails, and are chained. The card hardly portrays a sense of evil, but rather a passive, almost bored, acceptance of bondage or servitude.

Two hundred years later, in the early 1900s, the Rider-Waite-Smith Tarot deck portrayed the Devil with strong, hairy goat legs, a menacing goat face, massive curled horns, and large, unfurled bat wings. The naked humans chained to the pedestal have small horns and curving tails. The female's tail ends in a cluster of grapes (perhaps an allusion

Card 15, *Le Diable*, from the Tarot of Marseilles by Jean Dodal, circa 1701–1715

The Devil card, major
arcana 15, from the
Rider-Waite-Smith Tarot
deck, illustration by
Pamela Coleman Smith,
1909

to wine, intoxication, and the Pans) while the male's tail is tipped with flames (a possible nod to Hades, god of the Underworld).

Academic and mystic Arthur Edward Waite (who designed the deck with illustrator Pamela Coleman Smith) likens the male and female to Adam and Eve after they leave the garden. "The figures are tailed," he writes, "to signify the animal nature, but there is human intelligence in the faces, and he who is exalted above them is not to be their master forever."[6]

While the Devil image is more menacing here than in the earlier Marseilles deck, the chains upon the human figures are notably looser—so much so that the male and female could easily remove them. As Waite notes, the Devil need not be one's master forever, for we are free to loosen our bonds as we choose.

At first glance, the Devil may seem a dark card for it can signify our addictions and obsessions—our secret fears and secret desires, and all that we do not want to see about ourselves. But that is why it's such a helpful card, for it reveals clues about what we allow to enslave us as well as what we try to enslave.

Just as the Devil card may reveal personal Shadow, the Devil writ large holds collective Shadow, all that heavy emotional baggage—lust, anger, fear, guilt, shame—that we reject, deny, or deem evil. But by recognizing our chains—by identifying what we feel controlled by or are trying to control—we can begin to remove them and release the emotional holds.

While creating an animal-themed tarot deck many years ago, I sent detailed notes about their design to my illustrator. We discussed the images, postures, background, and symbols to be used, as well as the overall energy of each card. I chose Goat to represent the Devil and titled it Shadow God of Liberation. Around the goat's neck is a necklace with chains on one side, flower blossoms on the other—a nod to the ancient scapegoat and a suggestion of how we may choose to transform and release our bonds.

"This is probably one of the most powerful cards in the Major Arcana," I wrote, "for it asks us to go into the depths of our psyche to see what enslaves us. While it's a card of great fear for some, it speaks to enlightenment for others. The energy should be both dark and light: it is up to the viewer to decide which 'side' of Goat he or she chooses to follow." Indeed, how we relate to the Shadow God is a choice: Do we remain enslaved to our shadow material or recognize it as a powerful means to liberation?

Shadow God of Liberation, major arcana card 15 in *Spirit Animal Tarot* by Dawn Brunke, illustration by Ola Liola. The message of this card: "Embrace your shadow, liberate your life." Courtesy of CICO Books

How we see the Devil (in a tarot card, a religion, or the world) reveals a lot about ourselves. The Devil shows us what is not working: small-minded beliefs, destructive habits, control issues, and more. Humans created the Devil to hold that which is stubbornly denied within ourselves.

A handy repository for all that our ego dislikes and judges, the Devil is the communal scapegoat we love to hate. Just as Azazel is a confused conglomeration of demon, god, and goat, our ideas about the devil grew from our confusion and denial of what we feared and misunderstood. It is easy to blame something we do not understand on something that we think we do; thus, scapegoats are created!

The Shadow God challenges us to confront our Shadow. It prods us to investigate our presumptions and projections, to acknowledge that what we judge in others is what we judge inside ourselves, that what we fail to acknowledge as part of us is what we twist and project onto the world around us. If we disregard this, we will meet our Shadow at every turn.

Denied Shadow is the Devil out of control. It speaks in myriad ways: temptation, indulgence, anger, hate, anxiety, paranoia. That is why it pays to look closely, to reflect and ponder patiently. For the devil is in the details.

WHAT'S GOT YOUR GOAT?

To get one's goat is to anger, irritate, or annoy. It's originally an American phrase sometimes traced to horse racing and the belief that a goat in a stall next to a skittish thoroughbred will calm it before the big day. To get one's goat was a sabotage whereby an opponent would steal the goat and upset the horse.

What is it about humans and stealing goats or heaping them with sin and sending them into the wilderness or lending their sweet faces to devilish imagery!

Goats engage their natural fascination with life when exploring their environs. Perhaps we might engage a similar spirit of inquiry to investigate what we have cast upon Goat—our superstitions, our sins, our sly abdications of responsibility.

Both stable and agile, Goat is an excellent guide when traversing tricky terrain in the psyche. Are you game to explore? We can adopt a lighthearted and investigative approach to the Shadow by embracing Goat's curiosity and independent spirit to look within. As we identify the inner devils that enslave us, we can begin to reclaim responsibility for our projections.

By accepting our role in social scapegoating we can forgive others—and ourselves—for the stubborn, continual, unthinking habit of projecting. Goat is a life-affirmer who encourages us to see clearly, to honor ourselves as well as each other—including the horned, hoofed, and hairy. As we stop projecting blame and fear out onto the world, we not only unburden the scapegoat, but begin to retrieve lost and abandoned parts of ourselves. Thus we lighten up and move more freely with joy.

Thank you, Goat!

◆ ◆ **Exercise** ◆ ◆

Reclaiming Our Projections with Goat

This exercise—and most of the remaining exercises in this book—
begins the process of retrieving shadow material in more conscious ways. In order to do this, we first need to identify our
Shadow and the many ways it routinely shows up in our lives.

"Openness doesn't come from resisting our fears but from getting
to know them well," writes Pema Chödrön. She suggests we begin gently and honestly, by acknowledging our aversions and cravings. As we
pay closer attention to ourselves in daily life, identifying our triggers
and holds, we may also notice the strategies and beliefs that we used
to build our walls of defense and separation in the first place. "What
are the stories I tell myself?" Chödrön asks. "What repels me and what
attracts me? We start to get curious about what's going on. Without
calling what we see right or wrong, we simply look as objectively as we
can. We can observe ourselves with humor, not getting overly serious,
moralistic, or uptight about this investigation."[7]

Robert Bly maintains there are numerous ways to retrieve our projections or "eat the shadow." Make holes in your habits, he suggests;
deliberately shift things up a bit and watch what happens. Use "care-
ful language"—accurate, clear, intentional words—in conscious ways
to invoke, invite, and acknowledge projected shadow substance.[8]

Perhaps you observe a person who is reflecting some aspect of
your Shadow. *You've got my goat!* you might cry aloud in a joking
way. Simply noting it quietly to yourself is fine as well. Either way,
by acknowledging that a situation reflects something dark, heavy, or
hidden about ourselves we begin to open and learn more about who
we really are.

Bly notes that shadow retrieval involves "activity, imagination,
hunting, asking. 'Always cry for what you want.'"[9] You might sketch,
paint, sculpt, or journal about shadow carriers you observe in the
world. You might approach someone who seems to hold your Shadow
and engage him or her in conversation. You might wear clothes or jewelry that reflect the shadow animals you are working with. Seek out
what smells or feels or tastes of Shadow to you. Consider everything,

Consider everything.

Bly counsels. But at the same time be playful and curious—like a goat.

If you are a visual person or enjoy crafts, you might create or buy a little goat statue, perhaps even tying a red ribbon around its horns or neck, placing it somewhere in your home where you will see it daily—a reminder to summon awareness for the scapegoats who wander through your life.

Or, if you are an adventurous, intuitive person who enjoys inner exploration, you might choose to journey into the wilderness of your psyche. Using meditation, drumming, or daydreams, search for your goat—the one whose horns you have wrapped in red cloth, the one you have loaded with guilt and shame.

Maybe that goat has been gone so long it hardly looks like a goat anymore. Maybe it has taken on a demonic countenance. Can we be brave enough to sit beside it, to ask it how it is doing after all this time? Do we dare ask what can we do for it? Can we appreciate all that it has done for us?

These are just a few ways—and there are many, many more—that can help us sense where we are stuck, where we have given away our power or projected denied emotions onto another. *What's got my goat?*—it can be a mantra, a plea, an exclamation of investigation!

By identifying our triggers as well as our habitual, knee-jerk reactions that only serve to make our world smaller and tighter, we can begin the process of retrieving our Shadow.

Each journey is different, unique. There are no rules. But every frustration, anger, sadness, or fear offers a clue.

What part of ourselves have we exiled to the remote wilds of the psyche—distant, abandoned, removed from consciousness? If we want to know, it is well worth trekking into that wilderness, taking time to learn the terrain, wandering or sitting quietly, patiently watching. What approaches: a devil? a goat? a god? Thus begins the process of bringing ourselves—all our many selves—home.

Satyr Boy with Goat in Landscape, oil painting by Ludwig Knaus, circa mid-1800s to early 1900s

7

Nightmare

Because you have to face your nightmares, Jack. You have to unpack them like you would open up a gift. You must take your nightmares out of the box you've stuffed them into so you can learn what are lies and what is the truth.

JACQUELINE EDGINGTON, *HAPPY JACK*

The origin of the word *nightmare* has nothing to do with mares, or female horses. Rather, the word derives from the Old English *mare* meaning "a goblin, demon, or evil spirit" that sits or lies upon the chest of sleeping humans. It was only later that *night* was added to *mare,* emphasizing that the scary creature comes at night in a dreamlike manner. Over time, a nightmare came to mean a frightening dream.

There are several versions of the mare in other cultures—fearsome spirits perched upon the torsos of sleeping humans, bringing strange and terrifying visions. In some legends the mare presses down upon the limbs and chest of the human, eventually suffocating the individual to death. In other folk tales the mare rides a horse or shapeshifts into another animal to bring terror at night.

Although horses are not linguistically linked with nightmares, there is a connection nonetheless. For nightmares often behave like runaway horses, causing us to feel distressed, panicked, out of control.

Held sacred by many cultures, horses once served as divine vehicles for heroes, warriors, gods, and goddesses. When associated with

The Nightmare, oil painting by John Henry Fuseli, 1781

the wind—the breath of spirit—horses were linked to inner journeys, mystical encounters, and astral travel. For a long time horses were our only form of long-distance transportation, so their association with the way we travel in our dreams makes a kind of horse sense. As a means of transport, Horse can help us move swiftly through a variety of realms.

Domesticated some 6,000 years ago, horses connect us not only with the land and our ancestors, but also to deepened states of being. The wild, untamed power of Horse mirrors our yearning for the far reaches of something distant and unknown. Horse awakens the adventurous spirit, encouraging us to explore. Thus we might ask of our nightmares: Why are our horses running away with us? What part of ourself is out of control? What might be achieved by relinquishing control? What does our nightmare want us to find? Where does Horse want us to go?

Ancient Horse Goddesses

Epona: Celtic fertility goddess and protector of horses, ponies, donkeys, and mules. From the Celtic *epos* meaning "horse," and *ona* meaning "on," Epona was almost always depicted riding upon a horse. The patron goddess of mares and foals was also associated with nurturing and abundance, as well as journeys to the underworld.

Bas-relief of
Roman-Celtic
goddess Epona,
second or
third century CE
Photo by Owen Cook,
CC BY-SA 4.0

Rhiannon: Horse goddess in Welsh mythology sometimes associated with Epona. But while Epona was most often single, Rhiannon was a wedded queen. Mysterious and calm, with a slow riding style described as dreamlike and magical, she was sometimes shown as a mare alongside her son, Pryderi, imaged as a foal.

Demeter: Best known as mother and Greek fertility goddess of the harvest, Demeter once took the form of a mare to escape the unwanted pursuit of her brother, Poseidon. Impregnated by Poseidon in the form of a horse, Demeter gave birth to Arion, an immortal horse known for his incredible speed and ability to talk.

EARTH, SEA, SKY, AND UNDERGROUND

Humans originally hunted wild horses for food, but later realized they were more helpful as work animals. By riding horses we could travel quicker and cover greater distance. Horses carried our cargo, accompanied us onto the battlefield, and helped us till the fields by pulling a plow. Our alliance with Horse changed our world—though it came at a high cost to horses.

Plow horse, pack horse, carriage horse: there is a grounding aspect of Horse as it helps us work the land, explore new terrain, or travel in style and elegance. Companion, guide, and regal transport, horses carry wanderers and settlers, scouts and soldiers, kings and queens. Walking, galloping, charging, advancing over rivers and mountains to explore new lands—desert, forest, jungle—Horse awakens our spirit of adventure, our yearning for freedom, our desire to push beyond known barriers.

With Horse we not only move beyond physical boundaries, but imaginal boundaries as well. We intuit there is something *more* about horses, and so we envisage them in other realms, with special attributes.

Mythology informs us that Horse is not only a land animal, but connected to the sea and sky as well. In the Hindu tradition, a white, seven-headed, flying horse was created by the churning of the milky ocean, and later became the vehicle of kings as well as the sun god Surya.

Poseidon (known to the Romans as Neptune) is the Greek god of sea and sea storms, and—horses! Sometimes worshipped as a horse, he

Neptune's Horses, lithograph by Walter Crane, 1910

was called *Hippeios,* "belonging to a horse." In some myths Poseidon is a tamer of horses, in others the father of horses. He travels on a chariot pulled by galloping horses that race like rushing waves upon the sea.

The offspring of Poseidon and the Gorgon Medusa is Pegasus, the divine, white-winged horse that links sea to sky. Without Pegasus the Greek hero Bellerophon could not have slain the fire-breathing Chimera. Arrogant with his accomplishment, Bellerophon attempted to fly Pegasus to Mount Olympus and live among the gods. Zeus sent a gadfly to bite the horse, who reared and tossed Bellerophon to Earth. But Pegasus was allowed to reach his destination and later transformed by Zeus into the northern-sky constellation still bearing his name.

Flying horses—sometimes called sky horses—appear in legends all over the world. Four mighty horses spread their wings to draw the chariot of the Greek sun god Helios across the sky each day. The Buraq carries prophets to holy places as well as to the heavens and back in a single night. And the Norse Valkyries ride winged horses from Asgard to swoop up fallen souls on battlefields and take them to Valhalla.

The winged Buraq, reproduction of a
seventeenth-century Mughal miniature

Magical Horses

Many mythic horses are endowed with magical qualities. Some have wings or horns or extra legs. Some are sacred, some divinatory, and some capable of connecting us to otherworldly realms.

Sleipnar: The gray, eight-legged horse of the Norse god Odin, described as the best of all horses, was known for journeying to the afterworld.

Odin Rides to Hel, by W. G. Collingwood, 1908

Unicorn: Legendary horse, usually white, with a single, spiraling horn symbolic of heightened intuition and spirituality. Unicorns were connected to purity, grace, and innocence, and sometimes granted humans magical powers.

Hippocampus: From the Greek *hippos,* "horse," and *kampos,* "sea monster," the Hippocampus, also called a Sea Horse, typically had the upper body of a horse and lower body of a fish. In the ancient world, the creature resided in both fresh and salt waters, and was sometimes a vehicle for Poseidon.

Centaur: Half-human, half-horse, centaurs were often depicted as wild and untamed, but there were exceptions. Taught the art of herbs, music, and prophecy by the god Apollo, Chiron was celebrated as the wisest centaur and admired widely for sharing his knowledge. Chiron's students included the healer Asclepius, hero-warriors Ajax and Achilles, Kings Diomedes, and the god of wine, Dionysus.

A first-century Italian fresco shows Chiron
instructing a young Achilles about the lyre.

In the shamanic traditions of east and central Asia, the Wind Horse is a symbol of the human soul and may serve as a vehicle in shamanic voyages. Some suggest the Wind Horse was originally called River Horse or even Dragon Horse (for in Chinese mythology, some dragons arise from rivers), but in all cases it represents good fortune and well-being. On Tibetan prayer flags the Wind Horse is the central, pivotal element of four animals (Garuda, Dragon, White Tiger, and Snow Lion) that represent the cardinal directions. As the flags flutter in the breeze, prayers are carried to the heavens with the swiftness of flying horses.

Not only have humans connected Horse to land, sea, and sky, but also to that which exists below. The chariot of Hades, God of the Dead, King of the Underworld, is drawn by four black, immortal horses.

In Celtic lore the Black Horse was a symbol of death or dark energies, as well as a keeper of secrets and mysteries. In Danish legends a three-legged, black demon horse called the helhest is linked to death and illness. In some stories the Norse goddess Hel, who resides in the underworld, rides the helhest at night and breathes deadly fumes upon unsuspecting sleepers, sinking them into dreams of destruction.

THE NIGHTMARE HORSE

In ancient Greece it was believed that horses could foretell—or possibly bring—death. A sick person dreaming of a horse would soon

Bronze Wind Horse
figurine, Tibet,
nineteenth century
Photo by Clemensmarabu,
CC BY-SA 3.0

die . . . another way in which Horse is linked to nightmares!

In his tenth and last avatar, the Hindu god Vishnu appears as Kalki, sometimes imaged with a horse face (as on page 162). Other times depicted riding a white steed and carrying a fiery sword, Kalki signals the end of the Kali Yuga, the current age of war and discord, and ushers in the beginning of a new age.

In the book of Revelation, four horsemen dramatically signal the arrival of the end, the apocalypse, the final destruction of the world. First comes plague, pestilence, and infectious disease, represented by a man on a white horse with crown and bow. Second comes War upon a red horse, signifying the division of nations, fire, and the spilling of blood. Third is a food merchant upon a black horse, alluding to dark times of famine and malnutrition. And last is a pale horse, sickly and yellowish green, carrying a corpse, or Death, which foreshadows the disintegration of humanity.

Why should Horse play such a key role in signaling the end of times? Perhaps we sense a symbolic alignment with Horse as we ride into unknown territory. It's worth noting that the word *apocalypse* comes from the Greek *apokalupsis,* meaning "to uncover or reveal." Some scholars view the horsemen not as destroyers but rather as guides, their shocking warnings designed to awaken. Perhaps the wild horses of the apocalypse represent the shifting of our consciousness as we transition—running, racing, flying—from the death of one form of

The horse-headed Kalki with drawn sword, signaling his role to re-establish righteousness, gouache painting by unknown artist, circa 1825

Four Horsemen of the Apocalypse,
painting by Viktor Mikhailovich Vasnetsov, 1887

being into the birth of a new. In all cases Horse leads us deeper into the shadowy terrain of the collective psyche, helping us to uncover what we have lost, forgot, buried, or abandoned. The end may seem a daunting journey—worthy of a nightmare—and yet Horse is there for us, beside us, beneath us, as we travel onward.

Death on the Pale Horse. One of 241 wood-engravings designed by the French artist Gustave Doré for the deluxe *La Grande Bible de Tours,* 1865. The illustration is linked to Revelation 6:7–8 in which, after the fourth seal is opened, Death rides into the world.

BAT DREAMS

While growing up my sister and I rarely used the word *nightmare*. It was always a "bad dream"—anything scary, creepy, or unsettling—that we might occasionally report at the breakfast table. After many decades of working with dreams, I have come to appreciate that there is no such thing as a bad dream. Rather, all dreams, even nightmares, are helpful in some way, offering us clues, encouragement, advice, warnings, reminders, and sometimes even humor.

About a year after my Aunt Gini died, I dreamed that I was sitting with her at a small outdoor café, similar to ones we had visited in Amsterdam several years prior.

I ask her how she likes being in the spirit world. She laughs and says she loves it because "You can do anything here!" As if to prove her point, she takes an exceedingly long drag on her cigarette and smiles mischievously.

Then she tells me she has a new job. "What is it?" I ask. In answer she shows me her purse—the big purse she lugged everywhere while she was alive. As she opens the purse, I lean my head in to have a better look. But it is very dark inside—totally black—and I can't see anything. Suddenly, several black bats fly up and out of the purse. I am surprised and ask her what that is about: Why the bats?

She laughs and says the bats are meant to poke at people, that if someone is being lazy in life, or stuck in a belief system, or just not wanting to see something, then her job is to send them "a bat dream!" The bat isn't meant to scare, she explains; rather, the bat is meant to "give them a little kick in the butt." She laughs again with a gleam in her eye and tells me how much she enjoys this job. I can tell that she is proud of herself and quite happy with her new role.

I love this dream! On personal levels it offers reassurance from my aunt in the spirit realm. But so also does it speak of the clever ways our dream guides create "bat dreams" (bad dreams!) to nudge us out of complacency or denial. When shadow material is presented in a light-hearted way, we can more easily open to the idea of change.

The Sleep of Reason Produces Monsters, etching and aquatint by Francisco Goya, 1797–1798

Of course, nightmares are not usually lighthearted. More often these heart-pounding, muscle-twitching, sweat-inducing events wake us on galloping waves of terror. Plunging us into the dark recesses or yawning chasms of shadow territory, the Night Mare sits upon our chest and asks us if we are ready to uncover what we have been hiding for so very long.

WORKING WITH SHADOW DREAMS: SNAKE, LION, AND HORSE

Shortly after deciding to write this book, I had a dream.

> *I am outside, kneeling beside the foundation of my house. I use my hands to dig into the soil next to the house and after just a few handfuls, I startle as a large black snake comes out of the hole. It slides past me a few yards and burrows into the grassy ground. As soon as it disappears, a second snake comes up from the ground nearby. It slides past me in the opposite direction and slips into the hole next to the house from whence the first snake emerged.*

Some dreams are so simple and elegant! With just a few symbols—two black snakes, the foundation of a house, some holes in the ground—they reveal so very much.

The dream announces work with foundational issues. Digging at the foundation of her house (the home of self or psyche), the dreamer is startled by the emergence of a black snake. Snake is a classic shadow animal: both feared and honored throughout the ages, a powerful representative of wisdom, mystery, and transformation. Something enigmatic and not yet known—buried knowledge, perhaps, or untapped personal power—is coming to light. It is mysterious and not easily grasped, for the snake moves quickly before descending back into the earth.

For some the unexpected emergence of a black snake might evoke terror or disgust—a true nightmare. But dreams are unique to the dreamer, and at basic levels we must ask: What does Snake mean to you? For myself the snake suggests the creation of this book as inspired by my last—Snake rising once again as a transformative shadow animal and guide.

And then—a second snake! Repeated dream images are sometimes emphatic: *Notice this!* The second snake acts here as a mirrored return of the first snake's movement. Together, the two snakes illustrate a larger cycle: a reciprocity between personal stories brought up from the psyche and delivered to the earth—the collective foundation, and back again. The movement reveals a flow of seen and unseen, individual and universal: black snakes bringing shadow material to the surface for a short time and returning below. The snakes slide smoothly and reveal an elegance of well-timed comings and goings, gliding above the surface and then dipping below, an overview of how material for this book—as well as work with Shadow—might unfold.

The dream offers warnings as well. The brief time the snakes are seen may suggest a need to notice windows of opportunity, for shadow material is not always visible and accessible. So too does the opening of the dream suggest clearing one's foundation in order to discover what is buried or desires to emerge. Such work may be dirty. Are we ready to dig with our hands, in the earth, to find the clues we need to know?

The actions we take in a nightmare often reflect where we are in relation to our shadow material. Do we run away or hide? Do we stop and watch, or do we engage? Shadow animals may test us, presenting challenges and obstacles, or appearing again and again to determine if we are ready for their lessons. For if we are not ready, their teachings may be dangerous, exposing us to material we are not yet ready to see or integrate.

For several years I dreamed of big cats—leopards, cougars, panthers. In the beginning I was very frightened. The cats seemed menacing, ominous, unpredictable. But as the dream series progressed, I learned to calm my fear. And then I dreamed of lions.

I am in a large, curved room with floor-to-ceiling windows that open onto the wild. It is nighttime, and lions have come to the windows. I watch a male lion put its paw on a pane and press gently—I realize it is testing the glass. This makes me nervous and I check all the windows. I notice that one is open at the far end of the room. As I move to close it, a female lion enters with her cub. The lion walks toward me and I know I must calm my fear. And as she sniffs my body I realize that I am calm and need not worry.

As the lion walks on, I move past her to the basement door. I open the door and the lion walks down a few steps. I sit near her, on the top step, and together the mother lion and I turn our faces to the open house and telepathically call for her cub. It comes and I gently touch its body as it passes me. Following its mother down the stairs, the cub becomes a black jaguar and I realize, with a thrill, how extraordinary it is to witness this.

The wall of glass windows reveals a transparent boundary between the dreamer's home and the wild (the natural world? the wilds of the subconscious? the shadow realm?). As the male lion tests the strength of this boundary, the dreamer is apprehensive, alarmed that the fragile border may be broken and crossed. But the dream shows there is already an opening, through which a female lion and her cub enter. The scene clarifies: male energy will be held in the wild (for now), while feminine, feline energy can enter the dreamer's home.

The dreamer is already nervous by the window boundary being crossed, and now a second test, more intimate: a sniff test. It's a make it or break it moment. If the lion had smelled fear, a very different dream would have unfolded. But the dreamer passes the test by calming her fear, thus allowing the dream (and dream series) to evolve.

Now the dreamer leads the lion to the basement door—another boundary! The door is open and leads not to the wild, but to the basement of the dreamer's psyche. From the top of the stairs, both mother lion and dreamer psychically call for the cub. A telling moment, for shadow animal and dreamer are now aligned in a common task, via a shared mode of communication. The joining of forces reveals that something has been united. As the cub passes her to move down the stairs, the dreamer touches it and watches it transform to a black jaguar. Powerful! What is young and tawny becomes dark and mysterious, and the dreamer knows she is privy to a remarkable occurrence.

While there is much more personal information for the dreamer to unpack, on general levels this dream reveals how commitment to working with our dreams allows us to develop our abilities and even join forces with our shadow animals. Perhaps a future dream will allow the dreamer to explore the basement of her being with the lions (or jaguars) who live there.

By forming alliances with the shadow animals of our dreamworld, we open to further discovery about who we are. While many of these animals may initially appear frightening or aggressive, how we react in a dream can dramatically shift our perspective. Some nightmares don't need to involve large or scary animals. For sometimes the Shadow calls to us in small, despairing ways. One final dream:

> *I enter a special stable for abused or neglected animals and see a white pony in a stall. It looks battered and starved, possibly deformed. It seems wary of others and ashamed of itself. At first I feel uncertain toward it, but I open my arms and it slowly comes to me as if scarcely believing it real that I would embrace it. The longer I wrap my arms around this small horse, the stronger the flow of affection between us. It is deep and real and wonderful, and we both bask in the love.*

The special stable announces exactly what this dream is about: a notable encounter with something that is abused or neglected. In this case the shadow animal is a white pony, so physically and emotionally damaged that it is both wary of others and ashamed of itself. The dreamer need only ask: What is battered, damaged, abandoned, sick, or starved for attention within my self? What small, sad being is at last acknowledged as we open our arms to hold and love it? With care and attention, what might it become?

The Spotted Horse, painting by Paulus Potter, 1653

◆ ◆ **Exercise** ◆ ◆

Meeting the Night Mare

Our nightmares call to us. Alarming and unsettling, their engaging dramas arouse panic, despair, grief, trepidation—creating such indelible impressions that we rarely fail to remember them on waking. Perhaps this is why the shadow selves that seek our attention may appear in the guise of frightening dream animals. Circling us, sniffing us, they test our boundaries, our ability to engage and proceed. Sometimes we cannot see the invitation, for our anxiety is too great.

Nightmares are to dreams as shadow animals are to animal teachers: powerful guides that can help us awaken and evolve. Can we trust that our dream guides and shadow animals are not trying to harm us, but rather to enlighten us, to help us to discover what we need to know?

Some suggest that nightmares are unfinished dreams, interrupted at critical moments by overwhelming emotions. The nightmare challenges from our shadow animals may seem intimidating, but always they are asking: Are you ready?

When the answer is yes, consider reentering your dream to meet your shadow animal face to face. Consciously choosing to meet our nightmares is an excellent way to examine unresolved challenges, listen to fearful or angry selves, or reclaim lost, abused, or abandoned selves. You can access and reenter your dream in simple ways: through meditation or inner journey, or by deepening into a calm, contemplative space of being. If you are anxious at the thought of facing your fears alone, request support from a spirit helper or animal guide.

Horse can be an excellent dream ally for it has keen awareness of its environs and a heightened sensitivity to emotion. Indeed, since the classical times of the ancient Greeks, humans have noted the therapeutic value of aligning with Horse as a way to settle into deeper states of being.

Breathe deep, says Horse. *Walk with me. My hoofbeat is your heartbeat. Listen. Listen deep within. What calls to you? What seeks to be re-paired? Where do you need to go? I will take you there.*

Whether you reenter your nightmare alone or with assistance, use your breath to calm and center. If you journey with Horse, take time to feel your connection and the blending of energies as you move together.

As you travel inward pay attention to clues and insights that occur along the way.

When you face the critical moment in your nightmare—the one that calls to you, the one that rouses fear—open your heart and mind and being. Be brave and trust yourself as you meet the nightmare again. What does it ask of you? What is hurt or sad or frightened or misunderstood? Perhaps you feel a need to soothe your shadow animal by stroking its fur. Perhaps you sit beside it and ask what it needs from you. Perhaps you share why you are so afraid of it. There are innumerable possibilities that may unfold, for each encounter is unique.

To consciously meet our nightmare invokes a deepened relationship between Shadow and self. What we find when we face our fears is often surprising. For beyond the face of fear we encounter a deeper presence. There, in the dark mirror, we see ourselves. Previously misunderstood aspects of who we are gaze back at us, no longer cloaked by fear but illuminated with wonder.

Centauress, painting by John La Farge, 1887

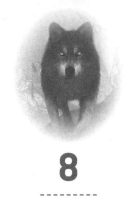

8

The Birds

Covering his head with his arms, he ran toward the cottage. They kept coming at him from the air, silent save for the beating wings. The terrible, fluttering wings. He could feel the blood on his hands, his wrists, his neck. Each stab of a swooping beak tore his flesh. If only he could keep them from his eyes. Nothing else mattered. He must keep them from his eyes. They had not learned yet how to cling to a shoulder, how to rip clothing, how to dive in mass upon the head, upon the body. But with each dive, with each attack, they became bolder . . .

DAPHNE DU MAURIER, "THE BIRDS"

In Alfred Hitchcock's 1963 film *The Birds,* the small seaside town of Bodega Bay is attacked by swarms of birds. Not just gulls, but all types of birds in the area—sparrows and crows, black birds and ravens and jays. "I have never known birds of different species to flock together," exclaims the elderly ornithologist Mrs. Bundy. "The very concept is unimaginable. Why, if that happened, we wouldn't stand a chance! How could we possibly hope to fight them?"[1]

From a young age I was fascinated with this film. Why did the birds show up so suddenly? What did they want? Why did they attack the humans? And why did they leave? Or did they? So many questions! What a mystery!

Hitchcock based his film on the 1952 story of the same name by Daphne du Maurier, who was inspired by her observation of a flock of gulls attacking a farmer in his field.[2] In the story farmhand Nat Hocken does his best to protect his family by boarding up their home. Although he cleverly observes the birds' cycle of attack and knows exactly when to race out to gather food and supplies, he is appalled when he realizes the assaults are happening not just in the British countryside, but also in London and possibly all over the world.

Both story and film end on an uneasy note. In the story Nat accepts the inevitable—that no matter the human preparations, the birds will come, making their way through glass and wood, diving and clawing and pecking out eyes. In the film the housebound family piles into their car and drives away. The last lingering shot is of birds everywhere—on the house, in the road, their calls growing louder. Hitchcock insisted the film finish without the typical "Fin" or "The End," a way of suggesting this was not an ending but the beginning of something more dire. His preferred ending (eventually abandoned since it was considered too

Gulls, often referred to as seagulls, are highly intelligent and keenly resourceful. There are approximately fifty species of this seabird and they inhabit all continents, including Antarctica, making them one of the most widespread bird families in the world.

expensive) entailed the family driving to San Francisco only to find the Golden Gate Bridge covered with birds.[3] In all cases the mystery of the birds—their arrival, their agenda, their dubious departure—remains.

WHAT IS IT ABOUT BIRDS?

We cage them and train them; we eat them and pluck their feathers for decoration or warmth. We admire their ability to fly—to dart and swoop and hover and sail—and travel incredible distances via well-established migration routes. They pollinate wildflowers and food crops, eat insects and spiders and worms, and help maintain ecological balance in our world. We listen to their calls—chirps and caws, shrieks and hoots—and marvel at the incredible diversity of their songs: cheerful, beguiling, mournful, haunting. They appear worldwide in fable and legend as guides and seers, offering insight, advice, warnings, and omens. Throughout history our relationship with birds has covered a wide range of ideas and experiences.

"The most important of all the creatures are the wingeds," notes Oglala Sioux medicine man Black Elk, "for they are nearest to the heavens, and are not bound to the earth as are the four-leggeds, or the little crawling people."[4]

Rising over the land, soaring through the skies, birds connect us with the heavens, helping us to commune with the divine. In the ancient world gods and goddesses were sometimes imaged as birds or with birdlike characteristics. The Egyptian god Horus had the head of a falcon, and Thoth the head of an ibis—though he was also worshipped as the great bird itself. Some deities were accompanied by their sacred birds: Hera with her peacock; Aphrodite with sparrow, swan, and dove. So too could deities transform into birds as needed. Thus the Norse goddess Freya becomes a falcon, Celtic goddess Fand a sea bird, the Irish Morrigan a crow, Zeus an eagle and ravaging swan.

From early times we depicted birds in mosaic and pottery, sculpture and painting. We wore their feathers, bones, and beaks. We placed their images on currency, stamps, emblems, and flags. We saw them in the stars and spoke their names: Corvus the crow, Cygnet the swan, Aquila the eagle.

Copper alloy statue of Thoth-ibis and devotee, Egypt, circa 700 to 500 BCE

We invoke the speed and daring of birds when naming vehicles, aircrafts, and sports teams. We name cities, streets, and businesses after birds, as well as our children: Robin, Sparrow, Starling.

Birds waft into our language through metaphor and simile. Thus we soar like an eagle, crane our neck, swoop like a falcon, have a lark,

Silver tetradrachm from Athens, circa 475 to 465 BCE. Tetradrachms, commonly referred to as "owls," were an extremely popular form of currency in the ancient world and were minted in Athens for over 400 years beginning in 510 BCE. They featured Athena, patron goddess of wisdom, on one side, and her sacred bird, the owl, on the back.

and seek a bird's-eye view. We call people chickens or vultures, dodos or cuckoos—though such phrases do not accurately portray the birds. We use the word *birdbrain* to denote a foolish or stupid person, yet birds as a group are incredibly intelligent, capable of making tools with their beaks and claws, of talking and mimicking and creating new songs. Like humans, birds are also able to deceive.

We define them: warm-blooded, egg-laying vertebrates with feathers, wings, beaks, and—usually—the ability to fly. We categorize and count them. We have identified at least 10,000 bird species, though a 2016 morphological study suggests there may be closer to 18,000 different species![5]

In many ways they are like us: traveling and socializing, eating and courting, mating and nesting and feeding their babies. Yet birds know a freedom that we can only imitate—that ability to transcend the earth, to rise above and soar. It is a human ambition, this desire for liberation, and so we are intrigued by the mystery of birds.

There was a time when we depended on birds to tell us when to

Sacred Geese, oil painting by Henry Motte, 1889. Sacred geese were kept as guardians in the temple of Juno. According to legend, while sentries slept and watchdogs dozed, the sacred geese awakened and alerted the Romans to the approach of the Gauls in 390 BCE, thus saving the republic.

plant and when to plow by observing their comings and goings. They foretold the changing of seasons. We created trade routes based upon their migration patterns and looked for them when we were lost at sea. Navigating not only by sun, moon, and stars, birds have an internal compass, accurate even under clouded skies. With keen instincts and avian knowledge, they guide us, lead us, advise us.

Symbol of freedom and adventure, Bird denotes travel, not only physically but via inner journeys and flights of the imagination. Throughout time and a variety of cultures, shamans and seekers have invoked Spirit of Bird to facilitate soul journeys and travel to other realms for wisdom and healing. Feathered cloaks, capes, robes, and headdress are often worn to connect with the power of Bird.

We may call upon Bird to view life from an elevated perspective. As teachers and celestial messengers, birds bring divine knowledge and mental clarity. Close to the heavens, Bird offers a connection to spirit— as well as freedom and the thrill of flight. In so many ways, Bird helps us better understand the mysterious journey of our own human soul.

Upon the Swallow

This pretty bird, oh! how she flies and sings!
But could she do so if she had not wings?
Her wings bespeak my faith, her songs my peace;
When I believe and sing, my doubtings cease.

John Bunyan, "Upon the Swallow,"
from Divine Emblems or Temporal Things Spiritualized, first
published in 1686. This illustration of a swallow
is from the 1867 version, artist unknown.

IN THE BEGINNING WAS THE EGG

Self-contained, sacred, and central to so many myths describing how the universe comes into being, the cosmic egg symbolizes the source, the start, the gestation of all that will be. Many creation stories begin with a divine bird—fire bird, solar bird, celestial eagle, great ibis, all symbols of rebirth and regeneration—laying the all-important egg. Our ancestors must have sensed the remarkable power of birds in associating them with the creation of the world.

In Egyptian mythology Geb and Nut—Earth father and Sky mother—lay the world egg that holds the sun. In some stories Geb is imaged as a divine goose.

In Indonesian lore bird spirits Ara and Irik float above a vast expanse of water in the beginning of time. Upon discovering two eggs in the water, Ara fashions sky from one and Irik creates earth from the other. They then shape bits of earth into the first people and wake them with the cries of birds.

Egyptian relief sculpture of a goose in limestone, circa 304 to 145 BCE. "Known as 'the Great Cackler,' Geb was said to have laid the cosmic egg that contained the sun and, thus, was honored as the father of the gods." Image and description from The Walters Art Museum.

Other creation stories feature ducks, swans, or other water birds plunging into the primordial ocean. Diving deep to the seabed, the bird gathers a ball of mud (another version of the egg!) and brings it to the surface to create land.

In Greek myth, Nyx, goddess of night—sometimes portrayed as a black-winged bird—hovers in a void of darkness and lays an egg that cracks in half. One half of the eggshell forms the earth, while the other half rises to become the sky. And from the broken egg of earth and sky emerges Eros, the golden-winged god of Love.

An origin tale from Egypt notes that as land rises from the primeval watery expanse, the first god appears in the form of a long-legged heron: the Bennu bird. As the Bennu cries out, its call breaks the silence and allows creation to unfold.

BRINGERS OF LIFE AND DEATH

Many birds represent fertility and new life, and in the West it is often Stork that symbolizes birth. While there are many threads to the origin

Ancient Egyptian depiction of the Bennu deity wearing a sun disk. The bird imagery is possibly based on the extinct Bennu heron, believed to be over 6 feet tall with a wingspan of almost 9 feet. Drawing on papyrus, circa 2700–1800 BCE.

The Stork, oil painting by Carl Spitzweg, 1885, depicts a stork about to drop a swaddled baby to a group of young women below, their aprons outstretched to catch the infant.

of this mostly northern European legend, trace it back far enough and you will find the widespread ancient belief that the human soul both arrives and departs in the form of a bird.

The Sumerians imagined the deceased as birds flying in the underworld, while ancient Greeks and Celts believed the dead could return to earth as birds. In the Hindu view birds are not only symbolic of the soul, but a soul may take the form of a bird in between human lives.

Some cultures express death by saying that one's soul-bird has flown away. The ancient Egyptians envisioned it as the Ba-Bird. Sometimes

The Ba-Bird hovers over its dead human body in a tomb. Illustration from an ancient Egyptian funerary text, circa 1550 to 1077 BCE.

depicted as a hawk with a human head, the Ba-Bird emerges from the body at death. Tombs had special shafts that led to open air so the soul bird could fly in and out. Journeying by night the Ba-Bird assumes any form it likes and travels wherever it chooses, but always returns at daybreak with food for the deceased.

The Great Recyclers

Some birds are associated with death and decay. Celtic war goddesses sometimes appeared as crows and ravens—likely because these birds gathered over battlefields to eat flesh from the fallen. The Valkyries were also known to shapeshift into ravens to carry dead warriors to Valhalla.

Several cultures honor carrion-eating birds for their valuable role in the cycle of life and death. In Zoroastrian communities offering the dead to birds is a sacred practice. The corpse is placed in a *Dakhma* or Tower of Silence, a circular structure raised from the ground built especially for this purpose. The birds come to feast upon the body, leaving only bones.

In Tibet a similar ritual called Sky Burial entails carrying the corpse to a mountaintop, where it is picked clean by vultures.

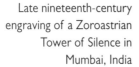
Late nineteenth-century engraving of a Zoroastrian Tower of Silence in Mumbai, India

Some birds announce life, some foretell death, some serve as guides to the afterlife, and some help heal. In ancient Rome a pure white bird with a long neck and yellow eyes called the Caladrius was known to absorb sickness into its body and then fly to the sun, where the illness would be incinerated. The Caladrius was also used to diagnose, for if

Caladrius, as depicted in a medieval bestiary, circa 1200. By looking at the sick man in bed, the Caladrius indicates that he will recover.

it looked into a sick person's eyes, he or she would live, but if it looked away, the patient was doomed.

Another mythological bird—the phoenix—appears in many times and cultures in a wide variety of forms. In Egyptian legend the phoenix lives in 500-year cycles. As the cycle ends the bird builds a special nest in which it spontaneously combusts. A young phoenix then arises from the ashes to replace the old. In some legends the bold red and gold plumage of the phoenix signifies it is born of the sun. Linking birth and death, the phoenix is one of the oldest and most widespread avian symbols of regeneration and rebirth.

This illustration of the phoenix from the Aberdeen Bestiary, circa 1200, may be interpreted in two ways. Perhaps the phoenix is facing the sun and beating its wings to fan the flames as it is being consumed. Or perhaps it is now rising from its own ashes, symbolizing resurrection.
Image and commentary from University of Aberdeen, Special Collections Library and Museum

MESSENGER, GUARDIAN, SEER, AND TRICKSTER

Harbingers and messengers: birds both advise and predict, warning of danger and offering secret knowledge.

In our legends birds sometimes speak in human language—or sometimes an individual acquires the ability to understand bird language. In Germanic tales the hero Siegfried slays a dragon and tastes its blood, whereby he is suddenly able to understand the language of forest birds, who guide him onward.

In older times it was believed that because birds fly everywhere, they are privy to world knowledge. Thus the Norse god Odin relies upon his ravens Huginn and Muninn (Thought and Memory) to travel during the day and return each night to reveal all that they have seen and heard.

Illustration of Huginn and Muninn perched on Odin's shoulders, from an eighteenth-century Icelandic manuscript

Agents of revelation, ethereal couriers of the divine, birds foretell the future and bring instructions from the gods. People once looked earnestly to birds for signs. Ornithomancy is the ancient practice of interpreting the movements, calls, and behavior of birds. Reading omens in avian sounds and actions was serious business and select humans honed their skills in observation and divination. Those connected to birds knew things—about the past, about the future—and were honored for their abilities.

Certain birds were believed to accompany pivotal events. In the Odyssey an eagle foreshadows the arrival of Odysseus, the dead dove in its claws signaling that the suitors of wife Penelope will soon perish.

Mighty birds—especially birds of prey—denoted courage and bravery and were thus claimed as symbols by kings and armies. Eagles were sometimes released at a ruler's funeral—a representation of the royal spirit taking flight—and many ancient tombs feature sculpted eagles as guardians and guides to the afterlife.

Eagle-headed deity, sage, or protective spirit, from a series of stone bas-relief panels found on the inner walls of the Northwest Palace of Ashurnasirpal II, located in the ancient capital of Assyria, northern Iraq, ninth century BCE

In Hindu, Buddhist, and Jain myths, Garuda is the divine king of birds and vehicle of Lord Vishnu. A protective, benevolent spirit, Garuda has the power to fly anywhere very quickly. Depicted in numerous ways—a giant bird, a crowned man with beak and wings—Garuda appears on flags and emblems in many Asian countries to represent strength and eminence.

"The function of the wing is to take what is heavy and raise it up into the region above where the gods dwell; of all things connected with the body, it has the greatest affinity with the divine," writes Plato.[6]

Freed from earthbound constraints, birds are linked to the heavens

Left: Garuda, holding a vase of divine nectar stolen from the gods to free his mother from a serpent goddess. From a series of 100 drawings of Hindu deities created in South India, circa 1825.
Right: Dancing Garuda with outstretched wings, as depicted in the national emblem of Thailand.

and often serve as emissaries of spiritual insight or advice. We imagine angels in similar ways, thus depicting them with large, feathery wings. Their name derives from the Latin *angelus,* meaning "messenger or envoy"—appropriate for spiritual intermediaries who protect and deliver important news from the divine.

Another well-known celestial messenger is the dove: symbol not only of peace and devotion, but also the Holy Spirit. Representing the mother goddess in ancient Near East and Mediterranean lands; sacred to goddesses of love and beauty Ishtar, Inanna, and Aphrodite; the dove is frequently featured in Renaissance art as a visible sign of divine presence or blessing. With its soft, rounded body and gentle cooing sound, Dove is often considered a bird of purity, innocence, and mystery.

Dove also stars in the story of Noah as a symbol of hope. After forty days on the ark, Noah sends a dove on three occasions to search for dry land. The first time the dove returns with nothing. The second time it returns with an olive branch, indicating that the waters have receded and land is near. And the third time it does not return, signaling that it has found home on a now-livable Earth.

The *Annunciation*, oil painting by Bartolomé Esteban Murillo, circa 1660. Surrounded by cherubs, Archangel Gabriel announces to Mary that she will be the mother of the Messiah. In the center of the painting, a white dove depicts the presence of the Holy Spirit.

But there's more to this story. For before the dove, there was the raven: the first bird that Noah sends from the Ark.[7]

Raven was a suspect bird in the Judeo-Christian world, sometimes noted to be one of the few animals that copulates on the ark, thus considered ceremonially unclean. In one legend raven's failure to return causes God to turn its feathers black. A similar theme in Greek myths has Apollo, god of prophecy, turning his beloved all-white messenger bird black for revealing bad news and divulging secrets of the gods. Clearly, Raven knows something of the Shadow!

Scavenger, creator, oracle, and nobody's fool, Raven is both hero and trickster for Native Americans of the Pacific Northwest. In various myths Raven creates humans, animals, and the land. He snatches the sun from the gods to bring humans light and warmth. Finding the hiding place where Creator keeps the stars and moon, Raven scatters them to the sky so people can have illumination even in the dark. In some Native stories Raven is a snow-white bird whose feathers turn sooty black while stealing fire for humans.

Wisdom keeper and spiller of secrets, Raven both holds and conveys

Noted for their remarkable intelligence, curiosity, and ability to problem solve, the common raven (*Corvus corax*) lives both in the wild and near humans. While some cultures revere ravens, others consider them pests—which may be why we sometimes call groups of ravens an "unkindness" or a "conspiracy."

mystery. Carl Jung noted Raven as an avian archetype of transformation, a powerful aspect of the deep psyche that can help us to complete change when we have reached the limits of our abilities. Raven is the dark angel, sent by the unconscious to present the necessary piece of the puzzle—the key message—that we cannot access on our own.

As noted in previous chapters, tricksters often reveal treasure by exposing our buried secrets. Like other shadow animals, Raven can help us be aware of the fullness of who we are, dark and light. By exploring our shadow self we bring our repressed secrets—our own dark angels—to consciousness, just as Raven brings the light of awareness to the world.

THE THING WITH FEATHERS

Helpers, guardians, divine oracles—birds swoop from the heavens to remind or recommend. They may convey wisdom, forecast future events, or announce the arrival or departure of a human soul. Symbols

A Crow and the Full Moon, by
Ohara Koson, circa 1900–1930

of rebirth, harbingers of fear, enigmatic tricksters, feathery descendants
of the long-dead dinosaurs—birds are a mystery.

"Birds will give you a window, if you allow them," writes master
birder and naturalist Lyanda Lynn Haupt. "They will show you secrets
from another world, fresh vision that, though avian, can accompany you
home and alter your life. They will do this for you, even if you don't
know them by name—though such knowing is a thoughtful gesture.
They will do this for you if you watch them."[8]

The first animals that revealed the secrets of telepathic communication to me were a group of small birds gathered on the bush outside
my office window. A soaring eagle once shared visual awareness, showing me the mountainous land below through its sharp, telescopic eyes.
So too did a group of ducks in flight share their experience of flock
consciousness.

While writing this chapter I encountered several birds in notable ways: a swallow darting inches past my nose as I lounged in the sunshine; a large raven sitting atop my car, watching me as I returned to the parking lot with groceries; a gull that glided conspicuous circles around my body as I stood by a river, edging closer and closer, until at last we simultaneously veered away. What do such visitations mean? What are the birds saying?

Each bird species has its own gifts and teaching. Through myth and folklore, we glean that Crane represents good health and fortune, Swan strength and elegance, Owl wisdom and knowledge of the dark, Vulture death and new beginnings. Such recognitions can offer helpful stepping-stones to knowledge. But to truly know bird we must become Bird, opening ourselves to a deeper mystery.

There are more than 225 owl species worldwide, from the tiny elf owl only 5 inches high to the great gray owl with a 5-foot wingspan. Most owls possess keen hearing, binocular vision, and specialized wing feathers designed for silent flight.

There comes a point in shadow work when words and concepts no longer serve. Trekking into the deep psyche, beyond the confines of logic and thought, we release old structures and much of what we thought we knew. Words and ideas may point us there, but deep down knowing is altogether different.

"Hope is the thing with feathers," wrote Emily Dickinson, perceiving an elusive, enigmatic bird that perches within the human soul, one that "sings the tune without the words, and never stops at all."[9]

Throughout the world bird feathers are a sign of something both delicate and powerful—that hollow shaft with its soft, silken, interlocking fringe, a distillation of the magic and mystery of Bird.

We assign meaning to the colors and shapes of fallen feathers, contemplating where or when or how they are found. We perceive that such feathers fall to earth as celestial suggestions and invitations, offering support, encouragement, or confirmation of our own intuitive insights. Sensing the connection between found feathers and gifts of spirit, we are reminded that messages may come to us in both strange and wonderful ways.

No matter the meanings we assign to birds—winged angels, wise prophets, dark messengers—their teaching both involves and invokes mystery. Birds invite us to know ourselves in a different way. But to step into that space of mystery requires something of us as well.

Feather found while
writing this chapter

◆ ◆ **Exercise** ◆ ◆
Becoming Bird

Author Jean Houston once observed an Australian Aboriginal woman of the Emu totem enter "into the body, mind, and spirit of the great bird so totally that for an instant her human form disappeared into the bird form. There was no emu present for her to imitate, but she had so closely identified with her totem that every movement and feature had become emu and nothing but emu. And whereas, previously, this woman had been silent and withdrawn, for a time afterward she became vocal and expressive and taught us much. When I asked her how this had happened, she told me, 'I caught my Dreaming—I was my ancestor.' She had become her totem."[10]

Since ancient times humans have invoked the Spirit of Bird in shamanic voyages, trances, and mystical states of consciousness. Sometimes a medicine man or woman becomes a bird—Eagle, Owl, Crow—traveling to different realms or dimensions to acquire knowledge and healing. Sometimes the spirit of a particular bird enters a shaman's body, helping to inspire and guide. Other times, human and bird share consciousness, traveling together as partners, learning from each other.

For this exercise embrace the challenge of becoming Bird. This is not a mental exercise, but rather a celebration of movement, embodiment, feeling, and creative expression. By taking on the appearance, behavior, and characteristics of an animal, we can deepen our sense of knowing. You can do this with any shadow animal, both to learn more about the animal and to explore your Shadow.

To begin, find a quiet, secluded space where you will not be disturbed. If you feel inclined, gather props that may help you to take on the shape and feel of your animal. For example, play a tape of bird calls or fashion a shawl into wings; wear feathers in your hair or place images of your bird before you.

Now, begin to move like your bird, calling out, singing its song, feeling the shifting weight of your body as you become more birdlike. Flapping, crowing, hooting, stretching, hopping, twirling, swaying, invite Bird to share its consciousness, to move through you. Allow yourself the unbridled freedom to open to the unique calls, gestures, and actions of your bird. Feel yourself becoming Bird.

If you find yourself blocked by thinking this is silly or stupid, notice how judgments from your shadow self prevent you from exploring. Could it be fear in disguise? While this exercise may initially seem whimsical, it is actually quite powerful—and a part of us knows that.

The key is to tap into the deeper mystery of Shadow by moving beyond our limiting ideas about it. By becoming our shadow animal, we can begin to embody its energy—resonating with it, aligning with it in ways that may surprise and illuminate.

When you sense the presence of Bird, invite it to move with you, through you, beyond you. Ancient guide, wise advisor, divine messenger, daring trickster, Bird leads us to adventure. Allow the mystery to unfold.

Welcome, Bird

9

That Which Swarms, Stings, Bites, Burrows, and Invades

From A to Z, they overwhelm us with their diversity: ants, birdwing butterflies, cockroaches, dung beetles, earwigs, flies, grasshoppers, head lice, inchworms, June beetles, katydids, ladybugs, mantises, net-winged midges, owlflies, periodical cicadas, queen termites, royal palm bugs, sawflies, thrips, underwing moths, velvety shore bugs, webspinners, xyelid sawflies, ypsistocerine wasps, and Zorapterans.

SCOTT RICHARD SHAW,
PLANET OF THE BUGS

Some we love: ladybug, firefly, butterfly. Some we scorn: wasp, mosquito, cockroach. Some we once honored as gods: honeybee, scarab beetle, mantis. Some we may never see or even imagine in our lifetime. And so many we are still in the process of discovering.

There are well over 1 million living insect species in the world. As entomologist Scott Richard Shaw notes, insect diversity and ecological success is so impressive that "it's not much of an exaggeration to say that they literally rule the planet."[1]

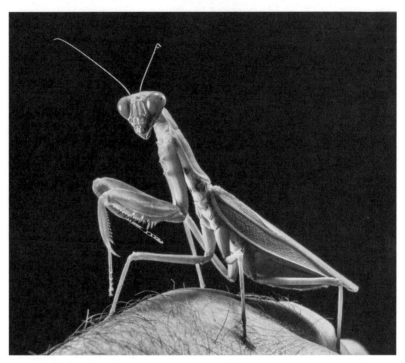

Trickster god and master of motion, Mantis gets its name from
the Greek for prophet or seer. Its large eyes, swivel head, and watchful
demeanor hint at clairvoyant powers, and its ability to spring swiftly
and elegantly into action has inspired several martial arts styles.
There are over 2,400 species of mantises worldwide.

We define them: air-breathing animals with hard-jointed
exoskeletons—shell-like coverings that comprise the outer body. We
observe adult insect bodies divided into three parts: the head, with one
pair of antennae; the thorax, including three pairs of legs and (usually)
two pairs of wings; and the abdomen, holding the guts and reproductive
organs. We divide class Insecta into just over thirty orders, the largest of
which is Coleoptera: beetles.

The Beetles

There are well over 350,000 known species of beetles, though we are
continually discovering new Coleoptera. Found nearly everywhere,
with an incredible range of shape and color, some of the largest

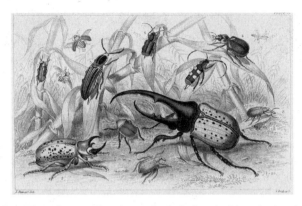

Engraving of several beetle species including the Hercules beetle
(*Dynastes hercules*, lower right) and the *Scaraebus tityus* (now known
as *Dynastes tityus*, lower left), as well as several ground and flying beetles
such as the striped click beetle, the beautiful capricorn beetle, and the
spotted lady-bird beetle, by natural history artist J. Stewart, circa 1850s.

(the size of a human hand) and some of the smallest (barely visible)
insects are beetles.

Ancient Egyptians viewed scarab beetles rolling huge balls of dung
(serving both as egg chamber and food) as physical manifestations of
the god Khepri (an aspect of Ra), who rolled the sun across the sky
each day. Thus, family Scarabaeidae came to symbolize awakening
and the renewal of life.

Limestone relief panel showing two baboons offering wedjat eyes to Khepri,
the newborn sun represented by a beetle. Khepri holds a disk with a star, sign
for the underworld, and beneath him there is a sun with rays, Egypt, 400–
200 BCE. Image and commentary from the Metropolitan Museum of Art.

The first insects evolved among the mossy soils of ancient trees over 400 million years ago. The versatility of six legs allowed them to creep, scurry, and climb, which is why they became such successful ground scavengers. Fifty million years later, the flying insects evolved—a game-changer! As Shaw notes: "When the insects invented wings there were no other flying animals—no birds, bats, pterodactyls, or gliding squirrels—and they completely mastered the air for more than 150 million years before any other organisms evolved the ability to fly or could chase them in the air."[2]

Insects live almost everywhere—from rain forests to deserts to high in the Himalayan mountains; on the land, in trees, under soil, and beneath the water. They live on plants and animals, on us and *in* us as well. Some have specialized to thrive in surprising places: salty lakes and pools of crude oil, algae and mud puddles, on the frozen tundra and in hot springs up to 95 degrees, and some walk on the ocean surface hundreds of miles from land.[3]

We are intrigued by their extremes: from stick insects over 14 inches long and butterflies with 12-inch wingspans to feather-winged beetles and fairyflies that cannot be seen without magnification. From locust swarms 28 trillion strong and super colonies of ants

Adult female fairyfly or fairy wasp, family Mymaridae, magnified

with over 300 million workers to the incredibly specialized: bird lice that live only in the pouches of pelicans, mammal lice that live only in the fur and nostrils of sea lions, and bloodsucking parasitic flies that live in bat fur.[4]

Entomophobia is the extreme fear of insects, a phobia that affects up to 6 percent of the U.S. population.[5] While some entomophobes fear all insects, some are more specific: apiphobia, for example, the fear of bees; myrmecophobia, the fear of ants; or katsaridaphobia, the fear of cockroaches.

There is often a fine line between fear and fascination, and when working with Shadow we may traverse that line numerous times. Insects offer millions of living examples of how we can be both intrigued and frightened by tiny creatures in the world. The following sections consider how several insect groups that "bug" us also help to reveal our Shadow.

THAT WHICH SWARMS

Swarmers include termites, ants, bees, and gnats, but the insect that creates the most spectacular swarm is the locust. Locusts are short-horned members of the grasshopper family, of the suborder Caelifera, which includes over 11,000 species of plant-chewing insects that have resided on our planet for more than 250 million years.

Symbol of good luck, health, wealth, and longevity, grasshoppers are generally considered messengers of joy. In various cultures they represent fertility, nobility, immortality, and souls of the deceased.

As teachers grasshoppers invoke intuition and inspire us to move beyond everyday limits. Powerful hind legs allow them to leap an impressive twenty times their body length. Thus Grasshopper is sometimes connected to astral travel and adventures across space and time. Their large legs become instruments of music when rubbed against their wings, creating chirps and songs—for some, an auditory medicine that opens pathways to alternate realities.

Not only are their legs extremely sensitive but also, surprisingly, the cause of what makes us fear locusts. Swarming begins when locusts crowd together. As locust legs brush against each other, the neurotransmitter

Grasshopper! Humans have granted grasshoppers a wide variety of descriptive names, such as the slender ground-hopper (*Tetrix subulata*), the grizzly spur-throat grasshopper (*Melanoplus punctulatus*), the white-whiskered grasshopper (*Ageneotettix deorum*), the wrinkled grasshopper (*Hippiscus rugosus*), and the obscure bird grasshopper (*Schistocerca obscura*).

serotonin is released into their brains. This causes changes in body color and behavior. Suddenly, the grasshoppers want to eat, meet, mate, and eat some more.

Banding together they join with other groups, forming even larger masses. As their population explodes the locusts begin to migrate, creating astonishing paths of destruction. This can happen very quickly—in only a few hours, billions of locusts may swarm over thousands of acres, feeding and breeding. They are strong fliers, too—clouds of locusts have flown across the entire Atlantic Ocean![6]

Locusts have swarmed for as long as we can remember. Ancient Egyptians carved and painted their images on tombs over 4,000 years ago, and locust plagues causing destruction, famine, and exodus are cited throughout Hindu, Islamic, and Christian texts.

Stripping foliage from plants and crops, locusts devour flowers, fruits, bark, stems, and seeds. From barley to buckwheat, melons to strawberries, plagues will attack almost anything: fence posts, cloth-

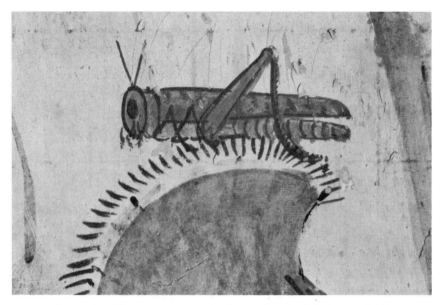

Locust detail from a large mural on the north wall of Theban tomb 78
for Horemheb, Egypt, circa 1422–1411 BCE

ing, and each other. The size of a swarm can be mind-boggling. The largest recorded locust plague occurred in 1875. Measuring 1,800 miles long and 110 miles wide, it included an estimated 3.5 trillion Rocky Mountain locusts ravaging crops from California to Minnesota. As one researcher put it, "Thousands of farm families threw in their shovels and gave up."[7]

While small groups of grasshoppers are peaceful, overcrowding causes behavioral change. At times we undergo a similar transformation. Just as serotonin causes locusts to swarm, elevated serotonin in our brain chemistry triggers anger and aggression—which is how crowds of otherwise pleasant, law-abiding individuals can suddenly turn frenzied and destructive.

The shadow aspect of swarming is about that which overwhelms. We may feel it in tightly packed crowds: a push to join herd mentality, to be swept up in something larger than ourselves.

On personal levels we may be swarmed by details. While any one on its own could be dealt with, the onslaught of so many particulars all at once can trigger fears of overload and suddenly we are inclined, like

A Swarm of Locusts, by Emil Schmidt,
chromolithograph illustration,
1882–1884

the midwestern farmers of 1875, to throw in our shovels and give up. The ability of the small to swarm and overwhelm is not only a powerful weapon of the insect kingdom, but an insidious way that shadow energy can overtake us.

THAT WHICH STINGS

Stinging insects include wasps, hornets, yellow jackets, fire ants, and bees. The stinger is the sharp, pointy organ that injects venom, usually located in the rear (abdomen), though one beetle species (*Onychocerus albitarsis*) delivers a sting from its antennae. Pain, swelling, itching, and redness may result, as well as allergic reactions; for some, a sting can be life threatening.

Many insects sting repeatedly and fly away, but honeybees have barbed stingers that lodge deep in the skin. When torn from its body the bee dies, though the stinger continues to release venom for several minutes.

Sting of a honeybee. Note barbed stinger at the end of
the bee's abdomen, neatly inserted into human skin.
Photo by Waugsberg, CC BY-SA 3.0.

Home for the honeybee is the hive: that iconic cluster of hexagonal-shaped cells created from their wax secretions. This is where honeybees eat, sleep, mate, raise their young, and support the queen—she who creates new life and assures continuity to the colony by laying up to 2,000 eggs a day.

Honored since ancient times, honeybees represent fertility, creation, royalty, and love. In Egyptian myth they are born from tears of the sun god Ra that fall upon the desert sand. In ancient Greece bees were considered divine insects, and before Apollo claimed the ancient oracle, the prophetic priestess at Delphi was known as the Delphic Bee. Sacred to Demeter and Artemis, goddesses of harvest and fertility, bees were honored for their diligence in pollinating crops and ensuring abundance. Goddess worshippers were called bees and some wore small metal bees as emblems of Artemis. Souls were imagined both as bees buzzing downward waiting to be born and whooshing upward as they departed the deceased.

Gold jewelry plaque depicting a winged bee goddess, possibly associated with Artemis, seventh century BCE

Bees form the bowstring of Kama, Hindu god of desire, and are similarly linked to Cupid, Roman god of love and affection. In a popular myth young Cupid steals honey from a hive and is stung by a swarm of bees. Crying to his mother, the goddess Venus, Cupid rages that such a tiny creature making such a delicious treat should cause such terrible hurt! To which Venus astutely observes that Cupid's form is also small and sweet, yet he too delivers the painful sting of love.

Sweetener, healer, and natural antiseptic; embalming agent to mummies; sacred libation to the dead; and the main ingredient in the ancient fermented drink called mead, honey has long been considered nectar of the gods and goddesses. To ingest honey is to take in the divine life substance and spiritual energy of bees.

But bees ferociously defend their honey, hive, and queen by stings. Most stings are protective, born of perceived threats. Stinging insects ask us: What treasure are you protecting? Do you perceive a true threat or are you projecting your fears?

We too may sting via sharp remarks and actions. Often our stings are barbed, not only inflicting pain on others but leaving a part of ourselves stuck in the wound. The shadow aspect of stings prompts us

Cupid the Honey Thief, by Albrecht Dürer, ink and watercolor, 1514

to heed the consequences of our actions, to perceive clearly and move through projected fears so that we can better enjoy and share the sweet treasures of life.

THAT WHICH BITES

While both insect bites and stings can be painful, there is a major difference between the two: stings inject toxins into the skin while bites are made to feed on blood. Most biting insects first insert an anticoagulant (and sometimes a numbing agent) through their saliva. Biting insects include beetles, ants, deer flies, horse flies, lice, fleas, bed bugs, and mosquitoes.

Mosquitoes are members of the fly family, their name deriving from the Spanish for "little fly." All mosquitoes feed on nectar, but the females of most species also require blood nutrients to produce their eggs. They accomplish this via their proboscis—a long, sharp-ended, tubelike mouth that pierces the skin and draws up blood.

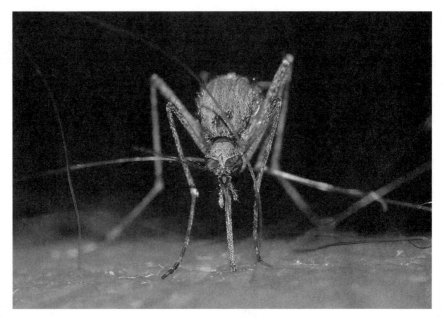

Female mosquito feeding. Once she has a full meal (her abdomen can hold
three times its weight in blood), she will rest while her eggs develop. After laying
them on water, she will seek another blood meal and begin the process again.
A female mosquito will typically lay three sets of several hundred eggs in her lifetime.

In addition to ingesting proteins, female mosquitos also take in any bacteria, virus, and parasites living in the blood. These can then be transferred via her saliva to another host. Mosquito-borne diseases include Zika, West Nile virus, yellow fever, dengue fever, encephalitis, and malaria. It is conservatively estimated that mosquitoes annually transmit disease to over 700 million people, averaging approximately 750,000 deaths, thus making them one of the world's most deadly animals.

While over 3,500 species of mosquitoes feed and breed worldwide, cultural myths about their origins are strikingly similar. In most cases, it begins with a demonic giant who loves to eat humans and drink their blood. A hero kills the giant, but the giant will not stay dead. So the hero cuts up the giant's body and burns it in a fire. But still the spirit of the giant affirms that it will not die. And so it is true, for a swarm of mosquitoes arise from the giant's ashes and take flight to travel the globe, eager to bite humans and suck their blood.

Mosquitoes are persistent! From their annoying hum to the

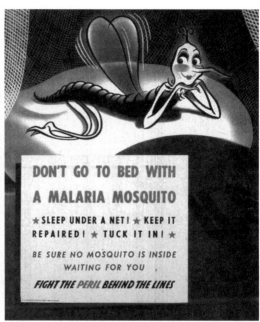

U.S. government posters warning of the dangers of malaria, circa 1944. Malaria caused considerable illness and death and was a major concern for soldiers throughout the Civil War, Korean War, Vietnam War, as well as World Wars I and II.

maddening itch of their bite, they remind us how significant small irritants can actually be. Are we overwhelmed with buzzing thoughts? What inside of us is maddened, troublesome, small yet exasperating?

Sucking out our lifeblood, mosquitoes invade epidermal boundaries and take without asking. So also can they spread disease as they unwittingly share pathogens from others.

From another perspective, our blood assures continuity of life for the mosquito world. The fact that only females bite invokes themes of mothering, nurturing, and protecting. Do we feel a loss of vital fluid? Is someone feeding from us only to nourish themselves? Or are we doing this to others?

Mosquitoes have influenced humanity to such an extent that they have significantly shaped the course of history. More than any other insect or animal, the tiny, ubiquitous mosquito brings illness and death—once again revealing the power of the small to create change in the world.

A mother nursing a child and a woman looking at them through a mosquito-netting bed cover, print by Kitagawa Utamaro, 1795

THAT WHICH BURROWS

Despite the pain and potential disease that biters bring, far more striking on the revulsion scale are the burrowers: blood-sucking insects that don't just remain on our skin but bore their way deep down to live and eat inside of us.

Botflies

Also known as warble flies or gadflies, botflies lay their eggs within mammal flesh to give their larva something nutritious to eat. There are about seventy species of botflies, but only one—*Dermatobia hominis*—affects humans.

Soon after a botfly drops her eggs upon warm skin, the larva hatch, burrow, and begin to feed. Because botfly larva have spines on their body, burrowing causes pain, and one sign of infestation is the eerie sensation of movement beneath the skin. While botfly infestation can cause skin lesions and infection, it rarely causes death.

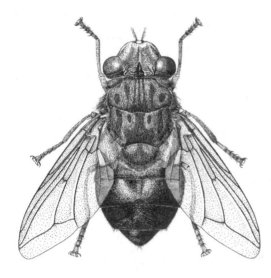

Illustration of an adult human botfly (*Dermatobia hominis*)

Extracted human botfly larva
Photo by Geoff Gallice, CC BY 2.0

Screwworms

Despite their name, screwworms are flies—the only flies, in fact, that consume live flesh as their primary food source. There are two types of screwworms: Old World (*Chrysomya bezziana*) living mostly in Africa and Asia, and New World (*Cochliomyia hominivorax*) found in the West. *Hominivorax* means "man-eater," which gives an idea of exactly what screwworms do.

Humans attract screwworms through open wounds or mucus-covered tissues such as eyes, ears, nostrils, and newborn navels. Even wounds as tiny as a tick bite can attract a female screwworm to settle in

New World screwworm
(*Cochliomyia hominivorax*)
Photo by Judy Gallagher, CC BY 2.0

and feed. There she may stay up to thirty days, expanding her feeding area by diving deeper into the tissue, laying up to 500 hundred eggs at a time. The eggs hatch within a day, and the larva burrow further into the wound to feed on living flesh. This can worsen the wound, attracting more flies to lay more eggs, and so the cycle continues.

Tip of a screwworm fly larva, as viewed through electron microscope
Photo by Commonwealth Scientific and Industrial
Research Organisation (CSIRO), CC BY 3.0

Fleas

Flea is the common name for the order Siphonaptera, which includes over 2,500 species of tiny, flightless insects that live by consuming blood from their hosts—usually mammals and birds. Although they lack wings, fleas have strong claws for grasping, mouths adapted to pierce skin and suck blood, and strong hind legs that allow them to leap up to fifty times their body length.

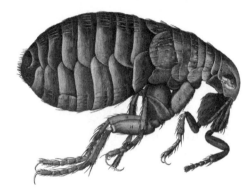

Illustration of a flea by Robert Hooke, the first to publish illustrations of insects viewed through a microscope. *Micrographia*, 1665.

Smallest among the fleas are *Tunga penetrans,* also called chigoe, sand fleas, or jigger fleas. The female burrows into the skin of a warm-blooded animal host—perhaps a dog, cat, rat, monkey, donkey, bird, elephant, or human. Angling herself proboscis-down, she takes a day to burrow almost all of her body, until only the anus, copulatory organs, and four abdominal air holes are exposed. Only then can reproduction begin. Her excreted feces attract male fleas, and after a two-minute copulation the

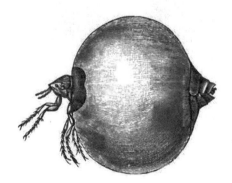

Illustration of female jigger flea with distended abdomen

male soon dies. With head still fully submerged, the female feeds on the host's blood as her abdomen expands, swelling to the size of a small pea, with thousands of eggs growing inside. Once the eggs are released the female dies, the eggs hatch, and the process begins anew.

Chigoe infestation can cause a serious disease called tungiasis, which not only results in pain, itching, swollen lesions, and ulcerations, but also desquamation—skin peeling. Left untreated, necrosis and gangrene can occur.

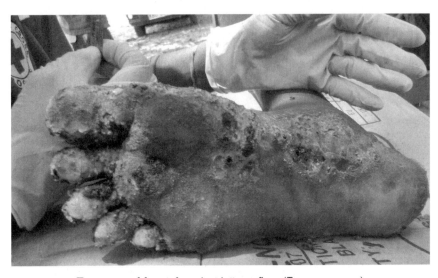

Treatment of foot infested with jigger fleas (*Tunga penetrans*)
Photo by R. Schuster, CC BY-SA 3.0

Burrowers ask: What has gotten under our skin? What is eating away at us from within? When shadow energy manifests as an internal parasite it causes pain and invokes alarm, demanding we take action. This aspect of Shadow cannot be denied, for if ignored it may attempt to eat us alive.

THAT WHICH INVADES

Widely disliked, often considered dirty and disgusting, the cockroach has a serious public-image problem. To call someone a cockroach is an insult, and yet there's so much about cockroaches—their strength, cunning,

American cockroach
(*Periplaneta americana*)

intelligence, and tenacious ability to survive—that we might admire.

Their English name comes from the Spanish *cucaracha,* their order Blattodea from the Latin meaning "insect that shuns the light." Of their nearly 5,000 species, only thirty are associated with human habitation and only four—the German, Asian, Oriental, and American (the largest of the common cockroaches)—are considered pests.

Survivors of the ice ages, witness to the emergence of *Homo sapiens* as well as the rise and demise of countless other species, cockroaches have been around well over 300 million years. As you might expect from such an ancient group, these insects are incredibly robust and hardy. With a tough exoskeleton that repels water and protects inner organs, they live abundantly nearly everywhere, from the tropics to the Arctic. They can eat almost anything: fruit, bread, glue, soap, paint, paper, hair, skin flakes, and fingernail clippings. Many can go a month without food, some can survive forty-five minutes without air, and some can withstand below-freezing temperatures by creating their own antifreeze. Even the severed head of a cockroach can wave its little antenna for several hours after death, while its body may wander around for a week or two.[8]

African and Caribbean folk tales champion the cockroach as a hero that outsmarts those who think they are in charge, though we of the West have generally demonized the cockroach. But why?

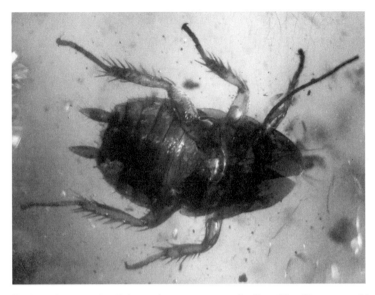

Cockroach encased in Baltic amber, approximately 40 to 50 million years old
Photo by Anders L. Damgaard, Amber-fossils.com, CC BY-SA 4.0

Living in basements and sewers, hiding in the dark and scuttling away when exposed to the light, cockroaches are prime examples of a shadow animal. Lurking in kitchens and bathrooms, invading our food and private spaces, they are fast and sneaky—unwelcome guests not easily persuaded to leave. Step on one and it will not only crunch but emit a latrine-like odor owing to the uric acid stored in its body.

While cockroaches do not carry disease, they can spread contaminants from their feces and molted skin. But they can't really hurt us—not like a burrowing flea or disease-transmitting mosquito. Yet for most people, a cockroach is far more repellent: creeping up on us, startling and surprising with their long, waggling antenna, their strange, alien-looking bodies and their fast bristly legs. Even more disconcerting is the realization that seeing one cockroach most often means others are near.

Defiant and prolific, cockroaches encroach and infest. Taking over our homes and lives, they intrude, evoking deep-rooted fears of invasion. We've long been trying to get rid of them. Insecticidal invocations, spells, and suggestions dating back thousands of years have attempted to banish cockroaches from bothering both the living and the dead.

Although we have tried our very best to eradicate them, the clever cockroach persists by thwarting traps, developing resistance to insecticides, and maintaining global survival.

We use the term *bug* to denote illnesses such as a virus. It's a curious yet apt connection, for virus-bugs invade our bodies just as cockroach-bugs invade our homes. Both come quickly, without warning, and when we finally notice it's too late. It's also fascinating that our depictions of aliens from other worlds often include bug-eyes, long antennas, and armored, insect-like bodies. A bug invasion frightens us—whether it occurs in our body, in our home, or on our planet.

Some entomologists speculate that of all the insects, it is Cockroach that humans fear the most. It is unpredictable, moves erratically, and in order to escape predators has evolved to be one of the fastest terrestrial animals on Earth. So also, it survives—no matter what we do. Thus the ancient Cockroach reveals some of our deepest personal and collective fears: invasion, violation, helplessness, and the realization that we are not really in control.

The mighty cockroach

THE BENEFIT OF BUGS

Without insects, the world we know could not exist. As biologist E. O. Wilson notes, "If all mankind were to disappear, the world would regenerate back to the rich state of equilibrium that existed ten thousand years ago. If insects were to vanish, the environment would collapse into chaos."[9]

Though we often think of bugs as problems, less than 1 percent of insect species are notable pests. The overwhelming majority are beneficial. Insects such as bees, butterflies, and moths pollinate the preponderance of our world's flowers, plants, and crops. Without these insects so much would be lost!

Insects are also amazing recyclers, breaking down waste into nutrients for plants. We need the saprophages—the beetles, wasps,

Butterfly sipping nectar from an Ixora flower

and ants that feed on dead or decaying plants and animals. Not only do they help to rapidly consume decomposing matter, but they create humus—that dark, nutrient-rich organic component of soil. So too, we need the coprophaghes—feces-eaters such as flies and dung beetles, whose activities clear away waste, aerate soil, and help plants to grow.

Ants

Since the time of dinosaurs, the intelligent, social-minded Ant has made itself at home nearly everywhere on our planet. We have classified over 12,500 species, most all of which work collectively to support their colonies. Because they have no ears, ants "listen" by feeling vibrations and communicate with each other via a sophisticated chemical language. Although small they are able to lift up to fifty times their bodyweight and can join forces to transport even heavier objects.

Worker ant, *Camponotus nylanderi*

When asked why he chose to study ants, world expert on family Formicidae, E. O. Wilson, answered: "The answer is that they're so abundant. They're easy to find and they're easy to study and they're so interesting! Each kind of ant has almost the equivalent of a different human culture. So each species is a wonderful object to study in itself. In fact, I honestly cannot understand why most people don't study ants!"[10]

Insects keep their population in balance by eating each other. And they are also a prime food source to countless species of fish, birds, reptiles, amphibians, and mammals. Dried, grilled, ground, or crispy fried, a wide variety of insects—grasshoppers, crickets, ants, termites, aphids, dragonflies, and more—provide nutritious sustenance for humans as well.

We take advantage of insect byproducts such as honey and silk, and use insects in medicine as well. Maggots have long been used to treat infection, and some cultures still rely on the pinched heads of large-jawed ants to stitch wounds. Bee venom is used to treat arthritis, muscular sclerosis, fibromyalgia, and more. And a great many insects—including locust, bees, wasps, beetles, fleas, ants, butterflies, moths, and mosquitos—are used in both traditional Chinese medicine and homeopathic remedies. Sometimes the healing power of insects surprises us. One homeopathic cure was discovered in the 1800s when an elderly man suffering extreme asthma suddenly felt better after accidentally drinking cockroach-infused tea.[11]

As a group, insects remind us about patience and persistence, teamwork and tenacity. But so also do they bug us! To view this as assistance rather than annoyance is a step toward cultivating a relationship with Shadow. Our irritations around insects can be incredibly helpful in revealing the underlying causes of our frustrations. Instead of destroying the irritant-messenger, why not explore it? Delving beneath our discomfort, we can inquire what it reflects to us, what it wants of us, how we might work with it, and so begin to release emotional holds that bind us.

Another Way of Seeing

Photographer Molly Holm notes, "I have never once felt threatened by a paper wasp. I admire their beauty so much and I always have a distinct impression that they are very intelligent. Something happens when I am filming them and other creatures; a feeling of being in love quietly takes over. They seem to sense that I am not threatening and we share a space for a period of time. Always though, the responsibility is on me to be a respectful guest. I have to make sure I do right by them as I steal their images with my camera. I just wish for others to see them the way I do."

Paper wasp
Photo by Molly Holm

What's Bugging Me?

This exercise focuses on identifying shadow irritants and reframing them with shifts in awareness. Choose an insect that reflects a shadow concern. For example, if you feel overwhelmed, consider a swarming insect. If you feel stung or invaded, choose a stinging or biting insect.

Print an illustration of your insect and fill in lines 1 through 6 as shown in the Ant diagram on page 218. Or simply use the accompanying image of Ant. Moving clockwise, answer the questions while observing the three parts of an insect's body in relation to yourself: head questions require thought; thorax questions trigger the solar plexus chakra of personal power and change; and abdominal questions request us to feel our emotions.

1. Who or what is bugging me?
2. Why does this bug me?
3. What emotions do I feel when this occurs?

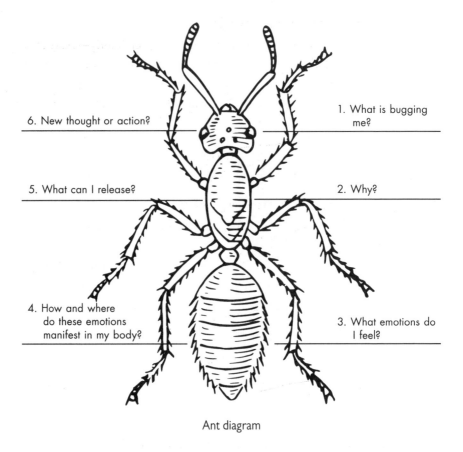

6. New thought or action?

1. What is bugging me?

5. What can I release?

2. Why?

4. How and where do these emotions manifest in my body?

3. What emotions do I feel?

Ant diagram

4. How and where do these emotions manifest physically in my body?
5. What is my role in this situation? What can I release? What can take flight?
6. How is what bugs me a clue to something in myself that prevents me from enjoying life? What new thought or action can replace the old?

Using the tools and insights you've gathered thus far, dive deep to explore what bugs you. Remember to be curious, creative, and playful, but at the same time respectful as you meet and begin to integrate this aspect of Shadow.

Invite the process to continue working through you by making a talisman or emblem of your insect. You might print an image, buy a small representation, or wear jewelry that signifies your insect. Such visuals serve as reminders of the change they've inspired.

Building Bridges with Ant: A Love Story

A friend who wishes to be anonymous—let's call her Sandy—read this chapter and completed the exercise. Her experience was so dramatically life changing that she offered to share it with readers as an example of how powerful investigating and addressing the small irritations in our life can be.

1. *What bugs me?* My husband when he zones out on his phone instead of talking with me.
2. *Why does this bug me?* Because he's ignoring me!
3. *What emotions do I feel?* Anger, annoyance, frustration. And beneath that, sadness and hurt.
4. *How and where do these emotions manifest in my body?* My head feels tense and my body feels restless—a little antsy (ha ha). When I sense deeper, I realize my heart and chest also feel heavy.
5. *What is my role? What can I release to lighten up?* Sometimes I get lazy and don't put energy into conversation. I think we've both fallen into a pattern of engaging our stupid phones instead of conversing. What I'd like to release is this and other ways of not relating.
6. *How is this a clue to what prevents me from enjoying life? What new thought or action can replace the old?* What I'm realizing here is that I'm angry and annoyed because I'm seeing a reflection of laziness and failure to engage in myself. I guess it's true that Shadow "bugs" us with things we don't want to see in ourselves. My new thought is to re-ignite curiosity within myself and pay attention to what excites *me* about life! Even if my husband doesn't respond when I talk, I'll be interesting to myself!

Sandy related that she chose ant as her insect simply because the drawing was included with the exercise. But after answering the questions, she thought of the query posed to E. O. Wilson and asked herself: "Why ant?" With research she discovered several intriguing facts that led to insights about herself (such as that ants build bridges to connect things—a metaphor of what she wanted to do communication-wise with her husband).

A week later Sandy emailed that the exercise had been a terrific success. As she shared her excitement about ants with her husband, he related that he had an ant farm as a child and that entomology had always interested him—something she had never known.

Several weeks later Sandy wrote again noting her surprise that something so small could bring such significant change. Relating that she and her husband now shared "a lively enthusiasm for the six-leggeds," she added, "I didn't do the last part of your exercise because we were talking so much about insects and there seemed no need for reminders. But it happened anyway, not only in a helpful way but in a heart-filled way. He gave me a present: an ant encased in amber! Every time I see it, I smile. At an ant! Sometimes it brings tears to my eyes."

The Power of the Small

10

What Lurks Below

In Brody's dreams, deep water was populated by slimy, savage things that rose from below and shredded his flesh, by demons that cackled and moaned.

PETER BENCHLEY, *JAWS*

In the 1700s most European scientists were convinced that an incredibly large creature dwelled deep in the cold waters of the North Sea. Sailors were terrified of the beast known to grasp a ship in its many long arms and yank it down to drown and devour all on board. The monster had a variety of names, but it was best known as the Kraken.

First noted in an 1180 manuscript by King Sverre of Norway, and mentioned in several Norse sagas of the thirteenth century, the Kraken was blamed for sinking ships off the shores of Norway, Iceland, and Greenland. Sailors claiming to have narrowly escaped the creature described their frightening encounters: From a distance it first resembled a group of small islands arising from the depths. But as it neared the surface, it appeared more mountain-like, measuring at least a mile and a half in circumference. Emerging last were its flailing arms, as high as a mast and strong enough to seize the largest of ships and drag it to the bottom of the sea. Even if vessels escaped its grasp, they were not out of danger, for as the Kraken descended such a great volume of water was displaced that it formed a colossal whirlpool capable of sucking entire fleets to a watery grave.

The Kraken, as seen by the Eye of Imagination, wood engraving
by Edgar Etherington for John Gibson's 1887 book,
Monsters of the Sea, Legendary and Authentic

In 1752 scientist and bishop Erik Ludvigsen Pontopiddan included the tales in his book, *The Natural History of Norway,* deeming the Kraken the largest and most terrifying creature in the sea. Even prominent biologist and father of taxonomy, Carl Linnaeus, officially recognized the Kraken in his first edition (1735) of *Systema Naturae* and gave it a scientific name: *Microcosmus marinus,* meaning "little world in the sea." (Later realizing it was an imaginary creature, Linnaeus removed its mention from further editions.)

For early navigators oceanic waters were a great unknown. Seafarers respected the power and unpredictability of the sea, mindful of the many ways they might sink, drown, or disappear into the deep. Glimpses of strangely shaped creatures arising from dark waters triggered fears and sparked imaginations. It is not difficult to understand how months at sea, afloat on a vast watery expanse, no land in sight, battered by storms, tossed by towering waves, might transpose shapeless monsters of the unconscious onto the open ocean.

The Kraken

Below the thunders of the upper deep;
Far, far beneath in the abysmal sea,
His ancient, dreamless, uninvaded sleep
The Kraken sleepeth: faintest sunlights flee . . .

ALFRED LORD TENNYSON, FROM *POEMS, CHIEFLY LYRICAL*

Giant Calamary Afloat, from *Monsters of the Sea,* 1887

Stories of the Kraken were likely based on sightings of giant squids (*Architeuthis dux*), some reported over 60 feet long. Like octopuses, squids have eight, sucker-lined arms; but unlike octopuses, squids also have two longer tentacles (the longest known of any cephalopod), which they extend to grab distant prey. While present in all the world's oceans, the elusive giant squids live in very deep waters (between 1,000 and 2,000 feet) and are difficult to study. Even now they largely remain creatures of mystery.

All head and arms, Squid and Octopus appear peculiar and alien to us. Lacking shell, claws, or other protection, they survive with their impressive speed, agility, and intelligence. True shapeshifters, they can alter their body form and color, blending or camouflaging as needed, and create inky clouds of distraction to escape predators. To encounter a deep sea squid—in the ocean or in one's subconscious—is to sense the formidable skills of confusion and transformation, as well as the cunning perceptiveness, that reside in the darkest depths. Thus Squid and

Giant squid holding sailor, illustration by Alphonse de Neuville, from the original 1870 edition of *Twenty Thousand Leagues Under the Sea* by Jules Verne

Octopus continue to rise as powerful, fascinating archetypes from our collective unconscious.

Sea monsters were once so widely accepted that expedition leaders, captains, sailors, medics, and even missionaries wrote personal accounts of seeing the fearsome creatures: Devil whales as large as mountains! Sea snakes 300 feet long that twisted tight around a ship and swallowed every last human before slinking back to the deep! Colossal, mighty, never-before-seen monsters with bulging eyes, wicked-sharp teeth, and snapping claws!

Tales blended as stories were told and retold, and the terrifying creatures that lurked beneath the ocean's surface grew bigger and more ferocious. Stories of the Kraken were told the most, and so it became the strongest, largest, and most gruesome sea monster, a repository of all the deep fears of the unknown abyss—both in the seas and in ourselves.

MONSTERS OF THE DEEP

Early mapmakers often illustrated uncharted ocean areas with images of water dragons, serpents, and sea monsters. Most of the creatures had lots of tusks and tentacles, fearsome faces, and strange—sometimes fanciful—bodies. These mapped monsters of the deep were perfect guardians, warning away the terrified and inexperienced while enticing the bold and intrepid with possibilities of new encounters and amazing discoveries.

Detail from *Carta Marina,* a large, detailed map created by Swedish cartographer Olaus Magnus in 1539, shows sea creatures dwelling in the waters between Norway and Iceland. In the middle left is the Pistr (also called the Pristis or Physter) known for powerfully spurting prodigious amounts of water from the crown of its head, enough to fill and submerge the largest of vessels in only seconds.

The earliest sea monsters reflected both our anxiety and curiosity about what lies below. A medieval story told in different versions for thousands of years involved the Aspidochelone, an enormous turtle, fish, whale, or spiny-backed sea creature that rises slowly to the

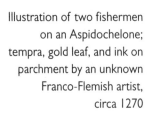

Illustration of two fishermen
on an Aspidochelone;
tempra, gold leaf, and ink on
parchment by an unknown
Franco-Flemish artist,
circa 1270

surface, accumulating a layer of sand on its back so that passing sailors mistake it for land. What happens next is in some tales simple misunderstanding, but in others a devious trick the Aspidochelone uses to secure its prey.

Beaching on the sandy shores, the crew gets comfortable and makes a fire to cook a meal. This hurts the creature (or signals successful entrapment), causing it to plunge downward and engulf the sailors in eddying waters that drag them and their ship below, never to be seen again.

Other tales involved the Leviathan, an ancient serpent sometimes depicted with many heads or as a ferocious, fanged dragon, said to dwell in the deepest waters of the abyss. In religious tales it represented chaos and was often paired with Behemoth, a chaos monster that lived on land. Both had incredible strength and were connected to battles at the End of Times. While some associated the Leviathan with deception and the devil, others opined that it had eyes of such extraordinary illuminating powers that to stare into the creature's face or eat its skin was a metaphor for enlightenment—a perceptive insight of what may occur when we are ready to face and eat our Shadow!

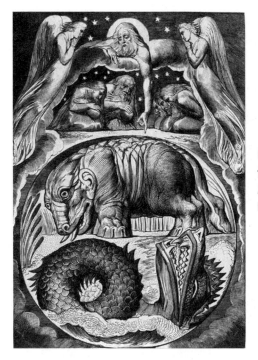

Detail of Behemoth and Leviathan, from the series, *Illustrations of the Book of Job,* line engravings on paper by William Blake, 1825

Ancient, primal, salty, amniotic—the sea is where life began! The seemingly bottomless depths of the dark abyss hold the oceanic memories of our planet and ourselves. From trenches 7 miles down (deeper than the tallest land mountains are high) submarine earthquakes are born, unleashing tsunamis of enormous power and chaos—no wonder this is where Leviathan dwells!

Oceans cover more than 70 percent of our planet's surface, yet more than 80 percent of the vast underwater world is still unmapped, unobserved, and unexplored.[1] Although we may no longer fear the Kraken, Aspidochelone, or Leviathan, underwater animals continue to call to us in odd, disconcerting ways: the ominous fin circling near, a gaping mouth rising from the depths, the faint brush of a tentacle in a dream. The collective fears of our seafaring ancestors still reside within us. And so too does the ocean—that deep, dark fluid world so different from our own—remain a convenient receptacle for shadow materials unconscious and unknown.

Just as maps of uncharted waters were once embellished with sea monsters to indicate pause for concern, adventurers of the deep self

Sea wonders and strange animals, as found in the countries at midnight, in the sea and on the land is one of the over sixty maps included in *Cosmographia*—an encyclopedic opus entailing six books and 1,800 pages, which took twenty years to compile— by German cartographer Sebastian Münster, circa 1544.

might be similarly warned: such voyages are not for the timid or inexperienced. And yet to investigate the deep sea of the psyche is to open ourselves to vast knowledge and treasure.

Lucky for the intrepid explorer, there are several helpful sea animal guides that may lend assistance in investigating the shadowy waters of the subconscious. As an example, let us consult an ancient sea-dweller: a powerful, sensitive, and highly discerning animal, often regarded as one of the smartest fish in the ocean . . .

SHARK

Before the first mammals—or even the first reptiles—appeared on Earth, sharks were already swimming in the seas. Fossils dating back 450 million years indicate they had elongated bodies, large triangular fins, and lots—

and lots—of teeth. Over hundreds of millions of years, sharks evolved into a wide variety of shapes, sizes, and temperaments. From the 7-inch dwarf lantern shark (*Etmopterus perryi*) to the immense yet docile whale shark (*Rhincodon typus*) up to 62 feet long, they are found in all seas and oceans. Swimming over sunny coral reefs or weaving through thick kelp forests, exploring icy green waters or skimming dark sea floors over 6,000 feet deep, sharks are true masters of survival.

Whale sharks (*Rhincodon typus*) are the largest fish in the sea. Living in warm tropical waters, they are filter feeders, mostly consuming plankton, krill, fish eggs, and crab larvae by swimming slowly forward with an open mouth. The bottom photo shows the relation in size between a small whale shark and a human diver.

In Hawaiian culture Shark is a highly respected animal spirit. Ancient legends tell of sharks helping the first peoples in their migration to Hawaii. For some humans sharks are a powerful ally: befriend shark and you will forever be protected in the ocean. For others, sharks are *aumakua*—personal or family gods—ancestors that take on the form of a living shark to protect and help their descendants, or appear as dream sharks to offer insight and guidance.

One of the main Hawaiian shark gods, Kamohoali'i, was known for his ability to navigate almost anywhere. Like Kamohoali'i, other shark guides could take on both fish and human forms. Some served as guardians to local bays and coastlines. Some helped humans escape predator sharks. Some offered safe travels, and some were known to save shipwreck victims and lead them to land.

What has happened that so many of us now malign sharks, deeming them aggressive predators rather than potentially helpful allies? As with most shadow animals, sharks are not generally understood, and thus they are feared.

ALL THOSE TEETH

One of our biggest fears about sharks is plain to see: all those rows of sharp, pointy teeth! Teeth to bite and pierce and chomp and chew. But one's chances of being bitten—or eaten—by a shark are incredibly low.

Sharks are rarely interested in humans as food, and worldwide shark attacks average only eighty per year, with about eight fatalities.[2]

Unlike many other fish, shark have teeth that can be replaced indefinitely. A single shark may produce up to 30,000 teeth in its lifetime.

In comparison, both hippopotamuses and elephants kill an annual average of 500 people, crocodiles about 1,000, and scorpions over 3,000.[3]

In startling contrast, humans kill a conservatively estimated 100 million sharks each and every year.[4] One of the main culprits is illegal shark finning, an appalling practice in which fishermen attempt to avoid declaring the full animal at port by cutting off the dorsal fins from living sharks, then dumping their mutilated bodies back into the ocean to die.

Of the nearly 500 shark species, only three are responsible for most fatal unprovoked attacks on humans: the tiger shark, the bull shark, and—perhaps most notorious—the great white shark.

The 1975 film *Jaws,* based on the 1974 novel of the same name by Peter Benchley, was about a great white shark terrorizing a seaside tourist town. While created for the thrill of a good scare, the popularity of both novel and film ignited a widespread and greatly exaggerated fear of sharks. As Benchley later commented, "Knowing what I know now, I could never write that book today. Sharks don't target human beings, and they certainly don't hold grudges."[5] Benchley spent his latter years advocating for marine conservation and shark protection.

SHARK'S EXPERTISE

As apex predators sharks have little fear of others in the sea. Intelligent and perceptive, they can quickly assess a situation and engage well-honed instincts to act with authority.

So too are sharks naturally curious, nudging unknown objects with their nose or gently "test biting" to learn more. With excellent eyesight and an amazing ability to detect odors (some sharks can smell a single drop of blood in water at one part per million), they are also sensitive to subtle vibrations, electrical fields, and electromagnetic currents, allowing them to detect animals that are motionless, in total darkness, or buried beneath sand.

As a guide Shark can help us to hone our senses so that we can discern quickly and accurately. Shark reminds us to rely on natural instincts but also to remain inquisitive, alert to the unusual and intrigued by what may be hidden below.

Sleek, hydrodynamic, and efficient, Shark has no need of the

Photograph of a great white swimming in Mexican waters. Also known as the white shark or white pointer, the great white shark is the largest predatory fish on Earth. *Carcharodon carcharias* (the name means "jagged tooth") can grow up to 23 feet long and weigh as much as 5,000 pounds. Eating a variety of sea animals including crustaceans, fish, and other sharks, as well as sea birds, sea lions, seals, and orcas, great whites can live up to seventy years.

Grey reef sharks (*Carcharhinus amblyrhynchos*) frequent shallow waters in the Indian and Pacific Oceans, often near coral reefs. Fast moving and agile, they are social with their own species, but aggressive to other species and may attack human divers if they feel threatened.

superfluous. There's nothing showy or arrogant either—no sign of a weak ego overcompensating. Rather, Shark emanates its own natural authority. It knows what it wants and how to get it.

Shark encourages us to eliminate the unnecessary, to streamline our focus in order to move smoothly, even in stormy seas. Indeed, Shark can help us to navigate turbulent inner realms with heightened awareness, to remain centered and emotionally stable, without being overwhelmed.

While it's beneficial to acknowledge and feel our emotions, we don't need to drown in them. Sensitive to shifting currents, Shark can teach us how to move through emotions such as fear, helping us to focus on what is rather than what might be.

Some fear is helpful, of course, for it informs when danger is near. But so many of our fears are projections: mistaken ideas or assumptions, worst-case scenarios, erroneous beliefs derived from unhealed shock or trauma—all of which become embedded in our physical and emotional bodies. Such fears keep us small, hold us back.

Because they lack a swim bladder (an organ that controls internal gases, aiding many fish to maintain buoyancy), sharks need to continually move forward or risk sinking. It's an interesting metaphor in trusting one's forward momentum. Shark reminds us to keep moving forward, to sharpen our perceptions and remain clear, so as not to be distracted, deluged, or held back by unwarranted fears.

At the core of shadow work is the paradox that what we fear is also what can help us conquer or heal that fear. With its stern demeanor, highly astute awareness, and all those razor-sharp teeth, Shark can trigger our fears. But every trigger is an invitation! If we are willing to stay present, Shark can help us to gain clarity in identifying emotional blocks that manifest irrational fears. And this is exactly why Shark is such an excellent shadow guide: an efficient, exacting, no-nonsense teacher for those who wish to face—yet not be swallowed by—their fears.

As an ancient inhabitant of planet Earth, Shark reminds us to tap into our primal depths. By releasing emotional projections, mistaken beliefs, and unwarranted fears, we open to a deeper sense of self. Thus we may begin to reclaim personal power, manifest our unique abilities, and express a more joyful curiosity about who we really are. Like Shark, we become master of ourself.

Pyjama shark (*Poroderma africanum*), also known as the striped catshark; this small (3.5 foot), nocturnal, bottom-dwelling shark frequents the rocky reefs and kelp beds of South Africa.
Photo by Guido Zsilavecz, CC BY-SA 3.0

Zebra sharks (*Stegostoma fasciatum*) have a caudal fin almost as long as the rest of their body. Only the young have vertical "zebra" stripes. As the sharks grow older, their stripes become wider and more diffuse, eventually appearing as spots. Averaging 8 feet in length, zebra sharks live in shallow, tropical waters. They are slow moving, gentle, and easily approached by respectful humans. Photo taken while diving off the coast of Myanmar.
Photo by Makolga3113, CC BY 3.0

FINDING TREASURE

Shortly after starting to write this chapter, I was awakened early one morning with an ache in my neck. Curious of the cause, I settled into my body, breathed deeply, and attuned to the pain. In just a few moments, I fell asleep and dreamed.

> *I am in a small rowboat. There is a rope around my neck that is attached to an anchor deep in the sea. I jump into the water and follow the rope down to the anchor, which sits beside an open treasure chest partially buried in the sand. Though it resembles an old-fashioned pirate chest, it doesn't hold jewels or gold, but mirrors! There are many mirrors of many different sizes and shapes. I pick one that is round and just a bit larger than my hand. A scrap of white paper in the mirror reads* Different Perspectives. *I wonder if the paper is inside the mirror. If not, then what can it be reflecting, for there is no paper around me. As if in answer to my wondering, the mirror bends outward and becomes a small globe. The glass cracks as the mirror changes shape, but all of the pieces stay on, and now it looks like a mosaic globe of reflections. I become very excited because I know this means something important. Just then I sense a large shape coming near: a shark! It swims close to me and very gently nudges the mirrored globe in my hand. I say out loud, "Different perspectives," and the shark opens its mouth in a wide—and very toothy—smile.*

I awoke with great excitement and rushed to record the dream in my journal. It seemed an inspiring explosion of synchronicities, insights, and clues. I marveled at the creative segue between waking and dreaming: of how my neck pain (and my desire to find its cause) was imaged as a rope around my neck, tied to an anchor that sat at the bottom of the sea. The dream was reflecting one of my key shadow themes: that in order to find surface cause, we must often dive deep and explore below.

By following the rope into the watery realm to locate the source of my pain, I descended into the subconscious. Isn't it intriguing that the anchor (the "hold" of the rope around the neck) sits next to a treasure chest? As if to make clear that as we begin to explore with serious intent that which holds us hostage, we may find our treasure is near!

The treasure is not gold or jewels or what we might expect from a pirate's booty, but rather mirrors: objects of reflection. Mirrors are truth-tellers, showing us what is—both what we want to see as well as what we don't want to see. (In many dreams mirrors show us what we need to see.) Choosing the hand-sized mirror indicates the dreamer may be looking at a personal (handheld) perspective. And here the dream is very specific with its message: *Different Perspectives!*

The dreamer ponders: Is this message inside the mirror (inside oneself?) or a reflection of something outside? As if in answer, the flat mirror cracks and rounds. Suddenly it is pregnant with possibilities, for there is no longer only one reflection, but many faceted reflections. Said another way, the handheld, personal mirror becomes spherical and collective: a global mirror. There is something powerful about a flat two-dimensional surface suddenly becoming round and three-dimensional, a mirror perhaps of our evolutionary shift from believing the world was flat to knowing it as round. Also interesting is that when the mirror bends and fractures, the pieces hold together.

And then the shark: a water creature of heightened awareness, discernment, and ancient knowledge. As it approaches the dreamer, it gently nudges the reflective globe, further emphasizing the importance of this object. In response the dreamer reads the words written in the mirror, transporting them into a new medium by speaking them aloud. And the shark smiles: a wide grin that is not at all threatening, but encouraging.

I have worked with Shark in many dreams, and for me, its appearance does not generally signal fear, but rather growth and evolution. However, every dreamer will have his or her unique experience with Shark or other animal teacher that appears in the dreamworld.

So, what does this mean? What answer does the dreamer receive in pondering the cause of her neck pain?

On personal levels I felt the dream was prodding me to acknowledge that getting stuck in any one perspective (especially one's favorite perspectives, the ones we are convinced are "right") can compromise flexibility. On physical levels getting stuck equals loss of movement, which may cause pain. On psychological levels it may reflect stubbornness and a refusal to see other perspectives.

The dream also reflects a timely, collective vision of a world fragmented with divisiveness. "Different perspectives" is an answer, a reminder, and a hopeful message, for the fragments of the mirror do not fall away, but are held together, united.

My interpretation is this: that by exploring our Shadow (both individually and collectively) we might rediscover the global treasure chest of mirrors. And by reflecting upon this gift of different perspectives, we might learn from each other—and all other creatures on this planet—by celebrating the remarkable richness of our diversity.

So, too, I sense a feeling of reassurance from the deep: the ancient Spirit of Shark smiling gently, reminding us that by facing our fear, we also find our treasure.

Spirit of Shark

◆ ◆ **Exercise** ◆ ◆

Exploring the Deep Psyche with Shark

What calls to you from deep within? What frightens or annoys, but you're not sure why? What hidden treasures gleam in the dark waters of your psyche? The following meditation invites Shark to help you look for shadow elements that may be anchoring waking-life fears, problems, or obstacles.

Plunging into the deep sea of the psyche is a unique endeavor for each of us. The five steps listed below serve as a template that you may expand as you like. Use what works for you by personalizing these basics to create your own voyage into the psyche.

1. Contemplate and Prepare

Contemplate what you would like to explore. Do you have a pain, problem, emotional hold, or frustration that plagues you in waking life? Perhaps you are feeling confused or anxious. Focus on whatever you would like to investigate at deeper levels. Write it down or say it aloud. Be clear and concise: the more specific your question, the more specific your answer may be. Once you have clarity and focus, prepare your space—a quiet, darkened room; a comfortable place to sit or lie; gentle background music; pillow or blanket if desired—to inspire a deepened state for you to relax and explore.

2. Float and Descend

Breathe deep and settle into your body. Make use of a favorite meditation protocol, calming ritual, or simply follow your breath as it flows in and out. Easing into relaxation, imagine yourself floating in the ocean. Notice the water—its color and scent and buoyancy. Take time for this step, allowing yourself to fully feel the fluidity surrounding and supporting you. And when you are ready, descend into the water in whatever way feels best: gently sinking or diving down, or perhaps following an anchor-line downward. Simply give yourself the suggestion to deepen and allow inner imagery to unfold.

3. Explore and Invite

As you approach the ocean floor, have a look around. Perhaps there are fish, rocks, plants, or coral. Or perhaps the environment is unlike anything you've seen before. The imagery you encounter represents the deep sea of your psyche. Take note! When you feel ready, invite Shark to join you as ally or guide in exploring your question. Notice your feelings and observe what occurs. You might swim beside Shark or follow at a distance; you might join consciousness and explore as if you are Shark. Perhaps Shark steers you toward a cave or an object protruding from the sand. Perhaps you feel your senses sharpening, attuning to subtle frequencies; perhaps you receive a sudden knowing. Each experience will be different, and all you need do is relax, be curious, and observe. Trust Shark to guide you, helping you to notice what you most need to know.

4. Acknowledge and Ascend

When you have received the answer to your quest (it may be an image, an object, a feeling, a realization or deep-down knowing), acknowledge it in some way. Touch it, hold it, or speak it aloud as a means to carry its import back to waking consciousness. As you sense your adventure coming to a close, thank Shark for its help. When you are ready to leave, simply focus on your breathing and begin your ascent—swimming or floating upward—to conscious awareness.

5. Record and Reflect

Back home in your body, take time to write or sketch your experience. How does your answer relate to your question? If unclear, what clues or insights might you pursue? Use dream interpretation skills to consider a range of possible meanings. Sometimes it's helpful to let our experiences sit for a day or two; when you revisit your notes, other connections and ideas may occur. If appropriate, make plans to reclaim or integrate the shadow material you discovered.

You may benefit from experiencing this exercise several times. You can explore with different animal teachers of the deep—Sea Turtle, Octopus, Squid, or Whale—or continue your adventures with Shark. Remember that focusing your questions with depth and clarity can help you discover specific insights, hidden aspects of self, and greater familiarity with what lurks below.

11

Metamorphosis

Into the ancient pond
A frog jumps
Water's sound!

MATSUO BASHŌ (1686),

TRANSLATION BY D. T. SUZUKI

Bashō's famous frog haiku has well over a hundred English translations. Add foreign language translations to the mix, and there are thousands of different versions, with just as many interpretations of the poem's meaning. How does such a simple three-line poem evoke such variation?

Matsuo Bashō was a respected teacher, poet, and intellectual in Japan during the 1600s. But in his late thirties, he gave it all up to wander the countryside, seeking inspiration and enlightenment in nature. For a time he studied with a master called Bucchō who, in the Zen Buddhist tradition, emphasized direct experience to perceive the true nature of self.

Japanese scholar D. T. Suzuki notes that Bashō's frog haiku arose in response to a koan that Bucchō posed about the origin of life.[1] A koan is a paradoxical riddle designed to bypass the constraints of logical thought and evoke enlightenment.

While Bashō's haiku may seem inconsequential at first glance—a pleasant poem about a frog and a pond—Suzuki maintains that it is actually a portal to a deeper state of being: an opening into the experience of no-thought, no-mind.

Suzuki relates that a haiku is not so much about ideas, but rather about images that reflect deeper intuitions. He imagines the pond, the frog, the sound of water, all in the compressed clarity of *satori*—sudden enlightenment—in which Bashō was transformed: "The old pond was no more, nor was the frog a frog. They appeared to him enveloped in the veil of mystery which was no veil of mystery."[2]

Confused? Such is the deep nature of koan, haiku, satori—for all present something seemingly simple yet potentially profound and trans-formational. Perhaps the ancient pond is the calm, receptive mind of Bashō's being. The frog jumps, the water sounds, and the sudden splash of satori invokes a metamorphosis of awakening.

Metamorphosis means to transform or change shape. It often refers to the growth of an immature insect or amphibian—such as a frog—into its adult form in several distinct stages. For humans it may refer to a deep change in one's being, such as Bashō's experience of enlighten-ment. Bashō before the splash is different from Bashō after the splash or, as Suzuki puts it, "Bashō was no more the old Bashō."[3]

So, is Frog the trigger to awakening? Could the splashing jump of a fish in the ancient pond have summoned the same response? Long before Bashō's poem, humans noted Frog in connection to spiritual awakenings. But why?

The Mandukya Upanishad, written several thousand years ago, is part of a collection of several hundred sacred Hindu texts exploring the nature of reality. *Mandukya* means "frog" in Sanskrit, and so this text is often referred to as the Frog Upanishad. It is noteworthy not only for being the shortest Upanishad, but also because its twelve compact verses are believed to offer a jump-start to spontaneous enlightenment.

Again: Why Frog? How did a small amphibian inspire this particu-lar Upanishad? One story notes that the secrets contained in the text were revealed to a Hindu sage who sometimes assumed the form of a frog and was accompanied in his wanderings by large groups of frogs. But others say the reason is deeper, more intrinsic, that Frog is unique in inspiring the leap to transcendent consciousness. By unlocking the key in the Frog Upanishad, one stimulates metamorphosis into a com-pletely new state of being: to know ourselves as we truly are.

Frog's secret

WHAT DOES FROG KNOW
THAT WE DO NOT?

Historically, culturally, symbolically, and mythologically, there are a wide range of human ideas about frogs. In India frogs symbolize the many forms a soul may take through reincarnation. For the Aztec and Maya, Frog was Rain Bringer, the one who summoned life-giving waters to the land. For the Greeks and Romans, frogs denoted birth and harmony. And in some Native American traditions, Frog Spirit invokes health, prosperity, and growth.

Frogs lay an abundance of eggs—depending on the species, anywhere from 2,000 to 20,000 at one time. Thus the ancient Egyptians used the image of a tadpole as a hieroglyph to denote 100,000 or any very large number.

Heqet, an Egyptian goddess of fertility worshipped over 5,000 years ago, was most often represented as a frog or frog-headed woman. Her role: to bless mothers-to-be and breathe life into every newborn baby.

For the Egyptians, Frog is a very old symbol of fertility, creation, and new life. Because their prolific offspring were born after the annual flooding of the Nile, frogs were closely associated with water. Khnum, one of the earliest Egyptian gods and known as the source of the Nile River, was sometimes depicted with a frog head or with many frogs surrounding him.

Later viewed as a divine potter who molded both gods and humans on his potter's wheel, Khnum worked with Heqet to bring all beings into existence. Khnum created the body and Heqet helped souls to enter it. When a soul was ready to leave its body, Heqet led it to the afterlife.

Frog was one of the earliest animals fashioned into an amulet. In Egypt frog amulets were worn by young women to encourage fertility, by midwives to facilitate easy births, and by pregnant women to request Heqet's protection. Frog amulets were buried with the dead, sometimes mummified, to invoke Heqet's guidance in reaching the afterlife. A frog's image was also added to the written name of the deceased so that he or she would be reborn and live again.

In Japan frogs were also viewed as links between the living and the dead. A small frog carved of jade was placed in the mouth of the deceased to ensure safe passage to the spirit world. (It was believed to have the added bonus of helping the dead speak more clearly with the living.)

The Japanese word for frog—*kaeru*—also means "return," so frog charms were carried by travelers desiring safe return home. Tiny frog amulets were sometimes kept with money so that if lost, it would return.

Ceramic frog amulet representing Heqet, frog goddess of childbirth and fertility. Such amulets were worn by pregnant women hoping for an easy delivery, and carried by both sexes to request successful rebirth in the afterlife. Egypt, circa 1380–1330 BCE.

Jin Chan, a mythical creature also called Money Frog, is depicted as a three-legged bullfrog sitting atop a pile of money with a coin in its mouth. In the feng shui tradition, a Money Frog statue or charm helps to attract and protect wealth.

Throughout much of Asia frogs are associated with prosperity, good luck, and happiness. In feng shui a frog figurine placed near the front door invites wealth and a flow of positive energy.

All over the world frogs announce spring with their croaks and chirps, squeaks and trills. Frog songs signal the rains, which revitalize the land and nurture the growth of new life. But so also are frogs connected with the cleansing and healing aspects of water. Frog medicine can help us to wash away toxic energies (through crying or sweating), to immerse in the curative powers of water (through bathing or soaking), to deepen into the emotional realm (through floating or swimming in lakes, rivers, or oceans), and to feel harmonized in the flow of life energy.

As frogs are sensitive to toxins in the environment, they often mirror the health of an eco-system. Residents of both land and water, frogs speak to our physical grounding as well as our emotional fluidity. Blend earth and water and you get mud—a very old healing modality used to remove toxins from the body.

Frog in Your Throat?

Having a frog in one's throat is an American phrase denoting a sore throat that gives rise to a croaky voice. The idiom originated in the late 1800s, though folk medicine connecting frogs and throats goes back much further.

Some believed that putting a small frog in one's mouth would draw out infection or transfer illness to the frog; releasing it would encourage the sickness to hop away. In the early 1900s frog logos commonly denoted medicine for sore throats.

The Frog in Your Throat Company was one of several manufacturers that used frog images as a way to market cough lozenges. Advertisement, circa 1906–1919.

TRANSFORMATIONAL MAGIC

There is a decidedly dual nature about frogs: they are amphibians, after all. The word comes from the Greek *amphi* ("both") and *bios* ("life"), meaning that frogs, like other amphibians, have two modes of existence.

Born in water, frogs eventually move onto dry land. Never living far from water, however, they remain creatures of both realms. The transformation of squiggling tadpoles to fully grown, land-hopping frogs is a slow magic that involves several very different stages.

It all begins with the egg! Female frogs lay their eggs in large clusters in the water, where they are fertilized by male frogs. Tiny tadpoles form and grow within the eggs until they hatch. Tadpoles have gills and long rudder-like tails to swim underwater. As the tadpoles grow larger they develop lungs, which replace their gills and allow them to breathe air. Tiny stumps appear on each side of their body, gradually forming into hind legs and forelimbs. And their once-long tail shortens and shrinks until it completely disappears. The process of metamorphosis from egg to tadpole to froglet to frog takes approximately twelve to sixteen weeks.

Male and female frogs with egg clutch

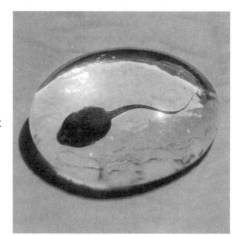

Tadpole in water droplet

Froglet

Because it bridges water and earth, Frog energy can help us to move between worlds, to navigate different realms, and to adapt, transform, and become more comfortable with variation and change.

Fear of Frog

For some, frogs have been linked to unclean spirits. They were the second of ten plagues described in the book of Exodus in the Old Testament. Some medieval views distinguished between land frogs as righteous and water frogs as sinful. The shift of Frog from healer to harmer was furthered in the Middle Ages when frogs and toads were connected to sorcery and used as ingredients in magical spells.

Detail from *The Second Plague in Egypt:*
The Plague of Frogs, color etching, circa 1775–1779
Wellcome Collection

The river shall bring forth frogs abundantly, which shall go up
and come into your house, into your bedroom, on your bed, into
the houses of your servants, on your people, into your ovens, and
into your kneading bowls.

EXODUS 8:1–4, NEW KING JAMES VERSION

Anura—meaning "without tail"—is the order of tailless amphibians that includes over 6,000 species of frogs and toads. Their diversity is amazing: from tongueless, toothless frogs to running, gliding, and flying frogs; from flattened toads to male midwife toads who carry eggs on their back. There are glass frogs and ghost frogs with transparent belly skin, brightly colored dart frogs with poison secretions powerful enough to cause heart failure in humans. While we may consider some of their features strange—spikes, hairs, horns, and side-bulging eyes—

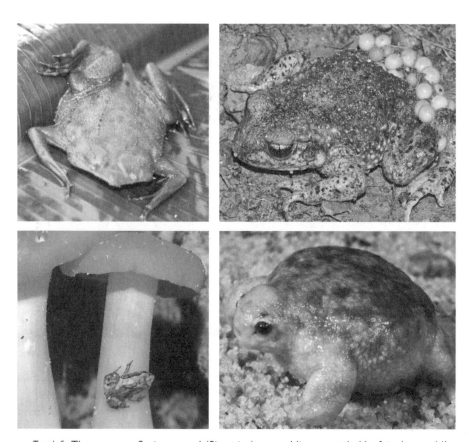

Top left: The common Surinam toad (*Pipa pipa*), resembling a mottled leaf, is the world's flattest amphibian.
Photo by Hugo Claessen, CC BY-SA 2.5.

Top right: The male common midwife toad (*Alytes obstetricans*) carries fertilized eggs on its hind legs.
Photo by Christian Fischer, CC BY-SA 3.0.

Bottom left: The Brazilian gold frog (*Brachycephalus didactylus*), also known as the flea frog, is one of the smallest frogs in the world, measuring less than ½ inch in length.
Photo shows an adult gold frog on a mushroom stalk.
Photo by Diogo Luiz, CC BY-SA 4.0.

Bottom right: The turtle frog (*Myobatrachus gouldii*), characterized by a small head, short limbs, and rounded body, lives in Western Australia.
Photo by Stephen Zozaya, CC BY 2.5.

frogs and toads have had over 250 million years to evolve and perfectly adapt to their environments.

While frogs and toads are of different families, there are many similarities and it is sometimes difficult to distinguish the two. In general, however, frogs have long legs; moist, smooth skin; and lay their eggs in clusters. Toads have shorter legs; dry, bumpy skin; and lay their eggs in strands.

Both frogs and toads periodically shed their skin, then eat it to reabsorb nutrients and remove evidence of their presence from prey. Both absorb water through their belly and blink their eyes to help swallow food. They have a similar diet of insects—though some can eat mice, baby turtles, smaller frogs, and baby snakes. And both undergo metamorphosis to transform from tadpole to adult.

Transformation involves both loss and gain. Gills are lost, but lungs are made. The wiggling tail, once so necessary for movement, vanishes, but four limbs appear that propel frogs onto land. Thus Frog is about change, transition, and liberation!

Because they possess transformational magic, frogs often appear in folklore and fairy tales. And most often their presence in such stories signals an invitation for change.

THE FROG PRINCE

In the olden time, wrote the Brothers Grimm, there lived a king with three beautiful daughters, the youngest being the most beautiful of all. When the day was hot, the young princess would walk through the forest and sit at the edge of a cool well. There she played a game of tossing her favorite golden ball into the air. One day she failed to catch the ball and it landed with a splash, disappearing beneath the dark water in the well. The princess began to weep.

May I help? a voice called from below. Peering into the well, the princess saw a frog stretching his ugly head above the surface of the water. Still sobbing, she explained what had happened. *If I retrieve your golden ball,* said the frog, *what can you offer in return?* The princess suggested pearls and jewels and even her crown, but the frog shook his head. *What I'd really like,* he told her, *is to be your beloved companion:*

The Princess and the Frog, illustration by Warwick Goble,
from *The Fairy Book,* 1913

*to sit at your table and eat from your plate and drink from your cup, and
sleep beside you in your little bed at night.*

What nonsense, thought the princess, but she readily agreed for she
was eager to have the golden ball back in her hands. And so the frog
dove down into the dark water and retrieved the ball. The princess was
overjoyed! Grasping her precious ball, she ran back to the castle, leaving
the frog by the well.

Although the princess forgot all about the incident, on the next eve-
ning's dinner there was a loud knock at the palace door, and there was
the hideous frog once more. When the king learned of his daughter's
promise, he insisted she keep her word. Thus the frog hopped into the
banquet hall and onto the table and crouched beside the princess to eat
from her plate and drink from her cup.

After the meal the princess hurried away but the frog called out,
reminding her of their agreement. The princess shrieked in dismay for
she was repulsed by the cold, horrible frog and did not want to share
her lovely bed. But again the king insisted she fulfill her promise to the
frog, who had helped in her time of need.

Prince or Frog?

Despising the ugly creature, the princess picked up the frog with two fingers, carried him up the stairs, and tossed him into the corner of her bedchamber. As she crawled into her beautiful bed, the frog called out once more, reminding her of the promise to sleep on the pillow beside her. Suddenly, the princess was seized with rage. Rushing from her bed, she grabbed the frog and threw him against the wall with all her might.

As the frog splatted loudly against the wall, what fell down was not a dead frog but a young prince with kind eyes. He explained how a wicked sorceress had bewitched him and no one but a king's daughter could release him from the well. In time, the frog-prince became not just the princess's companion but her betrothed.[4]

This story is very old, dating at least to the thirteenth century. It was first published by the Brothers Grimm in their 1812 collection of fairy tales. When translated into English in the 1820s, however, part of the story was changed: the frog was not thrown against a wall but kissed instead. And so many children grew up believing that bewitched frogs are transformed into princes by a kiss.

If this story was a dream (and all fairy tales are a type of collective dream), we might consider that the characters—princess, frog, king, prince, and even wicked sorceress—represent different aspects of the dreamer's psyche. The main dreamer is the princess, and her dream is about transformation and awakening.

While the moral tone of the story encourages honesty and keeping one's word, the shadow aspect reveals the princess's reluctance to face the "ugly" frog-like part of herself: that which she has judged and hidden away, banished to the bottom of the well. (Although we later learn that a wicked sorceress has bewitched the prince into a frog, she too is an aspect of the dreamer's psyche—a convenient way for the princess to deny responsibility for creating and banishing her Shadow in the first place.)

The action begins with the loss of the princess's cherished golden ball. Perhaps it represents her innocence or carefree youth. Sunlike and radiant, the small orb is playfully tossed into the air and caught—until it is not. The sudden loss brings angst, for now it is unreachable, having disappeared into the deep dark well.

And then from the well—the subconscious, the deep psyche, the shadow realm—a voice. How often do we listen to the whispers that rise from the well of inner knowing? The voice offers to help, but it requires something of the dreamer in return.

The Shadow has manifest as a frog—repulsive in the princess's eyes. And yet the frog possesses the knowledge and talent necessary to restore what the princess has lost. The cost? Nothing more than what the Shadow always wants: to be acknowledged!

The princess tries to escape her promise and rush away. Though she is self-absorbed and immature, her father the king—her moral compass, her inner wisdom—sees clearly and demands she keep her word. And so she complies.

But what a dance of emotions: avoidance, deception, repulsion, fear, frustration, and rage! All these emotions and more can appear as we sense our Shadow's presence.

The trigger to actually seeing our Shadow—to finally acknowledging its presence in us, as us—may come in a variety of ways. In the original story the princess catapults her Shadow onto the wall—*Splat!* In later versions she kisses or embraces her Shadow. In both cases transformation occurs: metamorphosis to a more awakened state of being.

There is no longer animosity between the dreamer and her Shadow, for the curse of judgment is broken. Transformation of the frog-prince leads to transformation of the princess, which leads to marriage, unity, wholeness. Finally, the dreamer sees the part of herself that was bewitched and banished to the deep well for what it truly is: part of her own noble self.

Most of us have at least one bewitched frog living inside our deep well. And it continues to call to us.

The invitation

DREAMING OF FROG

Many years ago I dreamed of a frog that revealed to me the power of facing our fear and acknowledging our shadow self. The dream began like this:

I walk into a mall and see a fishpond made of stone and built into a wall. As I walk past, I remember that I have a frog in my pocket. He might really like this pond, I think, and so I plop him into the water. I head to the center of the mall but then—in that fast-forward way of dreams—I find myself back at the pond. Now I see that there are many frogs in the pond and they are enormous, most the size of dinner plates!

I notice one incredibly huge frog, nearly the size of a man. I believe this is "my" frog—the one I placed there on arriving. The frog begins to crawl out of the pond. As I back away, he moves toward me on two legs, not fast or menacing, but with determination. Suddenly panicking at the sight of the huge frog walking like a man, I turn to run. But after a short distance I stop. How silly is it to be running away from a frog? *I ask myself.*

As my fear lessens, curiosity takes over and I wonder what the frog wants. Turning back to face it, I stand still and watch the frog coming closer, closer, until his dark green face is only inches from my own. He opens his mouth wide and I lean forward to hear him. As I do so, I feel a surprising fondness for the frog. I smile at him, and he says out loud, very gently, Thank You.[5]

This dream came just after I had the idea of writing my second book. The topic of the book had come swiftly, unexpectedly, and I was filled with many thoughts. To learn more I asked the Frog People—who I imagined as a group of frogs holding the wisdom that lives within all frogs—to offer insight.

They suggested that the small frogs in the pond represented my questions and ideas jumping wild with excitement, while the large frogs were the answers to the questions as they matured. The pond was an image of my brain as a container of thoughts. By plopping a small frog—a creative idea—into my brain it interacts with other frog-ideas and grows in size, complexity, ambition, and desire.

"Soon all of your ideas are larger," said the Frog People. "And then one gets big enough to have the courage and sensibility to crawl out of its container. . . . As it crawls out on its own, it becomes a different thing, a new way of being in the world. At first you are frightened of it—this big thing that has grown so much you can hardly recognize it. You are fearful as it comes to you. But why? Even you are not sure, except that this thing is no longer familiar. It has grown and changed, so different now that you can barely recognize it as still being a part of you."[6]

The dream frog comes after the dreamer to help her. Though initially fearful, she questions her fear, and turns to face the frog. Surprised by a rush of fondness, the dreamer smiles and listens, and the frog offers thanks. The Shadow has been seen.

Metamorphosis requires change. And we often fear change very deeply in our being. When something changes quickly or dramatically, it is especially suspect. A wriggling, water-breathing tadpole grows lungs and limbs and hops onto land; a bewitched frog becomes a prince; a tiny frog-idea matures and crawls out of its dream pond container. Metamorphosis can catapult us into a very different state of being. But when we stay present and centered, we realize, this too is who we are.

What Frog knows

◆ ◆ **Exercise** ◆ ◆

Frog's Mirror Meditation

Mirrors show us who we are. Like a potent koan or haiku, this simple mirror meditation can evoke insights that may lead to expanded awareness of self.

The setup is easy: find a quiet place where you can sit comfortably in front of a mirror. To begin, close your eyes and follow your breath to settle inside your body. Relax and be present. When you feel calm and centered, open your eyes and gaze at your reflection.

Let go of any judgments about your appearance—this exercise isn't about the outer self but rather about meeting our inner selves. To do that, we must be present.

Notice thoughts and emotions as they arise. There is no need to interpret or analyze. Allow them to come and go, observing them as you might observe clouds moving across the sky.

If something bothers you, stay present. Allow whatever comes to unfold and express itself, to show you what it needs you to see.

If something frightens you, stay present. Allow the feeling to run its course. By maintaining nonjudgmental observation, you may experience your fear shifting to fascination.

You may notice your features changing shape—blending, distorting, or transforming. Keep your vision soft, relaxed. These shifting shapes may represent deeper aspects of self. Facing them calmly, with an open mind and heart, can heighten our awareness of who we are.

You may see a child self, an older self, an abused or traumatized self, or a wise self: all of our many selves arriving in the mirror, ready to be seen by our consciousness. Some may want to talk. Some may want to journal afterward. Some may reveal a secret. Some may offer insights or advice. Allow. Listen. Be present.

Hold your gaze until you feel the experience is over. Afterward, take time to record your experiences.

You may benefit from doing this exercise several times over a period of weeks or months or years. As you become more comfortable with the technique, try variations—such as gazing directly into your eyes. Each experience will be different, and together they will have a cumulative effect.

This exercise can help us acknowledge and cultivate compassion for all of our many selves. As we begin to accept more of who we are, we lessen the need to push down fears or project unwanted judgments onto others. So too we may begin to retrieve and embrace our shadow selves. Like Bashō's poem, this exercise can open a portal, a magic mirror into our own ancient pond.

Frog's reflection

12

The Fear of Knowing
Who We Are

The snake was the most intelligent of all the wild animals that the Lord God had made. He said to the woman, "Did God really say that you shouldn't eat from any tree in the garden?" The woman said to the snake, "We may eat the fruit of the garden's trees but not the fruit of the tree in the middle of the garden. God said, 'Don't eat from it, and don't touch it, or you will die.'" The snake said to the woman, "You won't die! God knows that on the day you eat from it, you will see clearly and you will be like God, knowing good and evil."

GENESIS 3:1–5 (COMMON ENGLISH BIBLE)

The book of Genesis notes that there were many fruit-bearing trees in the Garden of Eden, but only one that Adam and Eve were forbidden to eat from: the Tree of Knowledge of Good and Evil. God told the couple that if they ate from this tree they would die.

But Snake, long-time guardian of trees, protector of sacred wisdom, and plainly noted as the most intelligent of all the wild animals, shared a secret with Eve: by eating the fruit she would not die; rather, she would see clearly and be like God, knowing good and evil.

The knowledge contained within the fruit must have been

Adam, Eve, and Snake,
stained glass window

powerful—perhaps so powerful that God deemed it dangerous and so invoked the fear of death. When Adam and Eve ate the forbidden fruit, however, they did not die. Just as Snake promised, their eyes were opened, and they began to see themselves in a new way.

Then everything fell apart: Adam blamed Eve for giving him the fruit, Eve blamed the Snake, and God cursed all three.

As Joseph Campbell notes, the first major turning point for Snake in world mythology occurs here, in the Garden of Eden story.[1] For at least 7,000 years before the book of Genesis was written, Snake inspired awe and respect. Wrapped around the cosmic egg from which the Universe was born, Snake was creator and protector of life, guardian of sacred knowledge, and agent of profound transformation.

How and why did a creature as supportive and life-giving as Snake become so maligned? What shadow elements were at work to so

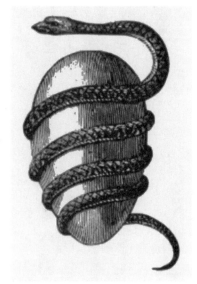

Orphic Egg from *A New System,
or an Analysis of Ancient Mythology*
by Jacob Bryant, 1774

dramatically shift our views that a once helpful and trusted ally was now feared, demeaned, and despised? And what knowledge was so powerful that God hid it in the fruit of a forbidden tree?

THE MOST POWERFUL OF CREATURES

From ancient Babylonia to Egypt and China, from the Mediterranean to South America and Australia, Snake is present in nearly all world mythologies. In Africa the snake god Damballah creates the stars and planets with his 7,000 coils. In India the thousand-headed snake Ananta uncurls his body in the cosmic waters and sets in motion the flow of life. And in tribal Amazonia humankind's ancestors arrive from the heavens in the form of a gigantic anaconda.

In the Australian Aboriginal dreamtime, Rainbow Snake traverses far and wide, pushing up mountains and ridges here, hollowing out valleys and waterholes there, giving shape to the land. Sometimes male, sometimes female, it lives on Earth as rainwater, rivers, and springs, and in the sky as rainbows and the shimmer of the Milky Way. Similar versions of a cosmic creator serpent span the globe. Descending from the heavens or arising from subterranean waters, Snake bridges realms, connects worlds, and joins that which seems separated.

With eyes that are always open, all-seeing Snake is linked to oracles and prophecy. Shedding its skin to revitalize and renew, it is thought to possess secrets of healing and immortality. Protector of gods and goddesses, Snake offers counsel to Zeus and Athena, wisdom to Vishnu and Shiva. And in Buddhist tales, the Snake king Mucalinda spreads his giant cobra head over the meditating Buddha to shield him from a week-long rainstorm.

Many early deities were depicted with a blend of snake and human features. In ancient Sumeria and Egypt, several goddesses had a cobra head, or serpent body with female head. The ancestors of Chinese civilization Nüwa and Fuxi were imaged as humans above the waist and snakes below. Why would we link our beginnings with Snake in such an intimate way? What human connection does Snake possess that caused our ancestors to imagine our origins intertwined?

Draped over shoulder, wrapped around belly or arm, Snake aligns with goddesses of wisdom Athena, Minerva, Isis, and more.

Silk scroll depicting the brother and sister creators of humanity, Nüwa and Fuxi, eighth century, China

Top left: Athena with Snake. This statue, found in fragments in the early 1600s, was repaired by Italian artist Alessandro Algardi. Some believe the statue may have originally depicted Hygieia (also aligned with Snake), but was restored to represent Athena, Greek goddess of wisdom.

Top right: Isis holding cobras, bronze statue, Egypt, first century BCE.

Bottom left: Minoan snake goddesses, reconstructions of figurines discovered by archaeologist Arthur Evans in 1903, Egypt, circa 1600 BCE.

Bottom right: Sculpted sunk-relief depiction of uraeus, inspired by the goddess Wadjet and typically worn on forehead at the third eye, Egypt, circa 746–335 BCE.

Priestesses and devotees danced with snakes to join with the energy of the Goddess—for Snake *was* the Goddess and physical snakes living representatives of her presence.

Some goddesses were imaged with a snake emerging from the forehead. In Egypt the cobra goddess Wadjet inspired the uraeus—a headdress worn by pharaohs as an emblem of wisdom and divine authority to rule. Snake's presence at the brow activated intuitive knowledge of the third eye and awakened higher consciousness at the crown chakra.

Ancient Egyptians feared the cobras that slithered through the grasses along the Nile as one careless step could lead to a deadly bite. Cobra was thus the perfect guardian of the pharaoh, for what better animal to protect a ruler than one that is greatly feared by the masses?

Facts
about Fearing Snake

There are more than 3,500 known species of snakes in the world, 600 of which are venomous. If you are bitten and envenomated, and if you fail to receive proper treatment, you may die or experience such horrendous pain that you wish you would die. Clearly, it is wise to be cautious and respectful around snakes, especially venomous snakes.

As noted by various medical groups, the number of snakebites that occur each year is very difficult to determine. Best evidence suggests that between 1.2 to over 5 million people are bitten by snakes annually, with up to 100,000 fatalities. While some countries have very high death rates from snake bites, others are quite low.

The Centers for Disease Control and Prevention (CDC) estimates that 7,500 people are bitten by venomous snakes in the United States annually. Of those, 30–50 percent will be dry bites. (Snakes can control whether to inject venom with a bite; dry bites are those that do not involve the injection of venom.) Because of good medical care and availability of antivenom, only 5 of those 7,500 people bitten will die each year.

For perspective consider that four times as many people in the United States will be killed by a horse or crushed by a cow every

The Western diamondback rattlesnake (*Crotalus atrox*), found in southwestern states, is both the longest rattlesnake species and responsible for the most venomous bites in the United States. It shakes its rattle in warning to keep humans away.

year, five times as many will die by dog attack, and over ten times as many will perish from a bee, wasp, or hornet bite.[2]

Protecting the Treasure

In addition to protecting gods and rulers, Snake is known for safeguarding hidden treasures—not only gems and riches, but also ancient wisdom

Naga Kanya is both a Hindu snake goddess and Buddhist guardian of sacred knowledge. In Hindu mythology nagas are supernatural snake deities that guard material treasures as well as esoteric teachings. As in this amulet from Thailand, Naga Kanya is often depicted with female head and torso, and the lower body of serpent. The crown of cobras above her head indicates the activation of *kundalini*.

and esoteric knowledge. Appearing as a fierce dragon or supernatural, many-headed serpent, Snake oversees the entrances to caves, pyramids, and temples where treasure is hidden, scaring away those who do not belong or are not ready to enter.

Within humans Snake guards one of our most precious treasures: kundalini. From the Sanskrit word meaning "snake," kundalini is a powerful energy that slumbers at the base of the spine. When stimulated through spiritual practice, kundalini awakens and begins to rise. Like a snake, it undulates, crisscrossing the spine, activating the body's chakras (energy centers) as it ascends to the crown, bringing enlightenment.

But so also does the sleeping serpent serve in its dormant state. Curled around the lower spine, Snake protects the potent essence of life energy, preventing premature awakening, and waiting for the appropriate time (if ever) to initiate the process of enlightenment.

In nature snakes intimidate with ferocious postures: bared fangs, raised body, unfurled hood, rattling tail. Spitting or hissing, they stand their ground, warning us not to move closer, advising us to avoid unfortunate interactions. In similar ways the kundalini snake appears frightening to those who are not ready for activation of its energy.

By appearing fierce and deadly, Snake protects us from recklessly triggering energies that might overwhelm or destroy normal consciousness. As a wise guide known for its expertise in precise timing, kundalini Snake stands guard, observing and testing us, making sure we are ready to face our fears before opening to this very special type of wisdom.

The treasure kundalini Snake protects is one of profound awakening—perhaps similar to the energy held in the Tree of Knowledge in the Garden of Eden. Parts of ourselves are so extremely powerful they are hidden from conscious awareness for good reason. Thus Snake tests us, for a certain degree of spiritual maturity and self-knowledge is needed to safely awaken the sleeping serpent inside.

In nearly all mythologies Snake both protects and initiates: frightening those who are not ready to face their inner fears, and welcoming those who are ripe to awaken. Once we are ready to see who we really are, Snake triggers transformation.

Asian cobra (*Naja kaouthia*)

BEHIND THE SCENES
AT THE SHADOW FACTORY

When Adam and Eve ate the forbidden fruit of the Garden, they did not die as God had threatened. But neither did they accept responsibility for their actions. Rather, Adam blamed Eve, and Eve blamed the serpent. The only character in this story who tells the truth is Snake.

In *Adam, Eve, and the Serpent,* historian Elaine Pagels notes that the Garden of Eden story had enormous impact on Western culture and civilization, for it ushered in a dramatic shift of how we would interact with the divine, the world, and each other.[3] This collective shift of consciousness continues to affect us today.

Most Bible scholars believe the book of Genesis was composed and revised between 1400 and 600 BCE, a time when northern conquerors who championed patriarchal views were attempting to replace Goddess-based cultures and religions with Sky Gods as divine rulers. The take-over followed typical patterns of conquering: slip the new gods in place while demeaning, denigrating, and destroying the old.

The writers of Genesis were males with a patriarchal agenda: discredit the Goddess (represented by Eve) and her ally Snake and install the Sky Father as supreme god. As Pagels notes, the Garden of Eden story was a foundational narrative used to justify the patriarchal paradigm. The story is cleverly crafted and so rooted in our worldview that most of us never think to question it. Thus we still routinely refer to deceivers or cheats as snakes, and imagine God as a father figure residing in the heavens.

Moving from a nature-based, matriarchal worldview to a hierarchical, patriarchal paradigm involved shifts in consciousness that resulted in escalating separation. Humanity moved from working in connection and cooperation with animals, land, and the natural world to manipulating and exploiting nature. Where there was once communal equality and a respectful pairing between male and female, there was now estrangement, domination, and the increasing devaluation of females, animals,

"*The serpent entwines itself around the body of Eve; it whispers in her ear. . . .*" Photogravure by Lemercier and co. after Walter Crane, 1899.
Wellcome Collection.

and children. The authoritarian, hierarchical view of life put the Sky God at the top, followed by self-appointed male rulers who oversaw political, military, societal, and religious arenas. More than that, the newly established patriarchal institutions and representatives reinforced their powers by claiming their rule to be divinely ordained.

Our perception of Snake shifted as well. Rather than regarding it as creator and protector, those in charge depicted Snake as tempter and attacker. No longer guardian of sacred knowledge, Snake was now a liar and obstructor of truth. From advisor to deceiver, healer to harmer, mentor and initiator to demonic destroyer, Snake became lower than low.

In one creatively controlled myth, the Garden story separated the Goddess (Eve) from Snake, pitting one against the other and portraying both in negative ways. No longer was Snake worshipped or draped around the necks of the gods—rather it was an evil creature to be fought and banished. Myths that once glorified goddesses aligned with snakes were reshaped and retold, with the goddess becoming a seducer and temptress, or made repulsive and chthonic. By extension women were demoted in society, viewed as spiritually unclean, untrustworthy, unintelligent, and less than—simple souls that needed the guidance of a strong male father, husband, and god.

The Mythic
Making of a Monster

The story of Medusa reveals how both Snake and Goddess were demonized through the reshaping of myths. Once beautiful and devoted priestess to Athena, Medusa is raped by Poseidon in the goddess's temple. Although Medusa pleads innocence, Athena is enraged and turns her beloved priestess into a gorgon—a monster— with a crown of serpents that turns any man who gazes upon her into stone. Exiled on a distant island, Medusa is later beheaded by the demigod Perseus (son of Zeus and half-brother to Athena), as depicted in this statue holding Medusa's head while standing upon her dead body.

Perseus with the head of Medusa, bronze statue
by Benvenuto Cellini, circa 1545–1554

The fall of Snake and Goddess has led us to over 4,000 years of separation from ourselves: an alienation between inner male from inner female, logic from intuition, conscious from unconscious, body from soul. This has affected all of us, male and female alike. It has affected our relationship with animals, the earth, the natural world, each other, and the divine.

When wholeness is replaced by separation, we are divided. Inevitably, one side is viewed as helpful, light, and right, the other suspect and dangerous. What we fear or deem dark becomes our Shadow. When Fear enters the picture, neither side wins.

Perhaps what bothers us most about Snake is its paradoxical nature: both creator and destroyer, healer and harmer, initiator and fierce guardian. Ironically, Snake is a master of transformation, capable of harmonizing and joining together that which is separated.

Testing us, guiding us, Snake prevents us from opening too quickly, ensuring we are ready to awaken. As the wise, ancient keeper of secret knowledge, Snake knows exactly when to activate energy that leads to transformation. By awakening dormant energy, encouraging its rise and

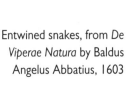

Entwined snakes, from *De Viperae Natura* by Baldus Angelus Abbatius, 1603

flow, Snake helps us to balance and integrate knowledge, wisdom, and experience so that we may know ourselves in a new way. By bridging realms, Snake joins sleeping self with awakened awareness when we are ready. And that time is now.

FACING THE GUARDIAN

Some fear is appropriate. But excessive or irrational fear can overwhelm and create obstacles that prevent us from knowing who we really are. We construct personal temples of fear early in life. Brick by brick, we build walls to keep away uncomfortable thoughts and feelings. Our temple seems to protect us, and we continually reinforce its power and praise its magnificence, thus making it ever stronger and grander.

The experience of being startled by a snake at a young age, for example, or hearing adults express their fear or hatred of snakes triggers an uneasiness that takes root. Nurtured in Shadow territory, our thoughts, feelings, and memories of the experience grow and mutate, instigating and reinforcing the belief that we don't like snakes. Over time it may convince us that snakes are evil, or trigger emotional and physical anxiety around snakes. Every time we read about a fatal snakebite we are reassured of our reasoning for disliking snakes. We close ourselves off and refuse to learn about snakes, thus preventing ourselves from ever really knowing Snake at all.

It is often the ancient lizard—Dragon, Snake, multiheaded Serpent, or Naga—that guards the deepest treasure within our psyche. Because its story is intertwined with our own, facing Snake at the entrance to our inner sanctum means facing what we fear most within ourselves.

To fully know ourselves means to see all aspects of Self, even (especially!) those that hide within the shadows. These are our unrealized selves: the unworthy and vulnerable, the abused and traumatized; those born from shame and despair, resentment and grief; the hurting, the hurtful; the angry, and all the fear-fueled monsters that rage out of control.

Ferocious guardian, loving protector: Snake is a premier shadow animal that calls us to embrace the aspects of Self that we have long denied, so that we may know the fullness of who we are.

Working with shadow animals such as Snake requires courage, honesty, and willingness to explore the deep self. The process involves seeking out our blind spots; examining what makes us feel uncomfortable; acknowledging our judgments, our conditioning, our rigid beliefs. We need to be detectives, observing patterns of frustration or anger, identifying the clever ways in which we attempt to disown our Shadow by projecting it outward.

We may need to take risks, to follow intuitive insights or unconventional hunches. We may need to persist in peeling back superficial layers of favorite thoughts or habitual feelings so as to expose the tangled roots below. We may need to enlarge our perspectives by considering ideas and views that are beyond our paradigm. What restricts or holds us back? Are we willing to think outside that box? Are we willing to realize that it is we who have created the box?

The transformations required by shadow work can be difficult. Change may involve crisis and catharsis, chaos and confusion. Not everyone is willing—or even wants to—embrace change. *Am I willing to change* is a question we must continually ask ourselves on this path. And only when we say yes can the deep re-pairing begin.

◆ ◆ **Exercise** ◆ ◆

Continuing the Quest with Snake

We can learn so much about ourselves by the questions we ask. To question is to quest, to seek, to deepen, and expand knowledge of who we really are.

When working with Shadow, some of the most helpful questions are born of yearning. By sensing beneath troubled thoughts or uneasy emotions, by considering puzzling or unpleasant dreams, we begin to ask the raw, eager questions that arise from within. Some questions are like magic keys, unlocking the perfect bit of advice or wisdom that we need next.

The following questions and observations offer both review and fresh perspectives for engaging shadow work. May they encourage you to continue the quest, to further explore who we really are in inspiring and enlightening ways.

Observe Emotions and Explore

Working with Shadow is an ongoing process, and life presents plenty of opportunities to enrich our explorations wherever we are. Observe

Opening to change

what angers, annoys, disappoints, or saddens—then question and contemplate: What do I sense beneath the surface of this drama? Am I willing to pull back the curtain to see? Am I ready to explore uncomfortable thoughts or feelings? If the answer is yes, consider: What am I not seeing? What am I hiding from myself? What frightens me about this potential opportunity to change?

Review exercises from:
 Chapter 1, Spider's Web of Intrigue (page 54)
 Chapter 9, What's Bugging Me? (page 217)

Be Receptive and Play

Answers come in so many varied ways: dreams, reveries, conversations, synchronous events, a look, a smile, a prancing horse, a soaring bird, a snake in a tree. When we are open, answers are everywhere. The world communicates useful information that activates the next insight. Am I ready to ignite my curiosity and engage life with childlike wonder? Look, listen, feel, intuit—then be artful and creative. Elaborate, untangle, arrange, and rearrange, play with what presents in fanciful, profound, elegant, or messy ways. Embracing play opens pathways to unexpected insights and further exploration.

Review exercises from:
 Chapter 2, Rat's Treasures, Three Ways (page 75)
 Chapter 8, Becoming Bird (page 191)

See Judgments and Accept Responsibility

What we judge or reject in the outer world offers a dark mirror of what we judge or reject in ourselves. What am I not owning but instead projecting onto others? How is what I wish could be different in another related to what I wish could be different in myself? Am I willing to acknowledge my faults, admit when I am wrong, and own my mistakes rather than blaming my spouse, my boss, the government? By accepting responsibility for our projections, we begin to reclaim energies we once ignored, let languish, or gave away.

Review exercises from:

Dig Deep

Every annoyance in life is an opportunity to dig deeper, every fear a potential turning point, a chance to probe further and learn more. Am I willing to entertain questions that provoke my emotions, short-circuit my sense of self, and speak to my soul? What would I most like to forget or flee from? When I act out in arrogant, angry, defensive, or self-justifying ways, what am I protecting? What parts of myself have I banished from conscious awareness? Am I ready and willing to dive deep and explore the dark areas of my psyche?

Review exercises from:

Re-Member

Shadow work involves finding and integrating what has been separated. Selves that have splintered away from consciousness may be hiding in shadow territory. We may not know much about these selves, but at times we sense their presence. We may then need to become quiet and aware in order to hear them, to feel them—all these troubled selves that have separated from our wholeness. This aspect of shadow retrieval can require persistence, patience, compassion, and a shift from doing to being.

Review exercises from:

The quest to know ourselves is a journey of deep exploration. As T. S. Eliot wrote,

We shall not cease from exploration
And the end of all our exploring
Will be to arrive where we started
And know the place for the first time.
Through the unknown, remembered gate
When the last of the earth left to discover
Is that which was the beginning . . .[4]

Part of Snake's expertise is linking endings and beginnings, harmonizing the discordant, and bringing together that which seems separated so that we can realign and awaken. The sacred marriage is a re-pairing of male and female, body and soul, dormant and awakened. When we see and feel no difference between ourselves and others, dancing gracefully between inner and outer realms, beholding the interconnectedness of all life, we begin to know ourselves—perhaps for the first time.

Re-membering

13

The Most Dangerous
Animal of All

*The time will come
when, with elation,
you will greet yourself arriving
at your own door . . .*
DEREK WALCOTT, "LOVE AFTER LOVE"

Hello, human. Most of this book was written in 2020—perhaps the most shadow-infused year we've experienced in recent history. We saw some of the worst behavior from our species, and some of the best.

It was a year of fear and confusion, rage and reactivity. It involved sudden job loss and rising unemployment; increasing polarization, mistrust, and divisiveness fueled by a deluge of disinformation; and worldwide projection of Shadow. The earth responded: record rainfall, hurricanes, floods, earthquakes, wildfires, drought, warming temperatures, and melting ice.

At home we suffered the last desperate year of a president who preferred to belittle, deny, and divide rather than unite. We faced the ugly truths of systemic racism, gender inequality, and sexual predation (notably by those with wealth, power, and celebrity status), and witnessed children pulled from their parents at border crossings. We fought for police and immigration reform, racial justice, and accountability in the media and government. At the tail end of 2020 Americans voted in record numbers for change, electing the oldest president ever to serve and the first female, first black, and first South Asian American vice-president. Even though we fired the old president, he refused to believe it was so.

But the biggest news was the global pandemic. COVID-19, an acute respiratory illness, found its way to every continent on Earth. We practiced social distancing, faced travel restrictions, and mostly stayed at home.

Disease is about disruption or disorder, the body's way of revealing what is amiss within ourselves. COVID reflected the global dis-ease of our species. Like a feverish dream it spread uncontrollably—scaring, disorienting, and isolating us. And yet it connected us too, pressing us to ask big questions about who we are and who we want to be.

The respiratory nature of this pandemic reminds that breathing joins us with each other and with the world. We breathe in the air molecules of those we know and those we don't know, all of us sharing in the sacred inhalation and exhalation of life. COVID required us to be more conscious of what we take in and what we release with our breath. We wore masks to prevent contagion, but so also did the coverings suggest that our words—increasingly combative, judgmental, and fraudulent—had become toxic. At the same time, an uprising of people all over the world questioned the agenda of those in charge and clamored to fight censorship, expose fraud, and reveal the truth. So what exactly was being masked? Was the ubiquitous mask—the global symbol of 2020—metaphoric encouragement to take stock, speak less aggressively, and listen more, or oppressive directive aimed at controlling, concealing, and silencing? Perhaps it was both—and even more, for as we would learn, mask wearing was simply the beginning of a long, chaotic journey with many surprising events and unexpected revelations.

The year 2020 was one for diving deep to face our Shadow, both personally and collectively. Life always presents what we need to see! Scandals and corruption were exposed as a plethora of secrets emerged—cloaked in fear and denial for some, inviting acknowledgment and change for others. It was a time of death, but also rebirth.

Pandemic!

The word *pandemic* comes from the Greek *pan,* meaning "all," and *demos,* "people." Global pandemics force us to recognize that what affects one individual affects all people.

Pan, the ancient nature god of primeval energies is present not only in pandemic, but also in panic and pandemonium. Clever and unpredictable, this trickster god sparks chaos in a world that is needful of change.

Pan, bronze sculpture by Andrea Briosco, called Riccio. Italy, circa 1510–1520. Less than 15 inches high, this statuette could be placed on a desktop for lighting or writing by adding oil or ink to the arm-held receptacles. Pan may trigger confusion although, as this sculpture suggests, he can also help us to see and understand ourselves more clearly.

Did the spirit of Pan manifest in our modern world as a tiny virus? Drawing upon the trickster's gift of shapeshifting, mutating microbes deep inside our bodies and spreading across the globe, Pan stirred panic, forcing us to wake up and pay attention. As spiritual medicine pandemics remind us that there is no "them," that it is all only us— one family, one world. Thus may we recognize the healing aspect of Pan, also present in a panacea.

We human beings are such incongruous creatures, saying one thing while thinking or feeling another. So too do our emotions, thoughts, and actions span a wild expanse of extremes. Part of us growls and bares its fangs while another part sings and swells with love. We flaunt and celebrate parts of ourselves, hide, repress, and deny others.

You know the pattern: whatever we reject or disown is mirrored back to us, showing up as a person, animal, dramatic event. Thus, as Jung put it, we "slowly come to recognize that we meet ourselves time and again in a thousand disguises on the path of life."[1] And so it goes— until we are ready to awaken.

Acknowledging our Shadow begins the process of releasing the ancient curses we have placed upon others and ourselves. It liberates the energy we've been using to dampen down uncomfortable thoughts and feelings, allowing us to use it in a more conscious, creative way.

There is a greater good too. By identifying and retrieving shadow energy, we prevent others from manipulating it to their own ends—and history reveals a very long list of unscrupulous dictators and politicians, business tycoons and media moguls, past as well as present, who have done just that. Shadow energy is incredibly potent—collective shadow energy even more so. When surreptitiously directed, it can be used to exploit, twist, and deceive, to allow skillful manipulators to seize power, take over countries, and turn its citizens against one another. As Robert Bly wrote over thirty years ago, "One of the things we need to do as Americans is to work hard individually at eating our shadows, and so make sure that we are not releasing energy which can then be picked up by the politicians, who can use it against Russia, China, or the South American countries."[2] Indeed, perhaps the most important individual, social, and spiritual work we can do is to recognize and retrieve our projections of Shadow onto the world.

So, how do we do that? How do we sit with uncomfortable thoughts and feelings as they arise in our everyday life? How can we prevent the unconscious projection of Shadow into the world? How can we move from anger to calm, from out-of-control spiraling thoughts to mindfulness, from hate to compassion? How do we find our center when we are caught in the midst of a maelstrom?

Working with Shadow in Everyday Life

1. *Acknowledge what is happening.* Consciously acknowledge the uncomfortable thoughts and feelings that affect you in a given moment. For example, someone interrupts you as you speak, abruptly expressing their opinion rather than allowing you to finish your thought. Rather than instantly reacting and casting blame, pause. Notice your feelings. By observing our annoyance or irritation, we can recognize that something deeper is happening here.

2. *Feel it fully.* What does the emotion—anger, sadness, betrayal, confusion—feel like in your body? What are the physical sensations (muscle tightness, nerve stimulation, heart rate, heat or cold) and where are they located (head, heart, spine, forehead, jaw, fingers). Observe your body's experience, sensing everything. We need to fully feel the emotion triggered by an experience in order to move through it.

3. *Let it flow.* Allow your body to tighten, flush, shiver, or shake. Stay present; feel the flow of these energies within your body. The trick is to observe but not identify—not get sucked into additional feelings of self-righteousness or victimhood. By staying present and observing the flow of your emotions, you may soon notice how they begin to dissipate or dissolve. You may feel yourself relaxing, softening, letting go. By allowing our body's emotions to flow naturally, we can move through uncomfortable sensations and release the triggers that hold us hostage to knee-jerk reactions and judgments. As Jung puts it, "Real liberation comes not from glossing over or repressing painful states of feeling, but only from experiencing them to the full."[3]

4. *Cultivate Awareness.* Invite a larger perspective by considering your role in the situation. What we see in others is less about who they are, and more about who we are. Investigate your thoughts, feelings, and motivations—without getting trapped in the rationalizing morass of why you were "right." Stay objective, as if analyzing a dream. Allow yourself to ask difficult questions, such as: How can I change what I see out there by seeing this more clearly in myself? Shifting inner perspectives shifts our perception of reality as well. It can help us move from the belief that life happens to us to the realization that life happens for us.

5. *Open to Joy.* Shadow work can be challenging. By paying attention to ourselves—noticing feelings of annoyance, vulnerability, aversion, frustration, and rage—we continue the process of getting to know all of our selves. People and events in the world may wittingly or unwittingly push our buttons. But with self-clarity and an open heart, we realize there are no buttons to push. And so we open to wonder and joy, both in the world and in ourselves.

OTHERING

In order to understand our relationship to the world, we categorize. We begin at a young age, recognizing ourselves as belonging to a group: family, friends, school, community. As we identify with our group we conform to its ideas and beliefs, thereby increasing our emotional connection to "us."

As we grow older we categorize further: race, gender, political views, social standing. We recognize our group as different from "them." *Them* is whoever is perceived as different from us: male, female; gay, straight; black, white; wealthy, poor; Democrat, Republican; Chinese, American.

Belonging to a group offers social identity. We sometimes attempt to elevate our group's status (and our own self-esteem) by projecting inferior qualities against "them." We may thus stereotype "their" behavior and mannerisms in negative ways that over time trigger distrust, fear, contempt, discrimination, and prejudice.

Merriam-Webster notes that the word *other* is increasingly being used as a verb, meaning to treat one group of people as fundamentally different from another group "by emphasizing its apartness."[4]

Othering can be highly infectious, spreading like a virus from one individual to another. What makes othering insidious is that by solidifying group cohesiveness and reinforcing shared beliefs, we begin to more vehemently believe that our perspective is the only one that is right.

Interestingly, the process of othering originates in the amygdala, the part of our brain connected to fear and aggression. As group mentality grows stronger and more exacting, our thinking brain—the prefrontal cortex (responsible for logic and perspective)—becomes more dormant. Thus, rather than discerning information for ourselves by researching facts, we gloss over accuracy and detail—which is how misinformation so easily proliferates on social media.

The very real danger—to each of us, and to our world—is that othering begets othering. While groups can offer us a sense of comfort and belonging—our family, our collective, our community—when fueled by fear and hate, group othering can spiral out of control.

In anxious, troubling times, we can become very quick to blame the other, to condemn and make wrong, to believe "they" are the cause of all our troubles; 2020 involved some vicious othering. We often failed to listen to those with views different from our own, our attention spans and patience dwindling to near nonexistence as we preferred to attack and build walls rather than think, find common ground, or create bridges of connection. Some politicians became very adept at casting suspicion, triggering othering, and twisting "facts" to suit their needs.

Othering is an easy fix for us to feel immediately better about ourselves, both individually and collectively. It seduces us into a dangerous fundamentalist viewpoint: we are right and they are wrong. And because our group believes so strongly that we are right, it must be so.

But othering is based on ignorance: on lack of information and truth; on failure to consider other views that might allow us a larger perspective; on a stubborn, small-minded insistence that we cannot be wrong. The sobering truth about othering is that what we do not know about others is what we do not know about ourselves.

THE TRICKSTER'S GAME

There are a wide variety of trickster archetypes in mythology. Some are playful and mischievous, some lustful and seductive, some malicious and malevolent. Some poke fun and use laughter to shake us out of rigid beliefs, while others unleash worldwide mayhem, forcing us to look upon all that we do not want to see about ourselves.

Find a trickster at work, and you'll find the presence of Shadow.

Eshu is a trickster god of the Yoruba tribe in Nigeria. Often imaged as a small man wearing an elaborate headdress, he is a very old and popular god. Known by a variety of names and worshipped in different forms across Africa, Eshu is frequently found at crossroads, borders, and gateways.

A fun-loving troublemaker who does not follow rules, Eshu uses trickery to teach lessons that need to be learned. In one of his most famous myths, Eshu promenades the boundary between two farms or through the middle of a village or town. No matter the setting, Eshu wears a large, unusual hat. After watching the god pass by, the farmers or villagers or townspeople always remark about that marvelous hat.

"What an amazing shade of red!" one farmer will say. "It wasn't red; it was sky blue. I saw it with my own eyes!" exclaims the other farmer. "No it wasn't!" "Yes it was!" The two farmers—formerly best friends—eventually become so angry they refuse to talk or even look at each other.

Yoruba wood carving of a kneeling Eshu-Elegba, Nigeria, Africa, late nineteenth or early twentieth century

Courtesy of the Brooklyn Museum, CC BY 3.0

Sometimes the entire village argues about what they saw: red hat, blue hat. In one story the villagers construct a stone wall through the center of town. One side builds a church where they worship a red-hatted god; the other side creates the same to honor their blue-hatted god. For years the village is divided, the people bitter adversaries.

One day Eshu returns, walking atop the wall that separates the two sides. This time he is wearing no hat at all, and the people clamor to set reality straight: "What color was that hat you were wearing when last you visited us?"

"Oh," says Eshu after a moment of recall. "I believe on that day I was wearing a hat that was red on one side and blue on the other." As Eshu saunters away, the villagers consider this new bit of information. In some versions of the story, each side refuses to believe the other could possibly be right, and so they remain a village divided. But in more popular versions, there is a laugh among the villagers—then another, and another, and soon the uproarious, communal laughter becomes so loud it shakes the earth and crumbles the wall to the ground.

No matter the subtlety or outrageousness of its antics, the role of the trickster is to facilitate change. By exposing our Shadow, the trickster loosens rigid beliefs and invites us to experience the world in a more expansive way. The trickster tricks us so that we can awaken.

DREAM DINING WITH
THE SHADOW TRICKSTER

In 2016 clinical social worker Martha Crawford noticed how many of her clients (as well as herself) were dreaming about Donald Trump. While presidents occasionally appear in our nighttime adventures, this was different, and Crawford began collecting the dreams. She was inspired by journalist Charlotte Beradt, who wrote *The Third Reich of Dreams: The Nightmare of a Nation,* which featured a collection of German people's dreams of Hitler after he became chancellor in 1933.

Both Beradt and Crawford's collections note the schism occurring in the world and within our dreaming psyche. "We're still fighting a civil war," said Crawford in an interview. "That's what these dreams show. We're splitting ourselves personally in half, and we're splitting ourselves collectively in half . . . I don't believe these dreams are about Donald Trump. I believe these dreams are about us. They're about some aspect of our own psyche that we haven't dealt with."[5]

For many years Donald Trump served as a collective Shadow projection, his constant media presence, never-ending tweets, and outlandish behavior a nationwide trigger. Some were appalled and disgusted as Trump revealed what we did not want to see about ourselves. Here—as our president!—was a boastful, obnoxious, self-absorbed man thoroughly entrenched in the belief that he is never wrong, willing to lie and manipulate to get what he wants. For others Trump's media cunning, showmanship, and celebrity status evoked Shadow desires to be like him: to have all the answers and never be afraid to speak one's mind. His self-aggrandizing gatherings stoked rage, indignation, and want, inciting his followers to vent their discontent by implying that rules can be broken without consequence or accountability.

Like the trickster god Eshu, Trump evoked divisiveness, pitting one side against the other, fueling hostility by emphasizing division. Red hat, Blue hat. Caught within the emotional chaos, most of us failed to recognize that the real problem is not the "other"; rather, it is in ourselves.

In many ways Donald Trump was the collective shadow self that refuses to look at itself. Always right, never wrong, avoiding any form of introspection, the badly behaved president revealed great reluctance to see—let alone explore—his Shadow.

Donald Trump was definitely my larger-than-life shadow projection. In my eyes he was an egomaniac and liar; a man lacking empathy and emotional maturity; an arrogant braggart who enjoyed belittling and manipulating others so as to avoid his own inner fears of insecurity and loss of control; a deeply defensive man unable to face failure of any kind.

Whether these perceptions are accurate or not, we can always detect the presence of Shadow when we encounter our projections with strong, insistent emotions—contempt, disgust, loathing. And then, alas, we must ask ourselves, as I so very often did, *What does my view of Donald Trump represent within me?*

I wanted to discover what was buried beneath the surface, to identify the haughty, manipulative, self-serving Shadow that lurked within my psyche. But so also did I repeatedly shy away from such exploration. I put off any meaningful attempts at analysis and deep probing of the psyche, always finding something else to do instead. In other words, I failed to take my own good advice to pause and look within.

I dreamed of Donald Trump several times. In one I went to great lengths to avoid him. In another I was secretly delighted as he was chomped in two by a Chinese dragon. Avoidance, happiness at another's demise—both dreams as well as several others revealed my great reluctance to face this tenacious shadow self of mine.

Then, near the end of 2020, a breakthrough dream:

> I live in an apartment in New York City. Although it's small there are few dividing walls, so it feels open and spacious. The apartment is painted gray—not a depressing gray, but a bright, elegant gray.
>
> Someone knocks at my door: Donald Trump has come for dinner. He walks in and sits at my kitchen table. Moving past him, I open the oven door and take out a huge pie. "What kind of pie is it?" he asks. "Humble pie," I tell him. I smell the pie as I set it in front of him—the scent is savory and delicious, and I can tell that it is very well made. I set a chef's knife beside the pie.
>
> As Donald Trump cuts into the pie, out comes a blackbird! It flies to the left of his head and starts pecking. Then other birds come out of the pie—ten, twenty, maybe thirty. They flutter around him, pecking all over his body. But he's not yelling and there's no blood. It's as if his body is a set of Russian nesting dolls. As the birds peck, thin chips of wood and paint and plaster crumble down in layers.
>
> When the birds are done, they fly out the window. I go to the chair and find a tiny Donald Trump, only an inch high. I pick him up and put him on the table.
>
> "What now?" he asks me. I consider for a moment, "Do you have it in yourself to change?" I ask. He thinks about it and then shakes his head, no. I sense this is true, that he does not have it inside of himself to make a change. So I tell him that he will need to ask for help.

Just then one of the blackbirds returns through the open window. It has a small gold-and-red embroidered mat on its back, and golden threads tied to its neck like a halter. It lands on the table and Donald Trump climbs upon its back. Settling himself on the mat, he tells me, "I'm going on an adventure! I'm going to learn to change and not be such an asshole."

Good luck with that, *I think in a sarcastic way. But as I say the words aloud, I hear them as genuine and heartfelt. As they are voiced, they become a blessing. And I realize with surprise that I am changed—that I truly feel joy to send him off with a blessing and, because of that, something inside of me has changed as well.*

A DEEPER LOOK

What a dream! I felt a lightness on waking, as if something old and heavy had taken flight. The feeling continued in the coming days, a calm easiness flowing through my thoughts, feelings, attitudes, and interactions with others. Something profound had happened in the dream, affecting me in the waking world as well. While there are many layers and intriguing references within this dream, let's look at just a few of the key elements that allowed for change.

The setting of a dream often reveals where we are within our psyche, a backdrop of our relationship to the dream's theme. An apartment in New York City—a small space in a large city—suggests the individual within the larger collective. The color gray indicates a perspective that is not rigidly black and white, but a balance or blend of opposites. Further, the gray is not depressive, but bright and elegant—perhaps the dream will present a clearer, more elevated, or enlightened point of view. This also fits with the description of the apartment—small without dividing walls, modest yet spacious and open. Perhaps the dreamer is now open-minded enough to receive the dream's message.

The action begins when Donald Trump arrives for dinner. Here at her door, the dreamer's Shadow representative of arrogance, defensiveness, and emotional immaturity has arrived to be fed. As her guest sits at the kitchen table (a type of altar, a space to meet or eat or reveal what we bring to the table) the dreamer opens the oven (a heating chamber, a vessel of transformation in which something raw is cooked and made edible) and brings out a pie.

The pie is huge—a telling reference to its importance, for although we don't know it yet, the circular baked creation holds live, hidden agents of transformation. The dreamer notes its scent is savory (salty or spicy as opposed to sweet and, as the word is also defined, morally wholesome or respectable) and that it is well made—skillfully constructed, suggesting it is perfectly created for this occasion. But so also is it "humble pie." While not particularly humorous in the dream, it is amusing and fitting that the dreamer's pretentious Shadow projection is served humble pie. To eat humble pie is to acknowledge our wrongdoings and be accountable.

Using the chef's knife (a tapered, pointed culinary tool used to pierce, slice, cut, or chop—though as a knife may also be used as a weapon, surgical instrument, or implement of self-sacrifice), Donald Trump releases what is concealed inside: a live blackbird! Birds can represent many things: the soul or spirit, a desire for flight and freedom, a medium between earth and sky. The black of its feathers indicates mystery, the hidden, the unknown. Perhaps it is like the trickster Raven, a dark angel sent by the unconscious to present a key piece of the puzzle that we are unable to access on our own.

Flying to the left (the feminine, intuitive side) of Donald Trump's head (signifying intellect, ego, or perhaps where this shadow self resides) the blackbird begins to peck (to strike, bite, or chisel—an avian version of the chef's knife). Soon more birds come: ten, twenty, maybe thirty—a possible reference to the old nursery rhyme featuring "four-and-twenty blackbirds, baked in a pie."

Inside the Pie

Sing a song of sixpence,
A pocket full of rye.
Four-and-twenty blackbirds,
Baked in a pie.
When the pie was opened

The birds began to sing;
Wasn't that a dainty dish,
To set before the king?

Drawing from *The Song of Sixpence Picture Book,* 1864

In the sixteenth century live birds were placed inside pies to be served at extravagant banquets for the wealthy. The trick was to keep the birds alive so they could fly out when the pie was cut.

In the first published version of this nursery rhyme (around 1745), however, the pie did not contain birds, but rather four-and-twenty "naughty boys"—a thought-provoking description of the badly behaved aspects of Shadow that may hide inside of us.

Just as tricksters reveal truth by exposing what we are desperate to hide, the birds peck away the superficial: paint, plaster, dust, all the layers of embellishment that cover up what is real. As if he is a set of Russian nesting dolls, Donald Trump is pecked away layer by layer, each crumbling veneer exposing the falsity of yet another "trumped up" facade.

Layer by Layer

Russian nesting dolls (also known as *Matryoshka* dolls) are a set of wooden dolls decreasing in size, all except the smallest opening at the middle so that each one can fit inside the next larger doll. The dolls date to the 1890s and are typically painted as females (*matryoshka* means "little matron"), though in the 1980s some were painted to look like Soviet leaders. More recent tourist versions also include Donald Trump dolls.

Donald Trump nesting doll set, carved, hand-painted,
and decoupaged at the Golden Cockerel workshop in
St. Petersburg, Russia
Photo courtesy of Golden Cockerel

It's worth noting that although Donald Trump has been served humble pie, he doesn't actually eat it. Rather, what's inside the pie eats him—an inverted reference to the process of eating the Shadow. The pie is the dreamer's creation, and cleverly tucked inside are the animal helpers who peck away—or eat—the Shadow on her behalf.

When the blackbirds are finished and fly away, the dreamer finds what remains: a 1-inch Donald Trump. Is this the "real" person within the facade, the small fraction of authenticity that resides within the pompous, larger-than-life persona?

Now that what is superficial, egotistic, and ostentatious has been pecked away, now that an authentic self is finally revealed, a question is posed: Do you have it in you to change? With uncharacteristic depth, Donald Trump ponders the truth and admits he does not have it within him to change. Thus, the dreamer informs, he must ask for help.

And then—unexpectedly, serendipitously—a blackbird returns! It's the dream's shout-out to the work of shadow animals, those who can help us find what is real by cutting us down to size. If we persevere, they may offer additional help—in this case, a means of transport.

Outfitted with a red-and-gold embroidered mat and golden threads (befitting what is "trump"—an alteration of the word *triumph*), the bird now serves as guide, vehicle, agent of change through travel and adventure. The rider accepts help by climbing aboard, stating he is going "to learn to change and not be such an asshole." But to do that requires something further. It is unclear if the dream Trump will succeed at his quest, for the scenario ends with what remains of the Shadow flying out the window.

The dream is not finished with the dreamer, however, for just as bird and passenger leave the building, there is one last surprise. What is sarcastic within the dreamer emerges as something genuine and heartfelt. A mocking thought becomes a blessing as it is spoken aloud, the meaning of the words transformed as they are voiced upon breath, the sacred medium that connects us all.

A BLESSING

A saying in Jewish folklore notes, *May the blesser be blessed.* By blessing our shadow selves, we too are blessed. And not only that, for the act of blessing proliferates. By engaging and working with our Shadow we begin to reclaim individual energy and collectively projected energy as well. Whatever activity we use to explore our Shadow—dreaming, writing, painting, dancing, conversing—helps not only ourselves but the entire world.

Shadow work can feel daunting at times: to descend alone into the dark depths of the psyche, to find—and know we need to enter—the formidable, dragon-guarded caves where we hide our shame and anger, our judgments and fears. We're searching for our own worst secrets, those we so very carefully conceal from others as well as ourselves.

Through our discoveries we may find abused, despairing, traumatized selves. We may incur the wrath of the cruel, callous, or extremely opinionated selves living within. But so too, as we reach out to them, we begin to sense their strengths and untapped talents, their whispers of wisdom and desire to love.

"Give wine. Give bread. Give back your heart to itself, to the stranger who has loved you all your life" writes the poet Derek Walcott. "Sit," he reminds us. "Feast on your life."[6]

May we listen to our hearts as well as our minds and feelings, expanding our awareness and deepening our compassion, not only for ourselves but for all the world.

May we learn from the many shadow figures—domesticated, wild, and human animals—who appear in our lives, invited or not, who lead us into chaos and desperation, anger and grief, who help us move through all the shadowy darkness until at last we find our treasures, our selves.

May we awaken to a larger understanding. May we find, and at long last embrace, the fullness of who we really are.

◆ ◆ **Exercise** ◆ ◆

A Celebration of Selves

Would you like to meet your shadow selves in a fun and meaningful way? Why not throw a party? It's a great way to loosen up, encourage conversation, inspire deeper layers of sharing, and celebrate—You!

Invite your shadow selves to bring their troubles and complaints along with their advice and abilities. The purpose is to learn more about these selves by listening and considering ways you can help each other. You might invite past selves who continue to hold shame, pain, or fear, as well as selves who have released their shadow aspects and now hold wisdom for others.

For example, a friend who helped develop this exercise invited the following selves to her party:

- 6-year-old self who witnessed violence and inappropriate behavior in her home and didn't know what to do about it
- 17-year-old self who felt scared but also excited and free as she

left home after her dad tried to beat her up and her boyfriend broke up with her

- 40-year-old self who married a man she barely knew, giving him all her money and property because she believed this was what she was supposed to do, and then felt devastated for ruining her life
- 42-year-old self who got a divorce, stopped smoking and drinking, and bought her first crystal sphere that launched a deep love of crystals, rocks, and stones
- 50-year-old people-pleaser and seeker of love who felt she needed to be perfect, especially to men
- 67-year-old strong self-healer who took control, found the right healing for her life-threatening illness, and realized she was not the same person she used to be

There are many ways to throw a party and you can be as physically, metaphorically, or metaphysically based as you like. For a tangible setting, prepare a table to seat your guests. Use place markers with names or images, or use stand-ins—dolls, statues, drawings, photographs, stuffed animals—to represent your invited guests. You might include party favors. An artist friend painted personalized watercolor cards as a way to honor and invite each self to the party. Another woman baked foods that each of her past selves had enjoyed.

You can also do this in the inner world, using your mind's eye to create a special meeting spot for your gathering of selves. If no specific selves come to mind, you might call upon shadow animals, using images or figurines to represent the various qualities you'd like to contact.

To begin the party, introduce yourselves. If you are physically seated at a table, you might move from chair to chair, settling into each "self," feeling its energy, emotions, and thoughts, and verbalizing your experience. You can also do this via meditation, visualization, or inner journey. Some questions you might ask:

Who are you?
How old are you?
What are your likes and dislikes?
What makes you sad or angry or scared?

Shadow animal gathering of selves. Guests around the table (a found intervertebral whale disc) include, left to right: Polar Bear, Explorer of the Dreamworld; Raven, Trickster and Master of Mystery; Kraken, Emissary of the Deep Psyche; Snake Goddess, Agent of Transformation; and Elephant God Ganesh, Remover of Obstacles.

What do you need?

What makes you feel safe?

What makes you happy?

How can we help you?

What are your strengths and abilities, your expertise or superpower?

Are you willing to share your knowledge and unique perspective to help other selves?

After everyone has shared, brainstorm ways to support each other. For example, maybe your belittling bully needs to be nurtured—perhaps he needs a comforting sweater or massage. Be specific and remember to follow through in waking life.

Sometimes selves are unable to share who they are or what they need. I once met a small spotted feline during this exercise. It seemed painfully shy and could not express who it was. By attuning to its energy, however, I remembered a dream of finding a cheetah cub hiding in my grandmother's closet. While I did not fully understand what this self represented, I felt its fear and vulnerability. The next day while shopping I found a cheetah print sweater. I happily purchased it and discovered that wearing it helped to coax this self into sharing more about who it was and what it needed. While on the surface actions like this may seem fanciful, on deeper levels they allow us to bridge realms and create pathways for communication.

Your party can be as small or large as you choose. (Some selves feel more comfortable one on one.) As you repeat the exercise over time, some selves may unexpectedly reveal themselves.

The importance of the exercise is to listen, support, heal, and integrate. So many of our shadow selves have unrecognized abilities. By helping them to express themselves in more balanced ways, all can benefit. The inner critic can become a discerning coach; the skeptic can help us avoid making rash decisions; the outspoken self can help us voice our opinion when appropriate; the sensitive empath can nudge us to see other points of view before behaving carelessly. All in balance.

Next time you are triggered by a shadow self—cynic, boaster, victim, manipulator—bring your best, wise, compassionate self forward. Breathe deep, listen, and feel. Sometimes what our shadow selves need most is to be seen, heard, and acknowledged. The more attention, consideration, and love you offer, the more you re-member who you really are. Welcome home.

Acknowledgments

Thanks to all the great people at Inner Traditions • Bear & Company for helping to make this book a reality. Special thanks to Acquisitions Editor Jon Graham for championing my proposal; to Creative Director Aaron Davis for the absolutely perfect cover; to Editor in Chief Jeanie Levitan, Project Editor Jamaica Burns Griffin, and Copy Editor Elizabeth Wilson for their exquisite attention to detail; and to Catalog Manager Erica Robinson, Book Designer Virginia Scott Bowman, Production Editor Eliza Homick, and Publicist Manzanita Carpenter Sanz.

Thanks to readers Cindy Lubar Bishop, Neal Bishop, Phil Kotofskie, and Karen Leach for their helpful insights and suggestions. Thanks to friends Barb Techel, Liberato Maraia, and Sheri Ray for sharing their stories, and to Molly Holm for the lovely photo of Wasp.

Thanks to my husband, Bob; daughter, Alyeska; dog-pal Deshka; and to family and friends for ongoing love and support.

And grateful thanks to all of the animals who have shared their thoughts, wisdom, and expertise through client sessions, informal conversations, unusual meetings, and in my many dreams. Thanks to all creatures, known and unknown, living upon this nurturing and beautiful planet we call Home.

Notes

INTRODUCTION: THE CAT, THE SNAKE, AND THE SHADOW

1. *Matter of Heart,* Film.
2. *Matter of Heart,* Film.

ANIMAL TEACHERS

1. Story excerpted from Brunke, *Animal Voices, Animal Guides,* 61.

SHADOW ANIMAL TEACHERS

1. *Pliny's Natural History* 3: 40–42.
2. Bly, *A Little Book on the Human Shadow,* 15.
3. Bly, *A Little Book on the Human Shadow,* 25.
4. Bly, *A Little Book on the Human Shadow,* 26.

WORKING WITH THE SHADOW

1. Bly, *A Little Book on the Human Shadow,* 27–43.
2. Bly, *A Little Book on the Human Shadow,* 38.
3. Bly, *A Little Book on the Human Shadow,* 42.
4. Bly, *A Little Book on the Human Shadow,* 42.

CHAPTER I. ARACHNOPHOBIA

1. Schmitt and Müri, *"Neurobiologie der Spinnenphobie,"* 352–55.
2. World Spider Catalog (version 22.5), *"Statistics,"* Natural History Museum Bern, online at wsc.nmbe.ch, accessed on January 8, 2022.

CHAPTER 2. HIDDEN TREASURES

1. Dean et al., *"Plague,"* 1304–9.
2. *"Rattus,"* Taxonomic Serial No. 180361, Integrated Taxonomic Information System (ITIS) (website), accessed January 8, 2022.
3. Lentini and Mouzon, "20 Things You Didn't Know about Rats."
4. Lentini and Mouzon, "20 Things You Didn't Know about Rats."

5. Panksepp and Burgdorf, "'Laughing' Rats and the Evolutionary Antecedents of Human Joy?," 533–47.

6. Emily Langer, "Jaak Panksepp, 'Rat Tickler' Who Revealed Emotional Lives of Animals, Dies at 73," *Washington Post,* April 21, 2017.

7. Bering, "The Rat That Laughed," 74–77.

8. Langer, "Jaak Panksepp, 'Rat Tickler.'"

9. Tobias and Solisti-Mattelon, *Kinship with the Animals,* 245, quoting Rachel Rosenthal, *Tatti Wattles: A Love Story* (Santa Monica, Calif.: Smart Art Press, 1996).

10. Margalit Fox, "Rachel Rosenthal, Bold Performance Artist, Dies at 88," *New York Times,* May 13, 2015.

11. Banksy, *Wall and Piece,* 95.

12. "Mice & Rats: The Essential Need for Animals in Medical Research," species sheet, Foundation for Biomedical Research (website), accessed January 16, 2022.

13. "Mice & Rats."

14. Sam Schipani, "The History of the Lab Rat Is Full of Scientific Triumphs and Ethical Quandaries," *S Magazine* (website), February 27, 2019.

15. "HeroRats and Their Trainers," FAQS: How would you describe the rats' nature?, APOPO.org (website), accessed January 17, 2022.

16. "Animal Welfare," FAQS: What happens to old rats that aren't working?, APOPO.org (website), accessed January 17, 2022.

17. Hillman, *Dream Animals,* 54.

CHAPTER 3. SUSPENSE AND SUSPENSION

1. Bill Finger, "The Batman Wars Against the Dirigible of Doom," *Detective Comics* #33 (New York: DC Comics, 1939).

2. Andrew Kness, "Bats and Pollination," Maryland Agronomy News (website), July 23, 2020.

3. Boyles et al., "Economic Importance of Bats in Agriculture," 41–42.

CHAPTER 4. THE KNOWER OF SECRETS

1. Brunke, *Animal Voices, Animal Guides,* 121–30.

2. "On Landing Like a Cat: It Is a Fact," *New York Times,* August 22, 1989.

3. Leslie A. Lyons, "Why Do Cats Purr?" *Scientific American* (website), January 27, 2003.

4. Mountain Lion Foundation (online at mountainlion.org); Bradley, "Mysterious American Cat."

5. Hillman, *Dream Animals,* 59.

6. Bly, *A Little Book on the Human Shadow,* 21.

CHAPTER 5. TRUST THAT TURNS

1. King, *On Writing,* 110.

2. Pinch, *ANUBIS: Handbook of Egyptian Mythology,* 104.

3. Ovid, *Metamorphoses,* 123.

4. Michael Worboys, "Dog Breeds Are Mere Victorian Confections, Neither Pure nor Ancient," *Aeon* (website), March 25, 2019.

5. Langley, "Human Fatalities Resulting from Dog Attacks in the United States, 1979–2005," 19–25.

6. Kenneth Maniscalco and Mary Ann Edens, "Animal Bites," National Center for Biotechnology Information (website), last updated September 28, 2021.

7. WLBT News, Jackson, Mississippi, "76-Year-Old Man Killed by Four Dogs in Attala Co.," last updated February 5, 2020; Scott Broom, "Woman Killed by Her Own Dog Was Engaged to a K-9 Officer," WUSA9 News, Huntingtown, Maryland, last updated June 22, 2018; WDTN News, Dayton, Ohio, "Infant Dies after Being Attacked by Family Dog in Dayton Home," last updated January 14, 2020.

8. "Pet Statistics," American Society for the Prevention of Cruelty to Animals, ASPCA.org (website), based on 2019 estimates, accessed January 12, 2022.

9. Jason Bittell, "Is the Gray Wolf Still Endangered? Depends Who You Ask," *National Geographic* (website), March 18, 2019.

10. Bly, *A Little Book on the Human Shadow*, 20.

11. Bly, *A Little Book on the Human Shadow*, 20.

12. Versions of this story are noted in both Bisagno, *The Power of Positive Praying*, 55; and Graham, *The Holy Spirit*, 131.

13. Chödrön, *The Places That Scare You*, 12.

CHAPTER 6. SCAPEGOAT

1. Leviticus 16:8–10 and 16:21–22.

2. *Merriam-Webster's Collegiate Dictionary* (online), s.v. "scapegoat."

3. Fortune, "The Rite of Pan," in *The Goat-Foot God*.

4. Matthew 25:31–46.

5. Commentary on satyr illustration from the *Liber de naturis bestiarum* (Aberdeen Bestiary), twelfth to thirteenth century, University of Aberdeen Special Collections, MS 24, folio 13r. Available on University of Aberdeen website.

6. Waite, *The Pictorial Key to the Tarot*, 128–31.

7. Chödrön, *The Places That Scare You*, 13–14.

8. Bly, *A Little Book on the Human Shadow*, 42–43.

9. Bly, *A Little Book on the Human Shadow*, 42–43.

CHAPTER 8. THE BIRDS

1. *The Birds*, Film.

2. Maunder, *The Facts on File Companion to the British Short Story*, 128.

3. Perry, *Hitchcock and Poe*, 62.

4. Black Elk, *The Sacred Pipe*, 58.

5. American Museum of Natural History, "New Study Doubles the Estimate of Bird Species in the World," press release, December 2019. Available on AMNH.org (website).

6. Plato, *Phaedrus and the Seventh and Eighth Letters,* 51.
7. Genesis 8:6–12.
8. Haupt, *Rare Encounters with Ordinary Birds,* 11.
9. Dickinson, "Hope Is the Thing with Feathers," in *The Poems of Emily Dickinson,* 140.
10. Houston, *Mystical Dogs,* xviii.

CHAPTER 9. THAT WHICH SWARMS, STINGS, BITES, BURROWS, AND INVADES

1. Shaw, *Planet of the Bugs,* 1.
2. Shaw, *Planet of the Bugs,* prologue.
3. Shaw, *Planet of the Bugs,* 3.
4. Shaw, *Planet of the Bugs,* 13.
5. Lockwood, *The Infested Mind,* 110.
6. Shaw, *Planet of the Bugs,* 3.
7. Carol Kaesuk Yoon, "Looking Back at the Days of the Locust," *New York Times,* April 23, 2002.
8. Choi, "Fact or Fiction?"
9. Wilson, "First word," 6; see also, E. O. Wilson Biodiversity Foundation (website).
10. "E. O. Wilson," E. O. Wilson Biodiversity Foundation (website), quote transcribed from video, accessed January 14, 2022.
11. Ray, *Blatta Orientalis Materia Medica,* 254.

CHAPTER 10. WHAT LURKS BELOW

1. NOAA, "How Much of the Ocean Have We Explored?," National Ocean Service (website), last updated February 26, 2021.
2. Statistics can be found in the International Shark Attack File, maintained by the Florida Museum (website).
3. Lydia Ramsey, "These Are the Top 15 Deadliest Animals on Earth," ScienceAlert (website), February 23, 2018.
4. Worm et al., "Global Catches, Exploitation Rates, and Rebuilding Options for Sharks," 194–204.
5. Valerie J. Nelson, "Peter Benchley, 65; *Jaws* Author Became Shark Conservationist," *Los Angeles Times,* February 13, 2006.

CHAPTER 11. METAMORPHOSIS

1. Suzuki, *Zen and Japanese Culture,* 239–41.
2. Suzuki, *Zen and Japanese Culture,* 239–41.
3. Suzuki, *Zen and Japanese Culture,* 239–41.
4. This story is paraphrased from Grimm and Grimm, "The Frog Prince," in *Grimm's Fairy Stories.*
5. Brunke, *Animal Voices, Animal Guides,* 131–32.
6. Brunke, *Animal Voices, Animal Guides,* 136.

CHAPTER 12. THE FEAR OF KNOWING
WHO WE ARE

1. As noted in Narby, *Cosmic Serpent*, 66.
2. Statistics in this box are from Andrew Durso, "The Truth about Snakebite," *Life Is Short, but Snakes Are Long: Snake Biology for Everyone* (blog), November 27, 2013; National Institute for Occupational Safety and Health, "Venomous Snakes," Centers for Disease Control (website), last reviewed June 28, 2021; Christopher Ingraham, "The Animals That Are Most Likely to Kill You This Summer," *Washington Post*, June 16, 2015, data based on 2001 to 2013 figures by CDC.
3. Pagels, *Adam, Eve, and the Serpent*, xxiv–xix.
4. Eliot, "Little Gidding," in *Collected Poems*.

CHAPTER 13. THE MOST DANGEROUS
ANIMAL OF ALL

1. Jung, *The Practice of Psychotherapy*, 321.
2. Bly, *A Little Book on the Human Shadow*, 43.
3. Jung, *Archetypes and the Collective Unconscious*, para. 587, p. 8606.
4. "Can 'Other' Be Used as a Verb?," Words We're Watching, *Merriam Webster* (website) accessed January 16, 2022.
5. Stephen Marche, "It's in Dreams That Americans Are Making Sense of Trump," *New Yorker*, March 29, 2020.
6. Walcott, "Love after Love," in *Sea Grapes*.

Bibliography

Banksy. *Wall and Piece*. London: Century, Random House Group, 2006.

Benchley, Peter. *Jaws*. New York: Fawcett, 1991.

Bering, Jesse. "The Rat That Laughed." *Scientific American* 307, no. 1 (July 2012): 74–77.

The Birds. Directed by Alfred Hitchcock. Universal City, Calif.: Universal Pictures, 1963. Film.

Bisagno, John. *The Power of Positive Praying*. Grand Rapids, Mich.: Zondervan Publishing, 1965.

Black Elk. *The Sacred Pipe: Black Elk's Account of the Seven Rites of the Oglala Sioux*. Recorded and Edited by Joseph Epes Brown. Norman: University of Oklahoma Press, 1989. First printed in 1953.

Bly, Robert. *A Little Book on the Human Shadow*. Edited by William Booth. San Francisco: Harper and Row, 1988.

Boyles, Justin G., Paul M. Cryan, Gary F. McCracken, and Thomas H. Kunz. "Economic Importance of Bats in Agriculture." *Science* 332, no. 6025 (2011): 41–42.

Bradley, Ryan. "Mysterious American Cat: The Mountain Lions of Los Angeles." *Virginia Quarterly Review* 92, no. 3, Summer 2016.

Brunke, Dawn. *Animal Voices*. Rochester, Vt.: Bear & Company, 2002.

———. *Animal Voices, Animal Guides*. Rochester, Vt.: Bear & Company, 2009.

———. *The Animal Wisdom Tarot*. London: CICO Books, 2013.

———. *Awakening the Ancient Power of Snake*. Rochester, Vt.: Bear & Company, 2020.

———. *Dreaming with Polar Bears*. Rochester, Vt.: Bear & Company, 2014.

———. *Shapeshifting with Our Animal Companions*. Rochester, Vt.: Bear & Company, 2008.

Bunyan, John. *Divine Emblems: Or, Temporal Things Spiritualized*. London: Bickers & Son, 1867.

Chödrön, Pema. *The Places That Scare You: A Guide to Fearlessness in Difficult Times*. Boston: Shambhala Publications, 2007.

Choi, Charles. "Fact or Fiction? A Cockroach Can Live without Its Head." *Scientific American*, March 15, 2007.

Dean, Katharine R., Fabienne Krauer, Lars Walløe, Ole Christian Lingjærde, Barbara Bramanti, Nils Chr. Stenseth, and Boris V. Schmid. "Plague: Human Ectoparasites and the Spread of Plague in Europe During the Second

Pandemic." Proceedings of the National Academy of Sciences of the United States of America 115, no. 6 (2018): 1304–9.

DiCamillo, Kate. *The Tale of Despereaux*. Somerville, Mass.: Candlewick Press, 2009. E-book.

Dickinson, Emily. "Hope Is the Thing with Feathers." In *The Poems of Emily Dickinson*, edited by R. W. Franklin. Cambridge, Mass.: Belknap Press of Harvard University Press, 1999.

du Maurier, Daphne. "The Birds." In *The Apple Tree: A Short Novel and Several Long Stories*. London: Victor Gollancz, 1952.

Edgington, Jacqueline. *Happy Jack*. Florida: Bowker, 2018.

Eliot, T. S. *Collected Poems*. New York: Harcourt Brace Jovanovich, 1970.

———. *Old Possum's Book of Practical Cats*. London: Faber and Faber, 1948.

Fortune, Dion. *The Goat-Foot God*. London: Williams & Norgate, 1936.

Graham, Billy. *The Holy Spirit: Activating God's Power in Your Life*. Nashville, Tenn.: Thomas Nelson, 1988.

Grimm, Jacob, and Wilhelm Grimm. *Grimm's Fairy Stories*. New York: Cupples and Leon, 1922.

Haupt, Lyanda Lynn. *Rare Encounters with Ordinary Birds*. Seattle, Wash.: Sasquatch Books, 2001.

Hillman, James. *Dream Animals*. San Francisco: Chronicle Books, 1997.

Houston, Jean. *Mystical Dogs—Animals as Guides to Our Inner Life*. Maui, Hawaii: Inner Ocean Publishing, 2002.

Jung, Carl G. *Archetypes and the Collective Unconscious*. Vol. 9, Part 1 of *Collected Works of C. G. Jung*. Translated by R. F. C. Hull. New York: Bollingen Foundation, 1957. Digital edition.

———. *Memories, Dreams and Reflections*. Edited by Aniela Jaffe. Translated by Richard and Clara Winston. New York: Vintage Books, 1989.

———. *The Practice of Psychotherapy*. Vol. 16 of *Collected Works of C. G. Jung*. Translated by R. F. C. Hull. New York: Pantheon Books, 1954.

King, Stephen. *Cujo*. New York: Viking Press, 1981.

———. *On Writing*. London: Hodder and Stoughton, 2000.

Langley, Ricky L. "Human Fatalities Resulting from Dog Attacks in the United States, 1979–2005." *Wilderness & Environmental Medicine* 20, no. 1 (March 2009): 19–25.

Lentini, Liza, and David Mouzon. "20 Things You Didn't Know about Rats." *Discover Magazine*, December 7, 2006.

Letakots-Lesa, Eagle Chief. "Introduction to the Pawnee Songs." In *The Indians' Book: An Offering by the American Indians of Indian Lore, Musical and Narrative, to Form a Record of the Songs and Legends of Their Race*. Recorded and Edited by Natalie Curtis. New York: Harper and Brothers, 1907.

Lockwood, Jeffrey. *The Infested Mind: Why Humans Fear, Loathe, and Love Insects*. Oxford: Oxford University Press, 2013.

Matter of Heart. Directed, edited, and produced by Mark Whitney. New York: Kino International, 1986. Film.

Maunder, Andrew. *The Facts on File Companion to the British Short Story*. New York: Facts on File, 2007.

Murakami, Haruki. *After the Quake*. Translated by Jay Rubin. New York: Vintage International, 2002.

Narby, Jeremy. *The Cosmic Serpent: DNA and the Origins of Knowledge*. New York: Jeremy P. Tarcher/Putnam, 1999.

Ovid. *Metamorphoses*. Translated by A. D. Melville. Oxford: Oxford University Press, 1986.

Pagels, Elaine. *Adam, Eve, and the Serpent: Sex and Politics in Early Christianity*. New York: Random House, 1988.

Panksepp, Jaak, and Jeff Burgdorf. "'Laughing' Rats and the Evolutionary Antecedents of Human Joy?" *Physiology & Behavior* 79, no. 3 (2003): 533–47.

Perry, Dennis R. *Hitchcock and Poe: The Legacy of Delight and Terror*. Lanham, Md.: Scarecrow Press, 2003.

Pinch, Geraldine. *ANUBIS: Handbook of Egyptian Mythology*. Santa Barbara, Calif.: ABC-CLIO, 2002.

Plato. *Phaedrus and the Seventh and Eighth Letters*. Translated by Walter Hamilton. London: Penguin Books, 1973.

Pliny. *Pliny's Natural History. In Thirty-Seven Books*. Vols. 1–3. Translated by Philemon Holland. London: George Barclay, 1848.

Pratchett, Terry. *The Amazing Maurice and His Educated Rodents*. New York: HarperCollins, 2001.

Ray, D. N. *Blatta Orientalis Materia Medica*. Homeopathic Recorder, 1890.

Schmitt, W. J., and R. M. Müri. "Neurobiologie der Spinnenphobie." *Schweizer Archiv für Neurologie* 160, no. 8 (2009): 352–55.

Shaw, Scott Richard. *Planet of the Bugs: Evolution and the Rise of Insects*. Chicago: University of Chicago Press, 2014. Kindle edition.

Silko, Leslie Marmon. *Ceremony*. New York: Penguin Books, 1977, 2006.

Steinem, Gloria. *My Life on the Road*. New York: Random House, 2015.

Stoker, Bram. *Dracula*. 6th ed. Westminster: Archibald Constable, 1899.

Suzuki, Daisetz T. *Zen and Japanese Culture*. Princeton, N.J.: Princeton University Press, 2010. First printed in 1938.

Tennyson, Alfred Lord. *Poems, Chiefly Lyrical*. London: Effingham Wilson, 1830.

Tobias, Michael, and Kate Solisti-Mattelon. *Kinship with the Animals*. Hillsboro, Ore.: Beyond Words Publishing, 1998.

Waite, Edward Arthur. *The Pictorial Key to the Tarot*. San Francisco: Harper & Row, 1971.

Walcott, Derek. "Love after Love." In *Sea Grapes*. New York: Farrar Straus & Giroux, 1976.

Wilson, E. O. "First word." *Omni* 12, no. 12 (September 1990): 6.

Worm, Boris, Brendal Davis, Lisa Kettemer, Christine A. Ward-Paige, Demian Chapman, Michael R. Heithaus, Steven T. Kessel, and Samuel H. Gruber. "Global Catches, Exploitation Rates, and Rebuilding Options for Sharks." *Marine Policy* 40 (July 2013): 194–204.

Index